Praise for *No Stones*

"*No Stones* is a timely work written from the perspective of one who has lived through the devastation of this disease. Marnie Ferree takes an honest look at sexual addiction, which is pervasive even among Christian women. She's taken a huge step in making it OK to talk about this difficult subject, which long has been taboo in Christian areas. This problem needs to be addressed now. Marnie presents the subject plainly and painfully, but I am encouraged by the hope and healing her story brings."

Robin Cato, executive director, Society for the Advancement of Sexual Health

"*No Stones* is a history-making book. Finally, Christian women who struggle with their unhealthy relationships or sexuality have somewhere to turn. Marnie tackles the issues with biblical accuracy and guts. I highly recommend this book to sexually broken women and to the pastors, counselors, or ministry leaders who care for them. God will use this book to change thousands of lives."

Russell Willingham, author of *Breaking Free: Understanding Sexual Addiction and the Healing Power of Jesus* and *Relational Masks*

"As I read Marnie's book I read my own life's struggle. She explains sex addiction with grace and compassion. *No Stones* offers me hope for healing and understanding, rather than the shame that my own mind heaps on me. The practical steps to healing sound scary, but they clearly outline a path to recovery and wholeness."

Barbara, recovering female sex addict

"Undoubtedly, *No Stones* is the best book available on understanding and treating female sexual addiction. Marnie writes from her personal experiences as an addict and a Christian counselor of women caught in the web of sexual addiction. This book is a comprehensive summary of all aspects of sexual addiction, which affects the woman, her husband, her children, and her faith. In this day of declining sexual boundaries even within the church, all should carefully read this book."

Anderson Spickard Jr., M.D., addictionist, retired director of Center for Professional Health at Vanderbilt Medical Center

"After fifteen years of marriage, I had become the male poster child for codependency. The shame I felt because of my wife' _____ _____ _____ with my own feelings of self-worthlessness, propelled my depress _____ _____ ly will *No Stones* lead readers to a greater ur _____ it also will accurately capture the emotional _____ an male co-addict. I wish I had had this book _____

Russell, husband of a female sex addict

NO STONES

WOMEN REDEEMED FROM SEXUAL ADDICTION

MARNIE C. FERREE

FOREWORD BY MARK LAASER, PH.D.

IVP Books

An imprint of InterVarsity Press
Downers Grove, Illinois

InterVarsity Press
P.O. Box 1400, Downers Grove, IL 60515-1426
World Wide Web: www.ivpress.com
E-mail: email@ivpress.com

Second Edition ©2010 by Marnie C. Ferree
First Edition ©2002 by Marnie C. Ferree

InterVarsity Press® is the book-publishing division of InterVarsity Christian Fellowship/USA®, a movement of students and faculty active on campus at hundreds of universities, colleges and schools of nursing in the United States of America, and a member movement of the International Fellowship of Evangelical Students. For information about local and regional activities, write Public Relations Dept., InterVarsity Christian Fellowship/USA, 6400 Schroeder Rd., P.O. Box 7895, Madison, WI 53707-7895, or visit the IVCF website at <www.intervarsity.org>.

All Scripture quotations, unless otherwise indicated, are taken from the Holy Bible, New International Version®. NIV®. *Copyright ©1973, 1978, 1984 by International Bible Society. Used by permission of Zondervan Publishing House. All rights reserved.*

The Twelve Steps of Sexaholics Anonymous on p. 263 are copyright ©1989 SA Literature. Used by permission.

Design: Cindy Kiple
Images: woman staring off in distance: Rebecca Parker/Trevillion Images
    pebbles: Victor Burnside

ISBN 978-0-8308-3740-3

Printed in the United States of America ∞

Library of Congress Cataloging-in-Publication Data

Ferree, Marnie C.
 No stones: women redeemed from sexual addiction / Marnie C.
Ferree; foreword by Mark Laaser.
    p. cm.
 Includes bibliographical references (p.   ).
 ISBN 978-0-8308-3740-3 (pbk.: alk. paper)
 1. Sex addicts—Religious life. 2. Sex addicts—Rehabilitation. 3.
Sex addiction—Religious aspects—Christianity. 4. Christian
women—Religious life. 5. Christian women—Sexual behavior. I.
Title.
BV4596.S42F47 2010
248.8'629—dc22

                                                                              2009042075

P	19	18	17	16	15	14	13	12	11	10	9	8	7	6	5	4	3	2	1
Y	26	25	24	23	22	21	20	19	18	17	16	15	14	13	12	11	10		

No Stones is dedicated with love
to my husband, David.

Grow old along with me!
The best is yet to be.

—Robert Browning, "Rabbi Ben Ezra"

CONTENTS

FOREWORD

Every author and speaker has a list of his or her most frequently asked questions. Over the last twenty years I've repeatedly heard, "Is sexual addiction only a male problem, or do women struggle with this too? If so, how many and how does it differ from men?" The book you are about to read answers those questions so much better than I ever could.

We live in a time of great cultural crisis about sexuality. The world would have us believe certain mythologies about sex, about men and about women. I fear that many women have been drawn into that darkness. It is time to remind ourselves of God's design for sexual integrity and for sexual wholeness. We have needed this book for a long time.

So many women have struggled with their sexual sins and temptations in silence. These women have longed for another person who understands their loneliness. By God's grace, sometimes there are moments in history when lonely hearts like these find a voice, a companion, someone who understands and puts into words what has for so long been shamefully buried. I believe that *No Stones* will be such a voice and companion for women. This is a deeply spiritual and personal book. It is also practical and points to the way out.

Like the story of the woman who came to the well of Samaria in the Gospel of John, many of you reading this book are ashamed of

your past. You are too guilty to allow yourself to find the fellowship
of others. You are lonely. You are thirsty for an affirming voice. You
long to be heard, to be cared for, to be touched and held, to be pas-
sionately desired for your mind and spirit, and to be embraced by a
loving God. You have heard the story of the prodigal son and wondered if there ever was a prodigal daughter. You perhaps have even
cried out to God, "Is it always about men?!"

Marnie has been at that well. She has also been that thirsty. She
has found that living water that only Christ can give. In this book
Marnie follows the example of that woman at the well who went back
to her village and told the message of salvation.

Writing a book is a journey. It is a journey of growth in knowledge. It
is a journey of gaining insight about what has been helpful to others. It
is a journey of spiritual maturity. It is a journey of tears. It is a labor of
love. For Marnie it has often been like the journey of being pregnant and
well past your due date. The child inside is the child of hope for others.
When will the child be born? Why is the waiting so long and the birth
experience so painful? Marnie has patiently stayed with the process.

It is a miracle to me that a woman who has not had a mother for most
of her life has been such a wonderful mother herself. It is that same
miracle that a woman who never had a sister has become such a sister to
others. These miracles show me the result of depending on God's love
more than on any earthly relationship. When we learn to be totally dependent on the heavenly Father, God transforms us into being able to
give to others that which we long for the most for ourselves.

It takes great courage to tell your story. Many of you will find your
own story in these pages. That will be sometimes frightening and
sometimes comforting. I believe that you will find this book a source
of great information and encouragement. There is hope!

It has been a joy to know Marnie as a friend and colleague and to
see what God has done in her life. As you get to know her heart, I
pray that you also will find the blessing of a friend who provides hope
and inspiration for your journey.

Mark Laaser, Ph.D.

LETTER TO THE READER

Dear Reader,

The book that you have in your hands is most likely the heaviest book you will ever read. Chances are you are reading *No Stones* because you or a close friend is a female sex addict. I can guarantee you that this book will not be an "easy read." I have grown up as the daughter of a female sex addict, and even though I know her story and her experiences throughout recovery, I still had a hard time reading parts of this book.

In reading *No Stones* you will see yourself as the little girl who was abandoned or abused. In these pages you will also see actions and thoughts that you could never put into words. I have faith that if you allow him, God will speak to you in an incredible way through this book. He spoke to me.

This book gave me insight that mere words could never express. I learned why my mom acted how she did and that she had no intention of hurting me, my brother or my dad. I learned that there is reason behind the madness. I learned that a person's past cannot simply be forgotten or written off as unimportant, because it truly has a significant impact on the future.

God's hand has been visible to me throughout the stages of this book. I've watched *No Stones* grow from an idea to a manuscript to this, its final form. I've seen my mom cry out of frustration and anger because she knew that it was God's will that she write *No Stones*, but nothing seemed to be falling into place. Through her journey in writing this book, I've seen that if something is God's will, it will happen on his timing.

My prayer for you, the reader, is that you read *No Stones* with an open heart and mind and that you prepare yourself for the journey you are about to start whether you are an addict, a co-addict, a codependent or a caring friend. If you have never stepped out of your comfort zone, you will once you turn the page. And even though this might be one of the heaviest books you will ever read, it will also be one of the most beneficial on the road to recovery.

Reader, I know that my mother thinks of you often and prays for you even more. Please know that you are loved by my mom, but more importantly, by your heavenly father. There is absolutely nothing you can do to make God love you any less than he loved you when you came out of your mother's womb. That is why he will never throw stones.

I also know that you can conquer this. My mom did and because of that she is an inspiration to me. The road ahead is a long, hard one, but a path has been cleared for you and written so that you can refer to it. Do that as often as necessary.

In the name of the One who heals,
Marnie's Daughter

PREFACE

I remember what it was like to fear that anyone who really knew me would be quick to throw stones. I knew such treatment was what I deserved: to be dragged into the dust. Shamed. Shunned. Stoned. I was a modern woman caught in adultery.

When I first walked into that Christian counseling center, I felt broken beyond repair. I identified with Rahab the harlot in the Old Testament, though I couldn't imagine God would spare any wrath toward me. I truly believed I was beyond redemption. I couldn't continue to live the way I was, and I was too afraid to die.

I wished often in those early days for a woman I could follow along this road of recovery. I longed to have a female who could understand the particular struggles and pains of my heart. I wanted to read about myself and my problem in a book filled with feminine pronouns and descriptions instead of the male ones I found. At that time there was no female voice or leader. No literature on how women too can struggle with sexual addiction. As I gained deliverance and healing, I prayed for the opportunity to provide that voice to other women who were stuck in sexual sin. I asked for courage and to be equipped for the task. I asked for the support of my husband and children.

This book is the answer to those prayers. In God's perfect calendar, the outline for this book poured forth on an airplane as I was returning from teaching about sex addiction. That day was the seven-year anniversary of my sobriety date. The symbolism of the date is significant to me. In biblical times, the year after seven cycles of seven years was determined by God to be a year of Jubilee, a period of resting and reaping from the fruits of the land. It was a time of celebration and renewal. To me, this book is a personal Jubilee. A bringing to fruition the seeds God planted seven years earlier in my heart.

After writing the initial outline, I spent two years completing the manuscript. When numerous Christian publishers rejected it, God used the rejections to humble my notions of fame, which was a necessary lesson. I chose to use a Christian self-publishing firm as a way to get the word out and offer a resource to women, and *No Stones* first appeared in print in 2002 as a self-published work. Now, after seven more years, I'm grateful to have the book accepted by InterVarsity Press, a major Christian publisher. It's a testimony of how far we've come in our understanding of sexual addiction, including among women. I hope this boost brings the book into the hands of more women who need it.

This new publishing opportunity has allowed me to update the book with the latest research and expand it in several key areas. Each chapter contains reflection questions which can be used either in a small group setting or for individual consideration. If used in a small group, I encourage participants to take no more than one chapter at each meeting. Each woman should read the chapter and answer the questions in advance. During the group meeting each woman can share her thoughts on each question and then the group can move into a general discussion of the chapter.

I include many women's stories in the book, and I appreciate their willingness to share their experiences. The stories are true, but the names and identifying details have been changed to provide anonymity. In some cases, the illustrations are compilations of several women's stories.

With a grateful, humble heart, I pray the reader will find hope and understanding within these pages. It *is* possible to experience healing. While I certainly have been imperfect in my walk of recovery, I have found answers, wholeness, peace and restoration of relationships beyond my wildest dreams. I give God the glory!

INTRODUCTION
MARNIE AND DAVID FERREE'S STORY

The great Western novelist Louis L'Amour opens his novel *Lonely on the Mountain* with this line: "There will come a time when you believe everything is finished. That will be the beginning." As a writer, when I first read L'Amour's line I thought it was a wonderful way to begin a book. Today, on a much deeper level I understand what those words really mean.

The "finished" state in my life and marriage came in the winter of 1990 when I received the devastating diagnosis of early stage cervical cancer caused by the sexually transmitted disease HPV (human papillomavirus). As I hung up the phone after the doctor's call, my mind raced with images of medical treatments, of figuring out how to care for my young children while I was ill, and especially of telling my husband. I knew that my secret life was about to be exposed.

David and I had married in 1981 (just a few weeks after Princess Diana), and for the first few years we'd been very happy. It was a second marriage for us both, but we'd each married young, neither of us had any children, and we both had divorced after only four years. We viewed our life together as an opportunity to start over after a serious misstep in our youth. David had an excellent position in a Fortune 100 company, and we had more money than we needed to be comfortable. Within a few years we were blessed with a beautiful, healthy daughter and son.

But underneath the veneer of tranquil, suburban, upper-middle-class life, I harbored a number of secrets. The darkest one—and the one most pertinent to my health issue—was a secret I'd successfully hidden for almost twenty years. Something I'd denied, rationalized and justified since the age of fourteen. A reality too painful to admit and so unrecognized in women that I'd never heard its name: *I was a sex addict.*

At the time of my cervical cancer diagnosis, I was intensely involved in an extramarital affair. It was only the latest of many similar relationships throughout both my marriages. In fact, my unfaithfulness had been the reason for the end of my first.

It was two more years before I heard that clinical diagnosis of sexual addiction, and even then, it was almost impossible to accept. A sex addict? What a horrible name! Surely that description didn't apply to me. I was a nice, conservative, church-going soccer mom with a college degree and a long list of accomplishments. I had an equally nice husband, though I'd come to quietly resent him over the years.

David worked hard and provided well. He was a kind, gentle man with a methodical head on his shoulders and a calm demeanor. He had a giving spirit and was a good father. He, however, was also unfamiliar with the landscape of intimacy. David was a practical man, not an emotional one. He didn't know how to talk about matters of the heart, and he wasn't able to show his feelings. Though I'd initially been attracted to his stability, I'd come to resent his lack of spontaneity and emotional presence. I viewed him as boring, shut down, and worse. I blamed him for the growing detachment in our marriage and for my growing discontent. I wondered how I'd again married the wrong person, and I believed that if I were married to Mr. Right, my life would be the magical one I'd always dreamed of.

I had little understanding of my own behavior and less understanding of my own story. I was a preacher's daughter who had been raised in the church. Our family looked perfect and was widely respected. I was raised with many advantages and was an excellent, popular student. Sure, we'd had our share of sorrow. When I was three years old, my mother had died from colon cancer, and my two older brothers and I were left to be raised largely by a grandmotherly helper who came to live in our home.

Our family spiritualized our feelings of grief, and we never talked about our loss. My father, brothers and I soldiered on, each lost in our separate pain. My father buried himself in "God's work" and gave little time to his family, which was the custom for his generation, especially for members of the clergy. As a grown woman with children of my own, I had no idea how deeply I'd been affected by my mother's death and my father's absence.

I had even less understanding of the rest of my story. Like most people, I viewed my situation as normal. Beginning when I was five years old, a dear family friend assumed a fatherly role in my life, and for the next fifteen years he was a central figure in our home. It was a very positive relationship in many ways as he taught me how to roller skate, encouraged me as a fledgling writer, and listened to my hopes and dreams. However, this friend also exposed me to lots of pornography (and himself), and he steadily groomed me as a sexual predator. In gradually escalating sexual activity, he exploited my loneliness, which he filled with fun activities during the day and long talks deep into the night when my father was away. I was ten years old before I realized that some of the things we were doing must be "sex," which, of course, was never discussed in my home. By the time we actually had intercourse when I was fourteen, the only way I could make sense of the sexual relationship was to blame myself.

My friend was gentle and "loving" with me. He spent time with me and was attentive to me. I loved him and sought his company. He said he loved me and that our relationship was special. How could I not be at fault for our sexual activity? I believed I had chosen (as a ten-year-old!) to be sexual with a man fifteen years my senior. Especially by the time I was fourteen and running my family's household, I thought I was old enough to choose to have sex with a man almost old enough to be my father.

And when I kept choosing to have sex as a promiscuous teen (desperate for the love and attention this man had removed), there was only one way I could frame my behavior: *I was a whore.* A horrible, terrible person. That identity was my internal self-description for the next twenty years, and I lived it out in a variety of ways.

I never told a soul about my double life, and I protected my secret with overachievement and perfection. I followed my father and brothers in pouring myself into church work. At the same time, I medicated my loneliness and shame with relationships that were both intense and sexual.

I thought that getting married would cure my promiscuity. Soon, though, I discovered my husband couldn't fill the gaping, black hole inside, which I could only identify as an aching, tender place within. Eventually, I resumed my pattern of looking for love in the arms of men. With each affair, I shrouded my heart in another blanket of shame. I knew my behavior was wrong, but I was powerless to stop despite my many attempts. At that point, I had no clue that what I was doing fit the classic definition of an addiction.

My diagnosis of cervical cancer caused by a sexually transmitted disease was God's wake-up call on my life. I was forced to confirm for David the affairs he'd long suspected and chosen to ignore. The diagnosis propelled us onto a path we had never dreamed we would walk. A path that today we view with immense gratitude.

At first we focused on my physical healing, and I went through three surgeries in the next twelve months. Eventually, the cancer was gone and my body healed. But I discovered my spirit and soul were still diseased.

Despite my good intentions, I continued in my latest affair. I knew my behavior (including unprotected sex) was literally killing me, and I was powerless to stop. Finally, with desperate thoughts of suicide bouncing darkly behind my eyes, I did something I'd never done before: *I asked for help.* I called a dear friend, poured out my truth, and received grace that was shocking and amazing. I started an intense period of therapy, and the healing began.

With the help of a gifted Christian counselor, I came to understand my story. I put the responsibility for my early sexual activity back on the abuser, which is where it belonged. I grieved the abandonment from my mother and my father, and I saw that my affairs were just false solutions to deep inner pain and legitimate needs. Eventually, I let others into my life when I became active in a Twelve Step group for recovery from sexual addiction. With the help of safe, intimate friends, I was able to end unsafe, sinful affairs. I learned what genuine intimacy felt like, and to my surprise, it wasn't sexual.

I learned that sexual addiction really isn't about sex at all, which is something I had intuitively always known. It is an *intimacy disorder*—a desperate search for love, touch, affirmation, affection and approval. Obviously, sexual addiction is false intimacy and a false solution for legitimate needs, but it's driven by pain and loneliness, not by physical gratification. The cry of the heart is for intimate connection with yourself, with others, and with God, whom I never believed could love or care for a "whore" like me.

The best part of the healing process was coming to know a God I'd never imagined—a God of pursuing grace who was fully able to meet my needs. I traded my rules-based religion for relationship-based spirituality. (Grace motivates in a way that shame cannot, and I longed to respond to God's love with obedience, rather than perform out of fear.) In every way, I became a "new creature."

Obviously, my marriage improved when I remained faithful to it. But David and I discovered after a few years that our healing journey was still significantly incomplete. Though David looked liked the much healthier one in our coupleship (after all, he hadn't had affairs or done the terrible things I had), our counselor gently identified his own areas of impairment. We realized David had his own demons to deal with, especially in the area of his profound, untreated depression, which crippled and isolated him.

David too was raised in a clergyman's family, though his upbringing was significantly healthier than mine. He was spared sexual abuse and other forms of recognizable trauma. He had loving parents and a brother who were positive figures in his life. But David's internal landscape was shaped in ways just as profound as mine. When he was a young child, his father had an extended hospitalization for catatonic depression, which in the dark days of mental health treatment in the 1950s was just as shameful as sex addiction is today. His family was embarrassed, and they never talked about their experience.

During their dad's hospitalization, David's brother went to live with family members 300 miles away, because his hyperactivity was too much for their stressed mother to handle. (No one knew of attention deficit hyperactivity disorder, ADHD, in the 1950s either.) David learned the best way to navigate life was to be quiet, avoid attention or conflict, ignore his own needs and wait for the hard times to pass. He struggled with an intimacy disorder—which was actually just the other side of the coin from mine.

Unknowingly, David and I were two wounded people who had each found another wounded person to dovetail with our pain. For each of us, the greatest (unrecognized) fear was abandonment, and we unconsciously believed we'd found someone who would never leave us like the key figures of our childhood. In David's stability, I thought I'd found security, and in my dominant personality, he thought he'd found someone resilient and strong like his mother. Sadly, we both were wrong.

Yet God gave our marriage a new beginning, one that didn't come until we thought the marriage was over. We were surprised to discover God had an amazing plan for our coupleship. From our deepest wounds, including the ones we'd inflicted on each other, our heavenly father forged our deepest healing. After two-and-a-half years of my sobriety from sexual addiction and significant healing from core trauma, we took a second major turn in the road when David embraced his own healing journey. He began to explore his story and how it had shaped the man he had become. He discovered crucial things about himself that had affected our relationship, and he bravely addressed them. He did so in his sweet, methodical fashion, which by this point I had come to appreciate.

David learned how to identify his feelings and fears and how to share them with me, which was very difficult for him. He risked stating his needs and engaging in healthy conflict. He did his own recovery work, including taking part in a Twelve Step program for co-sex addiction. He stepped up to the plate and assumed responsibility for his part in our relationship dance.

Slowly, we learned what it meant to be a genuinely intimate couple. We became emotional and spiritual partners, instead of just practical cohorts. The roots of our coupleship grew deeper and our bond stronger. I discovered that dear practical David, who for years had felt emotionally unavailable to me, was actually the one man in my life who had not abandoned me. And David found that despite the deep ways I had betrayed him, I was deeply committed to him and accepted him exactly as he was. We encouraged each other to develop into our healthy, true selves. We found that we greatly complemented each other's strengths and compensated for each other's weaknesses. Together, we became something neither of us could be alone.

Our journeys, separate and together, have moved past our personal lives and have evolved into ministry. At that "finished" point of coming to the end of myself, I thought God was through with me. How could I ever do anything positive for God after the profound ways I had failed him? In this area too I was graced with a new beginning. After a year or two of coffee-cup counseling, where I talked informally with other women who had similar stories, I returned to graduate school and earned a master's degree to counsel professionally. Quickly my practice centered on sexual addiction and sexual trauma. Before long I came to direct a Christ-centered, therapeutic workshop program for those affected by sexual addiction.

Bethesda Workshops now serves clients from across the country who come to Nashville for help and hope. In this effort David and I are a meaningful team. I'm the front person, the one visible and in charge, but David is a steady contributing force. He hauls materials to the workshop site and helps with anything behind the scenes that needs doing. He keeps the home fires burning when I'm gone for workshops or speaking engagements, and he supports me when I'm tired or discouraged. When we started affirming each other's natural gifts, we discovered how much we needed each other—and how fulfilling and fun it is to enhance each other.

A few years ago another tragedy provided a measuring stick of how far we'd come since our end and our new beginning. We were stunned when David was diagnosed with renal cell carcinoma—advanced kidney cancer. His prognosis was bleak.

One night we were rocking quietly in our darkened den, and David pulled me into his lap and held me close. "I want you to know that no matter what happens, it'll be okay," he promised. "I'm at peace with this situation, and I have no regrets. I'm grateful that we've had such a good life."

I looked at him incredulously. "A *good life?* Now I know you're really sick," I teased. "Where were you during all those awful years? How can you say we've had a good life together?"

David was quiet a few seconds and then responded in his typical understated way. "Yeah, we've had some hard times, I guess. But it took those tough times to get us where we are tonight, and I wouldn't trade being here for anything."

At that moment, I knew the outcome had been worth all the pain of the journey. L'Amour's promise was true: at the time you think everything is finished, that will be the beginning.*

---

*The introduction was reprinted from Mae and Erika Chambers, eds., *How Our Marriage Was Saved: 22 Couples Tell Their True Stories* (Hendersonville, Tenn.: Pass It On Publications, 2010).

PART ONE

THE PROBLEM
WOMAN CAUGHT IN ADULTERY

Jesus went across to Mount Olives, but he was soon back in the Temple again. Swarms of people came to him. He sat down and taught them. The religion scholars and Pharisees led in a woman who had been caught in an act of adultery. They stood her in plain sight of everyone and said, "Teacher, this woman was caught red-handed in the act of adultery. Moses, in the Law, gives orders to stone such persons. What do you say?" They were trying to trap him into saying something incriminating so they could bring charges against him.

Jesus bent down and wrote with his finger in the dirt. They kept at him, badgering him. He straightened up and said, "The sinless one among you, go first: Throw the stone." Bending down again, he wrote some more in the dirt.

Hearing that, they walked away, one after another, beginning with the oldest. The woman was left alone. Jesus stood up and spoke to her. "Woman, where are they? Does no one condemn you?"

"No one, Master."

"Neither do I," said Jesus. "Go on your way. From now on, don't sin." (John 8:1-11 *The Message*)

CHAPTER ONE

THE SECRET SIN

OF SEXUAL ADDICTION

Maria frowned as she pulled into the garage. It was 2:30 a.m.—much later than she'd planned to be out. She hoped her husband or children wouldn't wake up and realize she was just now getting home. She'd have to remember to tell the girlfriend she was supposed to have been with that she had stayed out this late just in case her husband mentioned it. She wondered if he had any clue about where she'd really been. Probably not, she reassured herself. He was pretty clueless in general, she thought. His dullness was why her life needed some excitement.

On the other hand, Maria felt guilty for deceiving him. All things considered, he was a decent guy. He didn't deserve what she had done in violating her marriage vows. Maria was ashamed she had again so quickly broken her promise to God that she wouldn't be with her lover again. Just last Sunday she had gone forward during the altar call. But she was bored in her marriage and her lover was so attentive. They had such a powerful connection! Surely it wasn't hurting her husband if he didn't know. After all, her other affairs hadn't harmed him, had they?

Maria tossed her head as if to shake off the competing thoughts.

At the moment, she had practical things to consider—like how to avoid her husband's detecting she smelled like another man's cologne. She decided to get up early and shower before he was awake. Her escapades sure were less complicated when she was single.

Maria vowed to make up for her sin by being extra nice. She resolved to be more patient with the children. She'd get up early and fix pancakes for breakfast. Maybe they could even go for ice cream after school. She'd work an extra shift at the church bazaar. She'd plan something special for her Bible class Sunday morning. She'd be on time and more responsible with the checkbook. She'd pull it back together somehow. She had to.

Maria sighed. The thought of her church friends made her shudder. What would they think of her if they knew? Everyone believed she was so together. So religious. She could never face them if she were discovered! The familiar, sick feeling washed over her. She felt overwhelmed with shame. Yet she felt so driven. So powerless to stop what she knew in her heart was wrong. *I'm nothing more than a hypocrite*, she thought. The self-judgment stung, but she couldn't deny it. *Why else do I do what I do?*

Tomorrow, she resolved. *I'll stop the affair tomorrow. I can do it this time. I know I can. I have to!*

You may be shocked by Maria's story. Or perhaps you view her situation as unusual. Surely only a handful of women are involved in this type of sexual sin. And, of course, none of them could be "good" women who go to church and are married and car pool their children and hold down a job. Women who sleep around must be different. Aren't they easily recognizable as the cheap women they are? Their hair is bleached blond or colored a brassy red. They wear figure-enhancing clothes. And figure-revealing. They swish their hips when they walk and bat their eyes seductively. They live in that bad part of town and socialize with questionable kinds of companions. They use vulgar language. They abuse alcohol and drugs. You'd never come in contact with them in your circle. Surely.

The truth is that Maria's story is painfully common. She represents thousands of women, including Christian women, who are involved in sexually sinful and addictive behavior. Maria could be your tennis partner, your lawyer, your child's teacher, your neighbor. She could have sung that beautiful solo in church last Sunday morning. Maybe she greeted you in the grocery store last night. She is any one of untold numbers of women who are trapped in sexual sin and feel there is no way out. Perhaps Maria describes even you.

Sexual misconduct is, by nature and necessity, a secret sin. If Maria were going to share her struggle with someone, where would she turn? Could she tell her pastor? The minister's spouse? Would she be comfortable confessing her affair to her small group or her Sunday school class? Would she dare to ask for the prayers of the church and specifically divulge why? Maria is afraid even to call the crisis hotline or visit a counselor. She doesn't think anyone could understand her struggle, much less help her. She doesn't trust she wouldn't be stoned for her sins.

Women like Maria (and perhaps like you) feel all alone. Because no one in the church talks about sexual temptations, especially among women, it's easy to believe no other female has similar issues. When was the last time you heard an honest, nonhumorous discussion among Christian women about their difficulties and struggles in the sexual area? Have you ever heard such a conversation? I believe that silence about sexual matters is a great shortcoming of the church. Have you gotten the message sexual problems are simply too bad to talk about?

Sexual addiction is a secret sin that has been around since biblical times, yet it has been denied, ignored, undiagnosed and untreated for centuries. Those within religious communities have been quick to condemn such sin, and rightfully so, but they also have been unwilling or unable to understand the sexual sinner and offer her the help she so desperately needs.

The shame associated with sexual mistakes is profound. Sexual sin has typically been considered somehow worse than other kinds of sins. When you think of King David, the sin of adultery usually comes to mind before his sin of murder. The fear of being discovered in sexual sin makes it especially difficult for strugglers to ask for help.

And when the problem has escalated beyond "just" a rare or occasional sexual slip into the realm of sexual addiction, the shame can be paralyzing.

Ignorance and misunderstanding about the concept of an addiction to sex is widespread. Knowledge and research is fairly new. Only in the last thirty years has attention been directed toward this area. The whole field is probably at the point where alcoholism was fifty years ago. Then, you may remember, people viewed alcoholism as simply moral failure. Most shamed the alcoholic and told her to "just stop!" Today, though, we understand much more about the disease of alcoholism, including the proven biological components. Now if someone admits to being a recovering alcoholic, she likely receives unqualified respect. Even within the church, the sober alcoholic often enjoys affirmation for facing the problem and turning her life around. Friends join her in celebrating her recovery.

But when someone admits to being a *sexual* addict, the reaction is quite different: "You're a what?" The response is usually horror and disgust. Or fear. Some sex addicts report people avoided them and kept their children away too. "My friends didn't want me around their daughters," one male addict said. "I've never considered being sexual with a child, but they immediately assumed I was some kind of pedophile." One female addict's church asked her to leave when she revealed she had struggled years before with sexual sin. She reported, "I felt like I had leprosy."

As if the shame of being addicted to sex isn't bad enough, the stigma of being a woman who struggles with this problem is particularly intense. I sometimes tease my male colleagues who are recovering sex addicts that my shame is greater than their shame. I honestly believe that's accurate. Our culture has the attitude that "boys will be boys" or that illicit sexual behavior is "just a male thing." A female who has a sexual addiction is considered especially perverted. After all, women aren't even supposed to like sex. We're the ones with the proverbial headaches.

The female sex addict quickly embraces an identity of shame, rather than seeing herself as created in the image of God. She questions whether God even loves her at all. How could she be a Christian and remain involved in sexual sin? The only way to make sense of that dual reality is to condemn herself. My own self-description (privately, at least) was "slut." I knew what I was doing was wrong; I knew I couldn't stop. The only conclusion must be that I was a horrible, terrible person. The label that matched how I felt inside was "whore." The juxtaposition of my heart for God and my lust of the flesh caused me to doubt my salvation. I was afraid of being stoned by God.

A common assumption is that sex addicts are nothing more than moral failures who are weak of character and will. Clearly they must lack faith and genuine commitment to God. If they would only try harder and be more intentional in their Bible study and prayers, they wouldn't sin sexually. These beliefs are inaccurate and only compound an addict's shame. Perhaps like you, most sexually addicted women have prayed about their problem and begged God to free them from its power. They've read God's Word and been convicted of their sin. They have tried to stop and have been unable to maintain abstinence from inappropriate sexual behavior. If the solution were as simple as taking these steps, far fewer women would remain enslaved. Failure to stop acting out, despite their best intentions, only increases these women's shame. To be judged as nothing more than morally corrupt adds to that pain.

While sexual addiction is unquestionably sinful behavior, to stop with this explanation alone is to miss other critical factors that are involved. Sexual addiction is also a disease. It's not an "either-or" issue. It is "both/and." If the question is, Is it a disease or is it sin? the answer is yes. My guess is that if you personally struggle with sex addiction, you already intuitively understand this idea.

I'll discuss thoroughly the disease concept of addiction in chapter three. At this point, please simply accept the challenge to look beyond a one-dimensional, moral explanation for what is, in truth, a complex and multifaceted problem. Accepting sexual addiction as a bona fide disease doesn't in any way absolve an addict from responsibility for her sinful behavior. She clearly must admit her immorality, become convicted of her status as a sinner before God, repent of her actions and lust, and turn from her behavior. Her recovery will be temporary and shallow, however, if she only takes these spiritual steps.

Perhaps a helpful illustration is to compare sexual addiction to the disease of diabetes. While no one denies the clear biomedical nature of diabetes, we also understand the patient's responsibility to implement life-long choices in managing that disease. It is the foolish diabetic who shrugs her responsibility to modify her eating and lifestyle habits because she "has a disease" and "can't help it." In a similar way, it's up to the sexual addict to seek treatment for her disease of addiction and follow through consistently with those measures that are necessary for sobriety.

If the church and individual Christians want to help sexually addicted women—those "caught in adultery" as Scripture describes the woman brought to Jesus—they must put down their stones of condemnation and offer a way out. I'm not recommending excusing or condoning sexual addicts' behavior. I'm simply suggesting Christians move beyond the barrier of judgment and discard their stones of shame.

Even the Master said, "Neither do I condemn you" (John 8:11).

QUESTIONS FOR REFLECTION
OR SMALL GROUP DISCUSSION

1. What label(s) have you applied to yourself?

2. Have you told anyone about your struggle? What reaction did you get?

3. What is it like to find a book devoted to female sex addiction?

MESSAGES ABOUT

BEING FEMALE

The couple who sat in my office was in their early thirties and had been married several years. They had no children. Both were professionals who were successful and well respected in their fields. The wife came to our sessions meticulously groomed and wearing the latest fashion. Each spouse had been raised in a religious home, and they claimed to embrace general religious principles. They attended a mainstream Protestant church with some regularity.

The presenting problem was a growing distance in the relationship and a lack of marital intimacy. The wife had recently ended an affair, which she had disclosed to her husband. Over several sessions we had discussed the husband's reaction to the affair, how it had happened, and what it meant to each of them and to the relationship. Both wished to remain married to the other, and they wanted help figuring out how to make their marriage work.

So far our work together had seemed fairly standard, though certainly sad. My surprise came when we began exploring what this couple wanted their relationship to be like in the future. Both spouses were clear that the kind of emotional attachment the wife had known with her affair partner was harmful to their marriage. In fact, they felt the emotional part of the affair was more damaging than the sexual part. That kind of connection, they agreed, was clearly off limits. But the wife went on to explain she saw no problem with occasional, "uncomplicated" sexual liaisons. No emotional messiness, mind you. But pure sexual encounters were okay. Her reasoning went like this:

> The idea of monogamy is out of sync with today's culture. It just doesn't work. I know the Bible talks about it, but the Bible was written in a vastly different time. Back then people didn't have as many options and didn't live as long. They wouldn't have spent 40 or 50 years with a spouse. When the Bible talks about sexual fidelity to one person, it's in the same category as telling women to have long hair to cover their heads. It just doesn't apply to our times. Long-term marriage, and especially long-term sex, with one person can become so boring. As long as the emotional, "love" kind of stuff doesn't get involved, I see no problem with occasional one-night stands. The attention of a different guy makes me feel pretty and desired, which is always great for my self-esteem. I'm a happier person when I know I look good and some man wants me physically. As long as I stay emotionally committed to my marriage, what's wrong with a little excitement every now and then?

To my dismay, her husband agreed. "I'm glad you brought it up," he said. "I wouldn't have dared suggest it, but I think your idea is great!"

Despite my challenge to their thinking, this couple left my office pleased with the "new freedom" they'd agreed to in their marriage. They believed it would give them the excitement they wanted—and were obviously unwilling to cultivate with each other. They cancelled their next appointment, and I haven't heard from them since.

In my view this young wife fell prey to the unhealthy messages that bombard her from our culture. She believes her "happiness" is what's most important. Equally alarming, she thinks her beauty and attractiveness are what will make her happy. She thinks she'll find her validation as a woman from being with a variety of men. This wife also buys the idea that sexual monogamy is boring and unrealistic. She's swallowed the "more is better" mentality. Her attitudes may appear extreme, but actually they're the sadly predictable response to her environment.

CULTURAL MESSAGES

Today's culture offers powerful messages about women and about sex. These pervasive beliefs are woven through Western society so insidiously that we often internalize them without being consciously aware. Consider the ways you've bought into the following ideas.

Sex equals power. Culture portrays sexuality as a woman's ticket to getting almost anything she wants. Advertisers use sex to sell everything from soap to coffee to automobiles. The media trains women to use their bodies to manipulate, influence or control. Females learn to use seduction to get attention or to avoid responsibility. To be beautiful and sexy is to have power.

Even before they go to school most little girls are already aware of the power they possess in their sexuality. They can't articulate it as such, but they know it's there. Watch any dance class for young girls, and you'll observe them being specifically taught to shake their chests or rear ends and to move seductively. Adults applaud these children for being provocative and laugh at how "cute" they are. Modern cheerleaders are the same way. It's not just the scantily clad ones that "cheer" for professional football teams. In almost any high school gym on a Friday night, you'll see young women purposefully strutting their "stuff." It's a clear expectation of cheering; the question is, *cheering what?*

Packaging and presentation are all-important. The image of the perfect female body is held up as the measure of what it means to be a woman. Perfection is to have flawless skin, gorgeous hair, big breasts, a small waist, curvaceous hips and shapely legs. The packaging is more important than the product. Throw in the right makeup, clothes and perfume and a woman can supposedly have the world at her manicured fingertips. This message is part of the insidious impact of pornography. The perfectly sculpted bodies, smiling faces and exotic settings enhance the lie that a woman's sexuality is her all-important feature. Women and men alike compare their own bodies and experiences to those portrayed in pornography, and the result is always disappointment, perhaps even despair. Women often view porn featuring other women because they want to compare themselves to the images, not necessarily because they're attracted to the same sex. Dissatisfaction with their bodies, which is greatly influenced by culture as well as pornography, leads many women into the dangerous world of eating disorders as they try to starve or purge themselves into matching the image of the "beautiful" female.

If ya' got it, flaunt it. Today's culture also trains women to be exhibitionists. You need only watch one of the television award shows like the Emmys or the Oscars to see this displayed. Females are dressed in less and less, with ever plunging necklines, higher and higher slits, and thinner and thinner material. The titillation effect is paramount. The press devotes a great deal of attention to describing these so-called gowns and the daring of the women who wear them. Mainstream news anchors also sport short skirts, oiled legs and low tops. It's the norm.

Exhibitionism, though, isn't limited to celebrities. Truck drivers report their high perch gives them a clear view of females who expose themselves to passing drivers. Women who show their bodies aren't naïve. They know what they're doing arouses lust.

Anita, a sex addict who was struggling in her recovery, admitted being obsessed with her own body. She would stand naked in front of a mirror and fret she didn't measure up to the women she saw in her favorite Internet pornography sites. She frequented a tanning salon and believed she was more attractive with even, darker skin. One day Anita decided to get some real sun by lying out on her back deck. She gathered her towels and lotions and arranged herself in the sunshine. She knew the neighbors on either side of her house weren't home, and she slipped out of her bathing suit to lie totally naked. But Anita wasn't expecting privacy. She was well aware there were telephone repairmen working high on the poles near her backyard.

She confessed she became very aroused by the thought of the men staring at her and masturbated several times while she was sunning. She admitted one reason she laid out naked was for the excitement of being seen. She explained she saw her actions as a kind of "gift" she could give the utility workers. "Everyone knows guys dream about that kind of thing," she said.

Part of Anita's acting out was due to her sexual addiction, but in this example she was also fulfilling her culture's message that men are always hungry to see female flesh and that beautiful women should be happy to oblige them.

Everyone is having sex. The notion of the ideal female, again greatly bolstered by pornography, also implies constant sexual availability. The modern woman has been freed from Victorian constraints and ushered into the age of the postsexual revolution. At every turn the media shows women being sexually interested and available. No matter how busy, how tired, how stressed, or how they're treated by their partners, women on TV and in the movies quickly put those concerns aside for a passionate encounter. Sex seems to be the medicine for all of life's ills.

Today's teenagers and young adults assume sexual availability is the norm. "Friends with benefits" describes people who have sex together without any pretense at romance. They simply agree to be sexual without any strings attached, and they view the interaction as mutually beneficial. Oral sex is the favored activity because it avoids the risk of unwanted pregnancy. Many teens and young adults, in fact, don't consider oral sex as *sex;* it's just something they do with their bodies. As long as it's consensual, there's no problem.

Culture tells women that any willing sexual partner, whether male or female, is okay as long as both are unmarried. Any social taboo against same-sex activity has been replaced with cultural endorsement. Women having sex with women is considered especially arousing for both genders. Same-sex experimentation is viewed as normal and rarely raises any eyebrows.

Sex equals love. Culture also defines the standard for romanticism. Popular movies, songs, books and television shows depict the "perfect" couple who enjoys the "perfect" relationship. A large part of that relationship is usually sexual. The passion is supposedly equal to the depth of the connection. Compatible couples aren't shown as sometimes disagreeing, or resolving conflict or compromising. The message delivered loud and clear is *if it's intense, it must be right.* What matters most is the giddy feeling of being "in love."

Many women, then, find themselves continually disappointed in their partners and their relationships. Real life just isn't like the media portrays it. This discrepancy may lead women to buy into one of Satan's most powerful lies: *I must have married the wrong man.* When the relationship hits rocky ground and requires hard work, women may be tempted to look for something easier. When you expect to live a fairy tale, forging through real life seems very bland. Many females first get involved in addictive behavior through chasing the butterfly of romance, looking for that perfect man who must be the right one.

RELIGIOUS MESSAGES

Secular culture isn't the only environment sending women faulty messages. Though much more subtle and often shrouded in "churchy" language, the religious culture delivers inappropriate messages, as well. Think of how you've encountered the following viewpoints from religion.

Women are inferior to men. The biblical view of the high place of women gets flipped into an unbiblical tenant about male domination and female "submission." While a full discussion of this idea is beyond the scope of this book, it's clear God didn't intend his crowning creation to become a doormat to men's needs or desires. The religious community often glorifies women the most for being servants. The church urges females to see caretaking as their most important role. Some pastors teach a woman's worth is based on what she does, especially for the men in her life. This programming creates a ripe breeding ground for dependent, unhealthy relationships where a woman is willing to do anything, including sexual things, to get and keep a man. So-called Christian romance novels contribute to the message that the male-female relationship is what's most important.

Sex is wrong. The religious world also sends mixed messages about female sexuality. It encourages women to look sexy but condemns them for having sex. The church preaches it's positive to be feminine, frilly and flirtatious, but it's wrong to be sexually active. Even within a Christian marriage, women receive few positive messages about the beauty, enjoyment and fulfillment of the sexual relationship. Wives are instructed to please their husbands, but they aren't given permission also to please themselves. Sex is considered a wife's duty, not her desire.

Sadly, this double message about Christian sexuality leads many teenage girls and young women into the realm of "technical virginity." Because of the strong teaching against premarital sex, which is certainly appropriate, females may observe the letter of the law but still engage in all kinds of intense sexual activity that doesn't involve intercourse. Many women, especially younger ones, believe that oral sex doesn't compromise virginity. Adolescent females may discover through experimentation that they do, indeed, possess strong, pleasurable sexual responses. As long as these responses don't lead to actual intercourse, the church remains silent about sexual behavior. Rosenau and Wilson address this issue in their excellent book *Soul Virgins: Redefining Single Sexuality.*[1]

The confusing double standard is that it's acceptable for women to want to be admired as beautiful and even to go after that notice as long as they don't "give in" to the attention in a fully sexual way. What a setup for sexual failure.

Christian marriages don't struggle with sexual issues. The church is sadly silent about healthy sexuality in marriage, and the assumption is that if both spouses are Christian, they'll automatically experience healthy sexuality in their relationship as long as both remain faithful. This premise, of course, hinges on both partners being virgins when they marry. If a husband and wife have both managed to keep that bottom-line boundary, they're home free. They'll be blessed with a fulfilling, no hassles sexual relationship—at least for the man.

Among other things, this message ignores the vast numbers of men and women who are sexual abuse survivors. We'll examine this trauma in detail in chapter eight, but this violation significantly affects a woman's view of herself, of her partner and her beliefs about sex. Sexual abuse taints and distorts your attitudes about relationships as well as sexual activity itself. Abuse has enormous effects that flood a relationship and drench a marriage bed.

As discussed in the first chapter, Christians seem to totally overlook the idea that women can struggle with sex and love addiction. Good, godly women just don't have those kinds of problems!

DOUBLE BIND

Clearly, culture and religion both dish out compelling and contradictory messages about sex and about what it means to be female. Kelly McDaniel gives a powerful description of these messages in her book *Ready to Heal: Women Facing Love, Sex, and Relationship Addiction.*[2] These clashing messages create enormous difficulty for women by setting up what's called a "double bind." That means the opposing messages create an impossible dilemma: You're doomed no matter which way you believe and act. In any scenario, you lose. You're caught in an impossible quandary without any solution. Kelly describes four cultural beliefs that mirror and overlap those we've examined.

I must be good to be worthy of love. From their earliest training girls are taught to be good. Especially in Christian homes, good is an exceptionally high standard. Girls are to be polite, conforming and self-sacrificing. They must obey parents, authority figures and men in general. Females must be capable in every area, yet remain humble. In this conditional environment if you're good enough, you'll earn love.

If I'm sexual, I'm bad. In this regard, culture echoes religion in condemning wanton sexuality. Being sexual is the automatic opposite of being good. This belief requires you to suppress or deny any sexual feelings in order to be acceptable. Sex is potentially dangerous, and you indulge sexual feelings and activity at your peril.

I must be sexual to be lovable. In conjunction with the already conflicting first two cultural beliefs, this third one creates an impossible catch-22. If you have to earn love and you do that only by being good; and if being sexual is bad, yet you must be sexual to be lovable, you're doomed in an unbearable predicament. It's a hopeless trap. Being lovable and loved is an innate desire of the human heart. It's

God-given and holy. Yet the only way to achieve this compelling longing is to do something that negates the very thing you're after. This impasse is unsolvable.

I'm not really a woman unless someone desires me sexually or romantically. Again, the premise of fairy tales, Hollywood and fantasy is that a woman is incomplete without a man. She must be pursued in order to be worthy. If she's not in a relationship or having sex, she doesn't measure up as a woman. She's flawed. Inadequate.

My guess is that you're well acquainted with the gridlock of these double binds. Whether from culture or religion, you're wounded by impossible, conflicting expectations. All women are affected. How much greater, though, is the shame of the woman whose sexual appetites and activities are out of control. My prayer is that this book provides a window into your shame and a pathway to your healing. Just as Jesus offered compassion and hope to the woman found in adultery two thousand years ago, he extends the same grace to the sexually addicted woman today.

QUESTIONS FOR REFLECTION
OR SMALL GROUP DISCUSSION

1. What cultural messages have affected you the most?

2. What messages did you get from the church about sex?

3. Which double bind(s) weighs heaviest for you?

4. How has your acting out affected your view of sex?

CHAPTER THREE

DEFINITION OF ADDICTION

The Bible isn't silent when it comes to addiction. Hundreds of verses, particularly in the Psalms, are cries for deliverance from brokenness. Many addicts find great comfort as they apply those confessions and pleas to their own pain. Some of the greatest Bible writers, including David and Paul, speak about their struggles. Romans 7 is a passage clearly applicable to any addict's experience:

> I do not understand what I do. For what I want to do I do not do, but what I hate I do. . . . For I have the desire to do what is good, but I cannot carry it out. For what I do is not the good I want to do; no, the evil I do not want to do—this I keep on doing. Now if I do what I do not want to do, it is no longer I who do it, but it is sin living in me that does it. . . . What a wretched man I am! (Romans 7:15, 18-20, 24)

If the apostle Paul, who was one of the greatest spiritual leaders and teachers of all time, was unable to stop "doing what I do not want to do," is it any wonder that Christians today are also unsuccessful? The reason, I believe, lies in the disease concept of addiction. While I've clearly established that sexually addictive behavior is unequivocally sinful behavior—indeed, the passage in Romans 7 discusses the "sinful nature"—that description alone is insufficient and inaccurate. Factors are at work beyond the "choice" to engage in sin.

At some point, a woman, even a Christian woman, can lose her capacity to make rational choices about her behavior. The Romans passage illustrates some of the elements that I'll explain are components of conceptualizing addiction as a disease.

We readily accept that alcohol can be addictive. After all, alcohol is a substance that's taken into the body. There's obviously a physiological, chemical reaction. But having sex or gambling doesn't involve ingesting a chemical. How could such behaviors become an addiction?

DEFINITION OF ADDICTION

Patrick Carnes, Ph.D., a secular clinician, has supplied one of the simplest, yet most helpful definitions of addiction. Carnes is considered the pioneer teacher and researcher in the field of sexual addiction—the "grandfather" of the recovery emphasis in this area. Most of the knowledge and understanding about this problem is based on his work. Carnes's definition is that being addicted is to have a pathological relationship with a mood-altering substance or behavior.[1] Two concepts, mood-altering and pathological, are critical.

All of us are familiar with altering our moods. We use a variety of substances and behaviors to either energize us or calm us down. Many use caffeine in the mornings to elevate their mood (I confess to being a recovering caffeine addict). Others use nicotine to mellow anxiety or tension. Maybe you relax by watching TV or going for a country drive. Runners get a "high" through exercise. We take deep breaths when we're feeling stressed. The variety of possibilities for mood alteration is nearly endless.

Pathological is the second important concept. To have a pathological relationship with a person, behavior or thing is to have a *diseased* relationship—an unhealthy or harmful one. That's a key point. Not all the ways we alter our moods are unhealthy. Many of us have found that music, for example, is a good way to alter our moods. I enjoy soft jazz when I'm feeling tense and need to unwind. On the other hand, when I'm feeling down and need a pickup, I choose upbeat praise and worship music. That's an appropriate way to alter mood.

Thinking about addiction in this light, then, we can understand that sex first skids toward being addictive when it's used primarily as a mood adjuster in an unhealthy, harmful way. Do you use sex to soothe the ache of loneliness? To release the heat of anger or quiet anxiety? Contrast that description of sexual activity with God's plan for sex to be part of the "one flesh" relationship between a wife and her husband. The sexual relationship is intended to be a celebration of the commitment and connection between spouses—a union that enhances the joy of the relationship. An intimacy that isn't tainted by either sin or negative consequences. Does that describe your sexual and relational behavior?

CONTINUUM OF ADDICTION

Next, it's important to understand that acting out can fall along a continuum of behaviors, which is illustrated in figure 1.

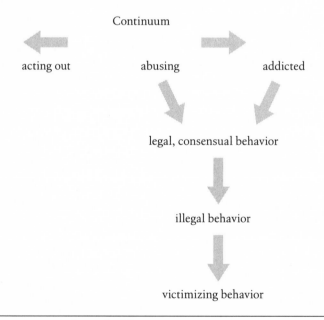

Figure 1. Continuum of sexual addiction

It's rarely possible to identify the discrete point when a woman's behavior crosses the line into being an addiction. For most women that progression can only be pinpointed with the benefit of looking back after some time in recovery. Even then, it's usually possible only to identify the pattern of decline and not one individual moment. To ask, *how much sex is required to be a sexaholic?* is like asking, *how much do you have to drink to be an alcoholic?* There's not a clear-cut answer.

In thinking about this continuum, consider what you know about drinking behavior. It's possible for a woman to fit the old-fashioned description *teetotaler* and never to consume alcohol at all. That's one end of the spectrum. Next, some women may drink socially or occasionally and do so responsibly. Then a woman may abuse alcohol at times by either drinking too much (binging) or too often. She may abuse alcohol rarely and drink responsibly the rest of the time, or she may escalate to abusing alcohol routinely. From the point of abusing, a woman can easily slide into the dependency of addiction.

Let's apply the continuum concept to sexual behavior. For the moment, think in objective terms simply about categories of behavior rather than considering the morality or appropriateness of the behavior. On the teetotaler end of the spectrum is the woman who doesn't engage in sexual activity of any kind, either with herself or with a partner. Next, would be the woman who is appropriate and responsible in her sexual behavior. (In Christian terms, this would be the married woman who is sexual only with her husband.) Neither of these expressions of sexuality is shown on the continuum.

The diagram begins at the next point. *Acting out* describes the woman who occasionally acts out sexually either alone through pornography or masturbation or with a willing partner who is not her husband. Next, she may come to *abuse* her sexuality through promiscuity or excessive sex with herself. From there, she may cross the line into sexual addiction. Just as with drinking behavior, sexual activity can fall anywhere along this continuum.

As illustrated, sexually addictive behavior has different levels in terms of legality. (Remember, for the moment we're ignoring the morality of these behaviors.) A first level is the woman who engages in legal, consensual behaviors. Examples include viewing pornography, masturbating excessively, being promiscuous or having affairs. A next level is engaging in behaviors that are illegal but seldom have serious legal consequences. Examples include exhibitionism, voyeurism or prostitution. Offending behaviors are the final level. These carry severe legal consequences and constitute sexual abuse such as child molestation or rape.

It's important to note that sexual addiction *does not* normally progress to sexual offending behaviors in either men or women. While many sexual offenders are sex addicts (especially regarding pornography use), there isn't a linear progression that implies a sex addict will go on to sexual offending if untreated. Sexual offending is a different category with its own characteristics and pathology, and the topic is beyond the scope of this book. The overwhelming majority of sex abusers are male. However, an increasing number of female teachers are seducing their students. A number of highly publicized cases involve middle or high school female teachers who are sexual with students. One teacher had the student's child, and they even married when she was released from prison. This kind of extreme boundary violation is victimizing and offending behavior.

SEXUAL SIN AS CONTRASTED WITH SEXUAL ADDICTION

For those readers who aren't from the Christian community, let me clarify my position about sexual sin, for it is the foundation for this book. From a spiritual standpoint, I unequivocally believe God's creation of healthy sexual expression is limited to one woman and one man who are married to each other for life. Therefore, I define unholy or sinful sexual activity as that which occurs outside the confines of marriage such as nonmarital or extramarital sex, prostitution, pornography, cybersex and so forth. However, it is *not* true that an affair or nonmarital sexual activity or occasional pornography use automatically classifies someone as a sexual addict. That kind of sexual activity is outside God's design, but it is not necessarily addictive. While all sexually addictive behavior is sinful, the reverse isn't always true. Sexual sin is not, by definition, sexual addiction.

CHARACTERISTICS OF ADDICTION

So what makes a behavior fit the definition of addiction? Clinicians and addictionists generally agree that certain elements must be present for a substance or behavior to qualify as addictive: compulsion, obsession, and continuation despite adverse consequences.[2] Many professionals add the element of tolerance, which I believe is accurate. Credit again goes to Patrick Carnes for outlining how sexual or relational behavior can fit the classic model of the disease concept of addiction.[3]

1. Compulsion. Because we better understand alcoholism, that addiction again provides a helpful illustration of these four concepts. Alcoholics report being compelled to drink, which means drinking even when they don't want to. You're familiar with the alcoholic who makes repeated promises to avoid getting drunk or spending her grocery money on booze. She sincerely intends to keep those promises when she makes them. She's not just mouthing words; her desire is strong. Yet when she takes the first drink, she finds she can't stop, and she continues drinking until she's done exactly what she promised she wouldn't do. The same is true for sexual and relational behavior. "It's like some force within me takes over," Carol explains. "I sit down at the computer just planning to check my e-mail and the weather forecast. Then, even though I've decided I won't give in any more, I feel this overwhelming urge to surf for pornography. I'm powerless to fight it. Just like poison ivy, it's an itch that absolutely demands to be scratched."

Compulsion also describes the desire to act out, not just the loss of control when you do. "Feeling driven" is the way many addicts describe it. "I know it's wrong and it's not good for me, but it feels like some automatic switch inside gets flipped, and I'm on this train I can't stop," Candace describes. "I just *have* to call my affair partner no matter how much I tell myself it's a bad idea."

Compulsion is key to any addiction. It's the defining characteristic that separates the sexual sinner from the sex addict. The addict simply can't stop even when she truly wants to, which is the element clearly described in the passage quoted from Romans 7. Compulsion means that you've lost control and engage in an activity or ingest a substance even if you've determined not to. While all addictions begin with an initial choice to use a substance or engage in a behavior, eventually addicts lose the ability to make rational choices in the moment.

2. Obsession. A second characteristic of addiction is obsession. To be obsessed is to be intensely, abnormally preoccupied with something. The object of the obsession is all-consuming. The addict ignores other areas of life and focuses attention on the person, activity, or substance.

Brenda, for example, was delighted when her husband got her the home computer she'd wanted for Christmas. She first explored sites of general interest like the weather, business news and shopping tips. Within a week, though, Brenda was obsessed with Internet sexual activity. "I don't even remember January and February," she confessed when she came for treatment in early March. "Those months are totally gone. I guess I cooked some and cared minimally for my kids. I know I went to work, physically, at least. But all I could think about was finding more pornography or hanging out in a sexual chat room. I was totally consumed."

For other women the problem isn't pornography or other sexual activity; it's a relationship. Melissa described it this way:

> I was totally obsessed with my affair partner. He was all I could think about and my whole world revolved around him. Before I got a cell phone, I wouldn't leave my house for fear I'd miss his call. I wouldn't take the kids to the park or go to the grocery store. When I did have to get out, I'd be angry and rush through whatever I was doing. When I first opened my eyes in the morning, I thought about him. I jumped every time the phone rang. I lived for the few minutes we could talk each day. When I went to sleep at night, I dreamed about him. He was the total focus of my life.

3. Continuing despite adverse consequences. It's the third characteristic of addiction that's hardest for most nonaddicts to comprehend. Continuing to do something that harms you just doesn't make sense, yet that's a hallmark sign of an addiction. In fact, this characteristic is the central feature of addictive behavior. Think of the alcoholic who's been arrested for two DUIs but continues to drink and drive. Eventually, all addicts suffer negative consequences because of their behavior, but they keep doing what they've always done. That kind of pattern seems crazy, and it *is* crazy. Obviously, there's a force of denial operating here. The addict seems to believe that this time the results will be different. This time she won't get caught or this time she won't get pregnant. In fact, a standard slogan from Twelve Step recovery programs describes this phenomenon: *To keep doing the same thing and expecting different results is the definition of insanity.* Kara's story illustrates this point well.

> I didn't think it would happen to me. I knew I shouldn't have unprotected sex, but it was so much hassle to use a condom. And most guys don't like them. Besides, if I carried condoms with me, that meant I was planning on having sex. I got a minor STD once in college, but after a big shot of penicillin, I was fine. I didn't really think about it anymore.
>
> I felt like I was being sexual with respectable guys. I didn't pick up men in bars or anything like that. I knew these guys. I went to school with them or worked with them. Some I even went to church with. Then one guy gave me herpes. That was scary, but I learned how to manage the outbreaks. It wasn't so bad. I knew I should probably stop sleeping around, but I never seemed able to quit.
>
> Now I'm HIV positive. I can't believe I was so stupid! Why didn't I stop being promiscuous when I first got an STD?

The inability to stop a behavior or using a substance is one of the clearest signs of an addiction. Paul describes it in Romans 7, quoted at the beginning of this chapter, as continuing to do what he did not want to do. The addict has passed the point of exercising choice. She's addicted and cannot stop, no matter how much she may want to or how much she tries. As Virginia explains, "Actually, I could stop. I just couldn't *stay* stopped. I probably broke it off with my affair partner 437 times! But within a day or a week I was back with him. I always reconnected, despite all the promises I made to myself and to God."

All addicts describe this element of *powerlessness*. It's the first step of the Twelve Steps of Alcoholics Anonymous: "We admitted we were

powerless over alcohol and that our lives had become unmanageable."
Female sex addicts report a variety of ways they've tried to stop, control or manage their behavior without success. Regardless of the negative consequences, which I'll outline in detail in chapter five, an addict
continues to act out when she's suffering from full-blown addiction.

4. Tolerance. In my view, an important fourth component of an
addiction is tolerance, which refers to a neurochemical process.
Again, alcohol provides a clear explanation. If a woman never used
alcohol, one drink could make her feel tipsy. Her brain chemistry
would react to the ingestion of alcohol to create that high feeling. But
if she continued to have a drink every day, quickly her body would
adjust so that one drink would no longer have the same effect. Eventually, in fact, she wouldn't feel the effects of one drink at all. It would
take two drinks and then three and so forth, to achieve the same result. That's the factor of tolerance at work.

Still, though, sexual activity is behavior. It's not like drinking alcohol
or taking drugs. How can behavior affect a woman's brain chemistry?
The answer requires that we look at the neurochemistry of addiction.

NEUROCHEMISTRY OF ADDICTION

Scientists and researchers are learning new things about human brain
chemistry every day. One of the discoveries is how behaviors affect
the chemical reactions in the brain. Two initial and leading researchers into this area are Harvey Milkman and Stanley Sunderwirth,
whose classic book is *Craving for Ecstasy: The Consciousness and
Chemistry of Escape.*[4] They first determined that sexual response is
as much a function of the brain as it is the genitals. Endorphins (the
body's natural painkillers), adrenaline, and various other peptides,
enzymes and chemicals are all affected by sexual activity.

Without going into detailed medical descriptions, let's consider an
elementary explanation of the neurochemistry of addiction. In simple
terms, sexual response is a function of the brain's nervous system. It's
an unconscious, automatic process like heart rate or respiration. During sexual stimulation certain chemical reactions increase in the
brain. For example, dopamine levels, which are tied to the feelings of

both boredom and depression, are increased by the influx of adrenaline that is part of sexual activity. When our dopamine level goes up, we feel better. (This reaction explains the stimulus-seeking nature of some addicts: They're after the adrenaline rush that boosts dopamine, and often they're using sex to induce it.) Likewise, when humans experience skin-to-skin contact, that touch releases oxytocin into the brain, which is associated with feelings of well-being, pleasure and attachment. This hormone facilitates bonding and connection, which, of course, is an important component of sexual activity. Further, the intense ecstasy felt during sexual activity is partially the result of opiate-like substances called catecholamines. These reactions are pure biology.

Do you see where I'm going with these examples? What woman wouldn't want to feel energized, stimulated or flooded with feel-good sensations? These neurochemical responses are obviously pleasurable. They also are governed by the concept of tolerance, which means that eventually more and more activity is required to get the same positive result, just as more and more alcohol eventually is necessary to achieve the same high.

And what a high it is! The pleasure center of the brain, the nucleus accumbens, processes ingested chemicals such as alcohol, nicotine, marijuana and cocaine—in fact, everything known to generate pleasurable feelings. All the neurochemical reward pathways run through a single pleasure center and operate according to similar reward principles. Researchers have proven what addicts have known for a long time: that sexual activity can provide a high equal to crack cocaine. The neurochemical process is identical. Doesn't that shed new light on the addictive nature of sexual behavior? Crack cocaine is powerful stuff.

These brain reactions are further affected by accompanying emotions such as arousal and fear. Obviously, arousal is a huge part of sexual activity. Fear may be a factor, as well, like when an addict is afraid of being discovered or takes greater risks in her sexual activity.

It's impossible to overemphasize the importance of this neurochemical component of sex addiction. And orgasm isn't necessarily required to cause neurochemical changes. Mere fantasy or preoccupation is sufficient. The addict literally carries within her own brain a constant supply of powerful drugs. She can get high on her own brain chemicals even without any specific physical or sexual behavior. Addicts thus become pharmacologists of their own brains as they seek to find escape, excitement or medication for their pain through sexual activity.

Prolonged sexual acting out can alter brain chemistry to the point that more activity is required to achieve the same high. The baseline level is reset, so to speak. Thus, sexual addiction is a progressive disease, where more and more acting out must be done for the addict to get the same hit. An escalation factor kicks in because of the phenomenon of tolerance.

Dr. Mark Laaser boldly asserts the implication of this physiological fact: *For the sex addict, there is never enough sex.* Tolerance demands more and more. As Laaser explains, that reality means that biological sexual desire can never be satisfied biologically.[5] For addicts, who are using sexual activity to alter their moods and medicate their pain instead of to celebrate a one-flesh union with a spouse, the sexual appetite is insatiable.

Neurochemistry, then, partially explains the discomfort addicts feel when they stop acting out. Although some of the distress comes from not medicating painful emotions with sex, part of that pain is a true neurochemical response. As the brain adjusts to decreasing levels of certain chemicals, the addict feels the changes. Many women report feeling anxious, moody, depressed, sad, angry and so forth, when they stop acting out. Some experience withdrawal-like symptoms. Sherry describes it this way:

> I literally thought I would die when I first tried to stop acting out. My whole body ached, kind of like I had the flu. I had awful mood swings and unexplained temper fits. I felt overwhelming anxiety to the point where I was afraid I was becoming paranoid. It was indescribable.

We'll explore withdrawal later in chapter twelve, but this reality sheds further light on why addicts continue to act out despite the negative consequences they suffer. The enticement of this neurochemical high, combined with the pain of withdrawal, pulls a woman repeatedly back into her behavior. The brain reactions are simply more powerful than the pain of external consequences, at least for a time.

The good news is that it's possible to override this neurochemical response. One of the first tasks of recovery is to go through a period of total sexual abstinence, which allows the brain to reset to a lower chemical threshold. I'll explain this process more in chapter twelve. The important point to understand for now is that sexual activity does, in reality, involve true physiological responses that contribute to addiction. In fact, many sex addicts who are also chemically addicted emphasize that getting sober sexually is much harder than becoming chemically sober.

ISN'T IT SIMPLY SIN?

Sexual addiction is clearly more than simply sin. Addressing the problem through only religious solutions is incomplete and doomed to failure. All the prayer, Bible study, church attendance and repentance in the world won't change the course of a life-threatening disease. Please don't misunderstand. I believe totally in the power of these acts of faith and commitment. I practice them regularly. They're key in my life and key to my sobriety and serenity. But these steps alone aren't what got me sober. In fact, sincerely performing these steps nearly every day for years didn't keep me from continuing in my addiction. Sobriety requires more.

I also don't want to discount or ignore the possibility of deliverance or supernatural healing from disease. However, to get drawn into that debate is to be detoured from this book's focus. In my experience, those who claim to have been delivered from a sexual addiction may, indeed, be technically sober (not acting out), but they're what alcoholics term a *dry drunk*. That means one or more of several things. She may be *acting in* or *white knuckling*, which will both be described further in the next chapter. The delivered person often hasn't dealt with the deep roots beneath the behavior. She usually isn't participating in healthy fellowship with others who know her whole story, and she isn't enjoying the benefits of true serenity and intimate connection.

Instead of delivering, I believe God blesses and empowers people with the intelligence and knowledge to address the problems in their lives. God has equipped human creation with the capability to split the atom, to travel to the moon, to build amazing structures and to cure diseases. It is insufficient—and indeed, I believe, wrong—to sit back and trust God to heal cancer or heart disease or addiction and do nothing to help yourself by taking advantage of the knowledge and tools available in treating those diseases.

Again, let me be clear. Labeling sexual addiction as a disease does not in any way remove one iota of responsibility from the addict. Just as it's irresponsible for my diabetic friend to do nothing more than pray about her condition and increase her Bible reading, it's wrong for the addicted person to claim lack of culpability because she has a disease. To take that stance is a form of sinful rebellion in and of itself. It's the height of victimhood and irresponsibility.

If our bodies are the temple of God, as they're described in 1 Corinthians 6:19, then we are responsible for doing everything in our power, including using psychological and medical tools, to maintain that temple as holy and pleasing to God (descriptions from Romans 12:1). To consider ourselves as God's vessels, in fact, *increases* our responsibility for healthy self-care and holy living, not decreases it.

RELIGIOUS BAND-AID®

When we use prayer, Bible study or other religious acts as the only weapons against complex life problems like addiction, I believe we're using these spiritual tools as impotent religious Band-Aids. God intended them to be expressions of devotion and vehicles of intimacy with him. They're not meant to be punch-tickets for removing pain.

I'm reminded of the story about the couple who was preparing to answer God's call to the mission field in a faraway land. Financial support was slow in coming and the husband was getting discouraged. Finally he told his wife he was just going to sit back and pray for God to meet their needs. She replied, "Well, while you're praying, I'm going to keep preaching about the cause and packing!" That's the perfect illustration of the balance between faith and action.

Addressing the problem of addiction requires a dual approach: using every spiritual tool available and using every medical, behavioral and psychological tool, as well. In fact, I believe to sit back and pray about an addiction without "preaching" and "packing" is the course of avoiding responsibility rather than of assuming responsibility. The disease concept of addiction does not negate the theological reality of sin.

Historically, the church has done an excellent job of exhorting Christians to practice valuable religious disciplines. The church has failed miserably, however, to encourage Christians to use other, more worldly tools to fight sinful behavior and addictive diseases. In fact, the church has often shamed those who used resources like therapy or medication or Twelve Step programs as treatment for their addictions. Rather than offering grace and help to struggling believers, the church has usually been quick to "shoot its wounded" as Charles Swindoll describes it.[6]

It's time (actually, it's way past time) for the church to stop throwing stones at women who are sexually addicted and instead, to encourage them toward informed approaches that are proven to help.

QUESTIONS FOR REFLECTION
OR SMALL GROUP DISCUSSION

1. Where do you place yourself on the acting out continuum?

2. How have you tried to stop your behavior? Describe the results of your efforts to stop—your successes or failures.

3. Describe how your mood alters when you act out.

CHAPTER FOUR

FEMALE PRESENTATIONS

OF SEXUAL ADDICTION

Often women experience great difficulty identifying themselves as being sexually addicted. In addition to the denial factor and the shame of accepting that label, there's confusion about the nature of sex addiction. Part of the problem is the belief that this addiction is about sex. In fact, it's not about sex at all. A Christian woman, married with young children and a teacher in a private Christian school, explains this truth best:

> Why is this called "sex addiction"? I hate that label! Don't you get that it's not about the sex! Sex is just what I have to give to get what I really want, which is love, and touch, and nurture and assurance I'm okay.

Some sexually addicted women don't even enjoy the sexual experiences. They either tolerate or endure the sex because of the larger payoff: the connection (however false and temporary) or the medication of emotional pain.

Women also often don't understand the myriad faces of sexual addiction, which makes it difficult to identify. "I'm not a prostitute or nymphomaniac," said one woman. "How could I be a sex addict?"

Her question is important. Again, in the early misconceptions about alcoholism, many people thought someone had to be a gutter drunk to be an alcoholic. We understand now the so-called functional alcoholic also has a problem. While there is a continuum to addiction with impairment ranging from mild to very severe, there are typical presentations of how sex addiction shows up in females.

UMBRELLA TERM

I think it's helpful to consider *sex addiction* as an umbrella term that covers a wide range of behaviors. In a similar way, we use *alcoholism* to describe that disease whether the drink of choice is wine or whiskey or champagne. While some clinicians and authors use different terms to delineate the differences in forms of acting out, I use the broad name *sex addiction* to refer to any or all of the presentations. At their core, I believe they all have the same roots and involve the same dynamics. Any differences are more about the specifics of the acting out behaviors themselves, rather than any substantial elements of the thought processes or the addictive experiences.

I encourage you to be gentle with yourself and not stress about whether you're sexually addicted or if so, in what form. Accepting a label isn't what's important. Healing is what matters. Try to consider the following descriptions with an open mind and see how one or more might reflect your experience.

1. Relationship or love addict. In general, females' sexual addiction is more relational than males'. Acting out usually involves another person. The story from John 8 that opened this book typifies the first kind of female sex addict: the woman who is an adulteress. Certainly, not every woman who has an affair is a sex addict, but a pattern of affairs or promiscuity can be a sign of addiction or potential addiction. Clinicians sometimes refer to this type as a relationship addict or love addict. (Again, I think those labels are accurate descriptions. For convenience I simply use "sex addict" as an all-inclusive designation.)

The relationship or love addict is the woman who repeatedly is involved in affairs or multiple relationships, whether she's married or single. These relationships are sometimes serial (happening in rapid sequence, one right after the other), or sometimes they are even simultaneous. One woman describes the complicated situation caused by her addiction:

> At one point I was involved romantically and sexually with the man who lived across the street and the man who lived next door. The man next door was supposedly giving me spiritual advice on how to break up with the man across the street. Juggling them both required the skills of an air traffic controller. I'd go in the back door of the house across the street and the side door of the house next door. I had to lie to both of them about where I'd been. Each was jealous of the other and suspected I was involved with them both. I was also married and had two young children. It was crazy!

While not all relationship addicts are this out of control, the pattern is the same. A woman goes from lover to lover trying to fill the awful black hole inside. When she becomes disenchanted with her current man, she goes looking elsewhere. Surely if she experiments enough, she'll find the "right" one. Her addiction is the manifestation of her desperate search for real love.

Sometimes these relationships are emotionally dependent but not necessarily sexual. For the woman who values reserving sex until marriage, this situation is frequently the case. Whether sexual or not, the relational addict forges an often desperate attachment to a partner, whom she views as her soul mate. She feels lost without him and burdens him with her expectations. She wants him to meet her every need, preferably before she asks. She expects him to read her mind, and she feels hurt or angry when he doesn't. She demands undivided attention and reacts in jealousy if he pursues a separate interest. She may smother him with her neediness or affection, and she punishes him if he pulls away. She's manipulative or controlling and confuses these behaviors with love.

Some women experience an especially painful push-pull dynamic in significant relationships. It's often described by the powerful, conflicting declarations, *I hate you! Don't leave me!* The woman may first idealize her partner and want to be immersed in him, then when he fails to live up to her expectations, she flips and decides she hates him. Even while filled with this intensely negative emotion, she is terrified of abandonment and is devastated if he leaves her. This pattern of relationship upheaval is a red flag for clinicians, who will work with a woman to determine if she may be suffering from an underlying personality disorder that warrants specific treatment.

These emotionally dependent relationships may be same-sex or opposite sex. Some women, especially those who have attachment issues with their mothers, which will be described in chapter nine, develop these obsessive relationships with other women instead of with men. An intense, same-sex friendship offers the nurturing a woman may have lacked from her mother. Because women can intuitively understand each other, another female may provide a unique bond that feels primal. Especially if the relationship isn't overtly sexual, it's often hard for a woman to identify it as problematic.

This kind of female-to-female relationship is different from the healthy connection that recovering women need as part of a supportive community. I'll discuss healthy relationships at length in chapter fourteen. The addictive relationship is possessive and consuming. A woman loses herself and places her focus on her partner. Similar to an unhealthy opposite sex relationship, a woman may be clingy, demanding or manipulative with a female partner. These relationships, whether same-sex or opposite sex, are often referred to as *enmeshed.*

Sometimes the intense emotional connection creates sexual feelings, and a woman may act out sexually with her female partner even though she considers herself heterosexual. She may wonder, then, if she's lesbian and this confusion often creates more shame. One woman said,

> I've always been sexually attracted to men, and I never thought I'd be in a lesbian relationship. I don't really think I'm gay. I just know I've never felt this way about anybody. Kathy listens to me and holds me and believes in me the way I've always wanted. The sex is good, too, because as a woman, she understands my body. But I feel like I've crossed a line. This is worse than the sleeping around I've done before, and it's harder to admit. I'd die if my parents knew what was really going on.

Intensity is the hallmark characteristic of addictive relationships regardless of gender coupling. Women frequently mistake intensity for *intimacy*. Some of the adjectives used to describe variations of this kind of unhealthy intensity include exciting, volatile, dependent, mysterious, powerful, dramatic, enmeshed, profound, passionate and haunting.

Remember, any relationship may at times feel intense or have some of the other characteristics described above. That's part of the normal ebb and flow of imperfect human interactions. The relationship or love addict has a pattern of these kinds of relationships that continues even when she recognizes they're not in her best interest, and she tries to stop.

2. Romance addict. Some women are more interested in the chase and intrigue of falling in love than they are in the relationship itself. These women are often called romance addicts. They're hooked by the seduction and excitement of pursuing or being pursued. One woman describes it this way:

> I loved going to bars, but it wasn't for the alcohol. Men were my drink. I'd walk back and forth to the ladies' room and count how many men looked at me. I got a high when they checked me out. It was even better when they hit on me, and we'd spend the night flirting. I rarely hooked up with anybody. I wasn't really interested in going home with somebody. I just wanted to know I could still turn a guy's head.

Some romance addicts date their partners for a bit, but after they realize they've succeeded in snaring their intended, the relationship soon fizzles. The early flush of excitement is compelling, but these addicts are uninterested or unable to sustain a relationship over time. The Prince Charming turns out to have warts, and these women send him back to the pond. It's simply easier, or at least it's more exciting, to find a new partner.

An entire genre of books, including within the Christian community, is devoted to feeding this addiction. The romance novels portray the excitement of pursuit and early love. The Christian version lacks the hot sexual descriptions and the couple doesn't have sex until after marriage, but the message is the same: A romantic relationship is key to a woman's ultimate happiness. And when the relationship is intense and compelling, it surely must be the real thing. The happily-ever-after myth is powerful, and the romance addict is easily susceptible. She doubts her worth as a lovable woman, and she needs the frequent reassurance of being chosen. She often is especially concerned about her appearance and may be considered high maintenance. Unconsciously, the romance addict wants the payoff of a fulfilling relationship without the hard work. In fact, she may believe that it can't be real love if the relationship isn't easy.

3. Fantasy addict. The fantasy addict is very similar. Her relationships, though, exist primarily in her mind. She creates elaborate fantasies about someone she knows well, barely or not at all. She falls in love with the guy next to her at the stoplight or the man she passes in a store. She obsesses about a man she knows and becomes convinced his normal courtesies toward her are a sign of his undying affection. She meets someone and within an hour she's daydreaming about the two of them married and living happily ever after with their adorable children.

The focus of this woman's life is the fantasy of the Magical Man, not reality. She compares any partner to the man in her head, and she lives in the world of "if only": *If only my husband would engage with me the way that man does with his wife, or if only my guy would do X-Y-Z, then I'd be happy.*

Compulsive fantasy provides a ticket out of a boring life or difficult relationship. These women live in their heads and prefer illusion to reality. They create life as they'd like it to be; they don't deal with life as it is. They also are chronically discontent, because they miss the positive things about a relationship since no human can live up to the fantasies.

Some women fantasize during sexual activity with their husbands. They imagine being with someone else (again, that Magical Man) and of what they would do together and how they would relate. Perhaps they fantasize being with another woman, instead, or they're only aroused when they replay pornographic scenes. Whatever the scenario, this addict is checked out during sex.

Almost all women, of course, occasionally entertain fantasies about a different partner or a more fulfilling life. The fantasy addict, though, camps out in her imaginary life. She isn't emotionally present because she's distracted by her fantasies. They interfere with her daily functioning and rob her of the joy of the moment. She may try to "take every thought captive," but she can't control her mind.

Many Christian women don't recognize themselves as fantasy addicts. They don't masturbate, much less act out with another person, so they never consider they have a problem. If, however, they fit one or more of the characteristics of addiction (obsession, compulsion or continuing despite negative consequences) the fantasy addict can be as powerfully addicted as the most active adulteress.

4. Pornography or cybersex addict. Today many female sex addicts are stepping beyond the mold of the relationship or fantasy presentation. More and more women, primarily younger women who've grown up in the media-saturated culture, are becoming addicted to pornography. In fact, many clinicians believe that culture is literally rewiring women's brains to be more visually oriented.

The main reason for the increase in female pornography addicts is the explosion of the Internet, which has opened a vast new domain for pornography. Key researchers describe the Internet as the crack cocaine of sex addiction because of its "Triple A Engine" of accessibility, affordability and anonymity.[1] For zero investment beyond the cost of a computer, a woman can access incredible pornography with a few mouse clicks from the anonymous privacy of her own home. She no longer has to worry about the distasteful or dangerous environment of a porn shop or X-rated video store; she simply takes a few steps to her computer.

Women's use of visual pornography surprises many who think only men struggle with sexual addiction. Yet, the statistics are startling: According to Nielson Net ratings, one in three visitors to an adult website is female. Christian women aren't immune, as a poll conducted in 2006 by ChristiaNet.com and Second Glance Ministries found that 20 percent of Christian women reported an addiction to pornography.[2] The power of pornography seems to be as equally strong for some women as it has traditionally been thought to be for men.

Female sex addicts who act out primarily with pornography sometimes feel extra shame about their behavior because it doesn't fit the relationship stereotype for women. It's brazenly sexual, which goes against the Christian picture of female propriety. Culturally, it's expected that males view pornography. For women, there's still a powerful cultural code of goodness, and it demands that nice girls don't look at porn. Reportedly, 70 percent of women keep their cyber activities secret.

Most women, though, are generally drawn to the relational aspects of Internet sexual activity. They get involved in chat rooms and connect with someone online instead of merely viewing pornography. Statistically, twice as many women as men favor chat rooms. These women develop intense online relationships, which are especially prone to creating false intimacy. Internet technology allows for an immediate (though artificial) sense of connection with another person. Without the challenges associated with face-to-face interaction, users are lulled into a false sense of safety that allows them to be vulnerable more quickly. Hiding behind a computer screen, women will type things they might not say in person. It's easy to develop an intense (there's that word again) bond with someone when you spend hours communicating online. Even if a woman is disappointed by an Internet partner, other possibilities are only a click away. The hope for the perfect romantic connection lures women around the next cyber corner.

Women's Internet relationships usually escalate to cybersex or phone sex. It's not unusual for women to arrange to meet their partners in person and physically act out with them. In fact, according to one study by Dr. Jennifer Schneider, a leading researcher in the field, nearly 80 percent of females who are involved in sexually-oriented chat rooms go on to meet their partners.[3] Women are far more likely than men to escalate from the illusion of online romance to real-life encounters.

The implications are enormous as women place themselves in potentially dangerous situations. A 2007 survey published in the U.S. journal *Sexuality Research and Social Policy* reports that one-third of women who meet someone online have sex on the first date, and three-quarters of these women do not use a condom.[4] Women who connect online believe *I know this person, and I'm sure he's safe.*

5. Masturbation. Masturbation, of course, is almost always in the picture of sex via the Internet. Self-stimulation is a huge part of cybersex, where the partners aren't physically in the same location. Even without pornography, though, female addicts commonly engage in masturbation. Sometimes this can be a result of molestation they experienced as they were prematurely introduced to sexual responses. Other times women discover masturbation innocently during childhood as a part of normal, developmentally appropriate self-exploration. In either case, if a woman chooses habitually to masturbate, it can become an addiction when used to alter mood in an unhealthy way.

Masturbation is a topic of a great deal of controversy among Christians. Opinions about its appropriateness vary widely. At the very least, masturbation often involves the use of pornography or unholy sexual fantasy, which are clearly outside God's boundaries for healthy sexuality. The issue is much broader than the simple guideline the church sometimes offers: "Married women shouldn't masturbate because they have a sexual outlet with their husbands, but it's okay for single women if they have to do it to stay celibate." A woman's marital status has little bearing on whether or not she can masturbate "appropriately," if such a practice is even possible.

One helpful Christian book on female sexuality, *The Secrets of Eve* by Archibald Hart, Catherine Hart Weber and Debra Taylor, outlines the conditions that clearly make masturbation problematic:[5]

1. When it is used to avoid sexual intimacy with your husband or to punish him by withholding sex. (This condition is an example of a concept I'll explain later in this chapter.)

2. When it fosters lust for someone other than your husband if you're married; and

3. When it is used addictively.

I will focus attention on the third item, though obviously the others are important in terms of healthy sexuality.

Again, the woman who only masturbates may find it hard to believe she's a sex addict. After all, she may never have looked at pornography or been physically unfaithful if she's married. But when a woman uses masturbation excessively, especially as a way of escaping her problems, soothing herself or avoiding true intimacy with her husband, she may be addicted.

As an example, I once counseled a female who was a virgin. In fact, she had never even engaged in what my generation calls "heavy petting." But she left her office desk and went into the bathroom to masturbate several times a day. "It calms my nerves and helps me cope with the stress of my job," she explained. Clearly, she was sexually addicted. Another woman became so adept at self-stimulation she could masturbate herself to orgasm without ever leaving her desk. The women who are involved with pornography and masturbation seem to align more closely with the stereotypical presentation of male sex addicts.

6. Exhibitionism. As described earlier, today's culture condones female exhibitionism. In fact, it's encouraged and applauded. Some women, though, exhibit themselves as a part of their sexual addiction. Actually, exhibitionism is best considered a subset of other addictive presentations like the romance addict or the addict who sells or trades sex, but I want to highlight it because it's such a common, if subtle, thread among women.

Obviously, the women who are strippers or pornography actresses (those who sell sex) are exhibitionists. While there is a definite economic factor at play because such jobs can pay quite well, these women may also be addicted to using their bodies for acclaim or attention. I'll describe later in this chapter the element of power, which is also part of this picture.

In less obvious ways, women flaunt their bodies through provocative clothes and movements. While females rarely expose themselves in the way male flashers do, they still can exhibit themselves in ways specifically intended to arouse lust. Much like the romance addict, some of these women become addicted to the rush of being seen and desired.

The woman who exhibits her body buys into the cultural value system about beauty. She believes appearance is the ticket to attention. Sex appeal equals femininity or even self-worth. Young women are especially prone to this kind of image management. Outside the modesty issue, this behavior becomes problematic when a woman finds that she keeps selecting attire that's inappropriate for the setting like work, and she doesn't respond to requests to alter her choices. She may also find she loves the high of exposing herself, and this payoff is worth the damage to her self-esteem that comes with objectifying herself.

7. *Addict who sells or trades sex.* Selling or trading sex is another form of sex addiction in females. This description doesn't just apply to prostitutes. Many female addicts will trade sexual activity for other favors, as this story illustrates:

> Carrie was a student at a Christian college that required daily chapel attendance. A worker visually looked over the rows from the top of the balcony and marked any vacant seats on a chart. Later an employee matched the vacancy to the person assigned to that spot. Carrie found she could skip chapel as often as she wanted by trading sexual favors with students who, in return, would occupy Carrie's chapel seat.

Another single mother with three young children described how she routinely slept with men who helped with her demanding responsibilities. She explained her relationship with a sexual partner this way:

> I don't particularly like the sex, and I don't really even like him. But he runs to the store so I don't have to haul three kids, or he rescues me when my car won't start or when the babysitter cancels. I figure he's earned sex. There's no way I'd break up with him, and if he breaks up with me, I'll find another guy just like him as fast as I can. I need the help. Don't you understand that?

People often assume that if a male pays for a date, the female will reward him with sexual activity. Because of the dependency of some women, they may feel they have no choice or that they aren't worth a man's attention if they're not sexual with him. A pattern of this quid pro quo behavior ("I'll do this if you'll do that") may indicate an addiction.

8. *Partnering with another addict.* Another common form of sex addiction in women is the female who attaches herself to other sex addicts. While she is also a *co-addict*, which simply means someone who is in relationship with an addict, some of these women are addicted themselves. At Bethesda Workshops, the clinical treatment program I direct, 15 to 20 percent of the women who come for help because their husbands are sex addicts struggle with the same problem in their own lives. Deborah was startled when she made this realization:

> I see now that I'm also a sex addict. Until I started therapy, I thought of myself as a co-addict. I knew both my husbands were alcoholics and in counseling I came to see they were sex addicts, as well. Most of my boyfriends between my marriages were too. I was shocked to learn I'm also a sex addict. I loved the sex in these sick relationships! I'd be just as into the pornography as they were. I'm the one who wanted more and more. I'm ashamed to realize my part. I thought the sex stuff was just about them.

When a woman who is sexually addicted becomes involved with a male sex addict, the relationship is usually both volatile and confusing. She often switches between the role of addict and co-addict within the relationship. This woman and couple need tremendous help to sort out the complicated dynamics of addiction and codependency.

A fine line, in fact, exists between sexual addiction and co-sex addiction in women. Many behaviors and dynamics are similar or even identical, and distinctions are mainly in the reasons behind the actions. According to Dr. Jennifer Schneider, the sex addict is driven by the "good feeling of the connection—the thrill of the chase and conquest, the sense of power over the other person, or the sexual high." The co-addict is out "to influence another person—to win them over, manipulate them, or keep them in the relationship."[6]

BINGE/PURGE PATTERN OF ADDICTION

Sometimes a woman goes through cycles of acting out. She may have periods of addictive activity followed by periods, perhaps lengthy, of refraining from inappropriate sexual or relational activity. Many Christian women describe alternating *good girl/bad girl* cycles, which Sara explains:

> Before recovery, I'd go back and forth between pornography and perfection. I'd spend weeks consumed with porn or chat rooms, then I'd feel so horrible I'd try to make up for it by being super good. I'd go back to the Christian student center and volunteer at church. I'd study more and clean up my apartment. I'd be disciplined about my daily quiet time and go out of my way to help other people. Unconsciously, I was trying to do enough good stuff to make up for all the bad. Before long, I was exhausted and discouraged because I could never do enough, and I went back to porn.

This yo-yo pattern is similar to what many eating-disordered women experience. Sex addicts may binge on sexual activity, and then starve themselves to make up for it. The starvation times are called *acting in* versus the binging times of *acting out*. Sometimes an addiction may be dormant for months or even years. The addict may believe she's cured, as Katherine explains:

> I distinctly remember my thirtieth birthday. I sat in my porch swing and thanked God I was over whatever had caused me to be promiscuous as a teenager and have affairs in my first marriage. I thought I had settled down. I hadn't acted out for almost four years. I had a good marriage and two wonderful toddlers. Then within a year it all started back up again. I quickly was more deeply involved in my sex addiction than I had ever been before. I was surprised. I had no idea that problem wasn't behind me.

SEXUAL ANOREXIA

Acting in sexually, which is called sexual anorexia, is the flip side of *acting out*. Think about eating disorders, which involve two main types of behavior: eating too much and eating too little. The anorexic restricts food; the overeater consumes too much (whether or not she purges). The behaviors are opposite, but they share a common element: Both have an unhealthy relationship with food. The same can be true for sex addicts. At one end of a continuum is the woman who acts out compulsively, and at the other end is the woman who is sexually anorexic, as figure 2 illustrates.[7]

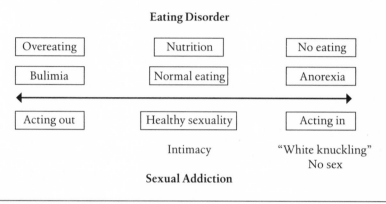

Figure 2.

This anorexic reaction may be confined to the woman's marriage. Most sex addicts describe a diminishing sexual relationship with their husbands. It's not unusual for a woman to be totally anorexic with her husband—that is, not to be sexual with him at all—and to act out a great deal with pornography, masturbation or with other people. Or she may be anorexic with her husband and be consumed with fantasy partners.

Other women are sexually anorexic without a history of acting out. Dr. Patrick Carnes devotes a whole book to the subject, which is aptly titled *Sexual Anorexia*. He describes this pattern as a dread of sexual pleasure and a compulsive avoidance of sex. It's often accompanied by distortions of body appearance and extreme shame about one's body or sexual experiences, which often include sexual abuse. Like sexual addiction, sexual anorexia is progressively unmanageable and distressing.

Clinical opinions differ about categorizing sexual anorexia. In simple terms, the behaviors are opposite, which is easy to understand. The underlying similarities, though, are striking, and both sexual addiction and sexual anorexia are usually considered subsets of disordered sexuality. Ironically, both addicts and anorexics are obsessed with sex. The first compulsively engages in sexual activity; the second compulsively avoids it.

Sexual anorexia is further complicated because it's sanctioned and even encouraged by the church. Many sexual anorexics become very rigid religiously. They may substitute an addiction to religion in place of their addiction to sex. Instead of being obsessed with sex, they become obsessed with outward religious symbols or activities that make them feel better about themselves. Their church leaders may applaud them for gaining control and consider them cured.

The problem is that this person hasn't really dealt with the issues and their underlying causes. My colleague Eli Machen describes the sexual anorexic as crossing from a ditch on one side of the road to the ditch on the other. As Eli says, "One hundred eighty degrees from sick is still sick." Sexual anorexia is not the cure for sexual addiction. To completely shut down her sexuality isn't the answer for the sexually addicted woman. Instead, she must learn how to live as the woman God created her to be and how to express her sexuality in God-ordained ways.

POWER COMPONENT

Female sexual addiction, especially for those women addicted to relationship, romance and fantasy, can involve an important element that's often overlooked: the incredible feeling of power. Jill describes it this way: "It's such an unbelievable high to walk into a room, pick out a guy, and know I can seduce him into going to bed with me. That's a rush all by itself. Talk about power!"

Again, in a culture that measures a woman's worth by her external beauty, this power factor is huge. When a man melts in the hands of a provocative woman, the power feels enormous. Though women have made great strides in achieving equal status with men, disparities still exist culturally and in the workplace. Sexually, though, women clearly have the power, and through wielding their sexuality, women can exert enormous influence and control that's otherwise out of their reach.

Female addicts can also be into the power that comes from being in a relationship with powerful people. A woman who becomes sexually involved with a United States president is a good example of a probable addict who attaches herself to influential men. This association, in turn, gives her power and influence of her own.

INCIDENCE OF SEX ADDICTION AMONG WOMEN

You may be tempted to believe this disease affects only a small number of women. (*Only me and no one else*, you may think.) Surely something this awful would be better known. The truth is the problem is widespread, at least according to anecdotal evidence. Research into sexual addiction, particularly as it affects women, has been quite limited. We know few definitive statistics. Carnes, the leading researcher in the field, initially suggested that 6 to 10 percent of the adult United States population is sexually addicted. Estimates now range as high as 45 percent.[8] Of that number, probably 40 to 50 percent are females. These figures aren't surprising to addictionists; they reflect the better-documented statistics on alcoholism. Remember, many first believed that women weren't alcoholics. I believe research will eventually document that women struggle with sex, relationship and love addiction at about the same rate as do men.

SIMILARITIES AMONG THE VARIOUS PRESENTATIONS

These descriptions of types of sexual addiction in women may seem more different than they are similar. Some involve solitary activities; others are done with a partner, whether heterosexual or lesbian. Some activities are between consenting adults; others are illegal like selling or paying for sex. The dynamics of the disease, however, are the same. All sexually addictive behaviors, no matter what form, share two important characteristics. The first is the element of powerlessness. Each woman feels powerless to control her behavior. As described earlier, she may have stopped a hundred times, but she can't stay stopped. Her life has become completely unmanageable.

SEX ADDICTION AS AN INTIMACY DISORDER

The second commonality is the loneliness these women feel. *At its core, sexual addiction is an intimacy disorder.* The supposed connection is false; the isolation is profound. Recall the words of the woman who opened this chapter: It's not about sex at all, but about the desperate search for love and touch and affirmation and acceptance. Those are descriptions of intimacy. God created us for intimate connection with him, with others and with ourselves. When those connections are broken or absent, which will be explored at length in chapter nine, women desperately seek a false substitute. Sex or an intense relationship offers the best stand-in for the real thing.

The one-flesh union God intended between a wife and her husband is about intimacy, not just about the coupling of bodies. When sex fails to provide the intimacy it was designed to create and celebrate, a woman is left feeling empty and alone, not cherished and connected. *Addicted sex is always empty sex.*

Many female relationship addicts may react strongly to that statement. They protest they're truly connected with their affair partners. I confess I thought the same thing when I was consumed by my disease. But sexual activity outside the parameters of God's design is, by its very definition, short of the mark of authentic, godly intimacy. Affairs are secret and clouded with shame, no matter how connected the partners feel. Shameful acts that must be hidden are hardly descriptive of true intimacy.

A further reality is that using sex addictively prevents women from experiencing true intimacy. They aren't able to be emotionally vulnerable with others. The duplicity and shame keep them from being truly known. They must keep the terrible secret, and isolation is the cost. Obviously, the female addict must hide her problem from her husband if she's married. It's impossible, then, for true intimacy to exist within that relationship because there's a lack of basic honesty. Many married females delude themselves into believing their addiction isn't harming their marriage as long as the husband is unaware. This reframe of sexual addiction as an intimacy disorder shows the fallacy of that belief. Even if the woman is single, her secret disease forms a barrier that keeps her friends at an emotional arm's length. If she's truly known, she's discovered in her sin. She's exposed as someone far worse than a flirt. She's judged a despicable failure. She's outcast and stoned.

The next chapter explains why the shame and loneliness of sexual addiction are still not enough to cause a woman to stop.

QUESTIONS FOR REFLECTION
OR SMALL GROUP DISCUSSION

1. What type of presentation(s) best describes your form of acting out?

2. Have you gone back and forth between acting out and acting in?

3. What part has power played in your behavior?

4. Describe your reaction to the idea of sex addiction as an intimacy disorder.

CONSEQUENCES AND CYCLE

OF ADDICTION

As explained earlier, a hallmark sign of addiction is continuing to act out despite negative consequences. For a disease like sexual addiction, the consequences women experience are often profound and devastating. In many ways the consequences of sex addiction for females parallel those experienced by men: loss of reputation and self-esteem or a negative impact on a relationship or family. Unlike men, however, women experience some unique consequences from their sexual behavior.

CONSEQUENCES OF FEMALE SEXUAL ADDICTION

1. Unplanned pregnancy. The most obvious negative consequence is unwanted pregnancy, which has long-term ramifications whether the woman chooses abortion, adoption or parenting the child. In most Bethesda Healing for Women workshops (for female sex and love addicts) there is at least one participant who has chosen abortion as a way of dealing with a pregnancy that resulted from her sexual acting out. Many have had more than one. With few exceptions these women are wracked with guilt over their abortions. The anguish they feel over taking a life multiplies tenfold their shame from acting out.

These women especially believe they deserve to be stoned for their sins. Their journey of healing and recovery is complicated and particularly painful. They are in critical need of accurate teaching about both addiction and grace.

Even without the complication of abortion, an unplanned pregnancy is a major crisis. The alarming incidence of pregnancy among unmarried or teenage mothers is likely due, at least in part, to the female's participation in sexual encounters as a way of obtaining love.

2. Health issues. The health impact alone of women's sexual behavior is enormous. Sexually transmitted diseases have reached epidemic proportions in our country. Again, in every Bethesda workshop for female sex addicts there has been at least one woman who was infected with herpes, in addition to others who had contracted less serious sexually transmitted diseases (STDs). Several women have been put at high risk for human immunodeficiency virus (HIV) infection because they've been sexual with infected partners.

One of the most shameful parts of my own story is having been diagnosed with cervical cancer caused by an HPV. My treatment required three surgeries within a year, and I had major hemorrhaging after the first surgery. My family was strapped financially because of the medical bills. *Yet I could not stop acting out.* Despite the extreme consequence of potentially losing my life, I continued to be sexual in ways that put me at ongoing risk for further health complications. I imagined my own young children growing up without a mother as I had done, and I felt overwhelmed with guilt at the devastation they would feel if I were to die from my disease. But I was powerless to follow through on my intentions to stop having affairs. The health consequences I experienced from addiction were great; the power of the addiction was greater.

3. Employment consequences. Often a woman's addiction can also affect her work performance. Consider Micah's story:

> I was an up-and-coming producer for a major record label until I was fired because of my sexual addiction. I slept with too many men at the company, and eventually they all figured out they weren't the only one. My boss got into my computer and found I was having cybersex

with one of the artists while I was at work. Then I became pregnant from a brief fling and ended up losing a lot of time at work. Eventually, my boss said enough is enough. I don't know how I'm going to support myself and my kids. I'm way over my head in debt too.

It's impossible to measure the lost productivity of women who spend work time obsessing, fantasizing and connecting with addictive partners. Sometimes they ruin their professional reputation along with their personal one. Remember the double standard about women whose sexual behavior affects their work as opposed to men who are in similar situations. Based on anecdotal experience, females seem more apt to experience employment consequences sooner and to a more extreme degree than males whose acting out is comparable. The public tolerated the probable sexual addiction of a recent U.S. president, for example. In fact, most people considered his sexual escapades a problem only when he was exposed in related transgressions like lying.

4. Family impact. A less tangible effect of sexual addiction among women involves the effect of a female's disease on her family. Of course, a male's addiction also harms his loved ones, but most men are ill-equipped to become the family's primary caregiver when their wives become consumed by an addiction. Children's emotional needs especially suffer when a man is the partner of a sex addict and must shoulder the nurturing role alone. These children are at high risk for their own addictive and codependent behaviors. They also are at high risk of being victimized by those who would exploit their vulnerable emotional state that arises out of their addictive family system.

One female addict shares a heartbreaking story in this regard:

> The worst part of my addiction is what it did to my children, especially my son. I still feel terrible guilt about what happened to him. He was only four years old and I was acting out all over the place. I wasn't there for him. But his stepdad wasn't there either. He was totally focused on me and what I was doing. He'd follow me and look for evidence I'd been with other men and then go into a rage. The reality is that neither one of us were parenting the kids.
>
> An older neighborhood teen babysat for us a lot and my son really

got attached to him. Then one day I discovered this teenager was molesting my child! I actually walked in on him and saw it. I nearly threw him out the window before I called the police.

I asked my son why he hadn't told me what was going on. He said I was never home for him to tell and that besides, this teenager was his "friend" who "took care of me." It broke my heart to see how my addiction had contributed to my son's abuse.

My husband and I got counseling for him and for all of us, and the teenager went to a treatment program for juvenile offenders. It's been several years and my son seems to be doing fine today. But I don't know if I can ever forgive myself for putting him at risk and for what happened to him.

Even if children escape specific abuse, they're usually confused about relationships, especially about the characteristics of a healthy marriage.

5. Emotional toll. The personal psychological and emotional toll suffered by a female sex addict is even more difficult to measure but certainly no less devastating. This consequence is deeply experienced by the love/relationship/romance addict in particular. She careens through the roller coaster of broken relationships and with each loss, her self-esteem plummets. Her negative core beliefs, which are outlined in detail in chapter eleven, are reinforced. Her acting out becomes a self-fulfilling prophecy that no one will love her or meet her needs.

For the heterosexual addict, even her relationships with other females are often painful. Women react strongly to other women who are promiscuous, for example, out of fear of losing their own male relationships. Women can be catty, judgmental and hateful. Christian women may ostracize a female who strays too far or too often beyond unspoken sexual boundaries. Because of her strong relational wiring, a female sex addict is usually devastated by her self-perceived failure at relationships. Shame and self-loathing become frequent emotional companions.

6. Spiritual effect. Perhaps ultimately more harmful is the effect on a sexually addicted woman's view of God. Because she has likely prayed and begged God to remove the obsession and he has not, an addict often becomes angry and disappointed with God. She believes he has ignored her cry or worse, turned his back on her. It's hard for her to trust that God does, indeed, love her and stands ready to help her. She's lost in a cycle of hopelessness. She may desert God and religious groups completely, even if she earlier had been very active in the church. In my experience, the once-religious female sex addict is the one most likely to seriously consider suicide. Without the hope of God's help, she feels there's no other way to end the pain.

WHY CAN'T I JUST STOP?

The cycle of addiction as first described by Patrick Carnes[1] sheds light on a key reason women are unable to stop sinful and addictive behavior even in the face of these kinds of destructive consequences. Consider the following story:

> Toni opens her eyes in semi-darkness. In that intermediate time between sleep and wakefulness, she's not sure where she is. The room is unfamiliar. The man sleeping beside her is equally unfamiliar. Slowly she realizes the furnishings and bedspread indicate a motel room, one of those medium-priced chains known for offering a complimentary continental breakfast. Quietly Toni slips out of bed and finds her clothes. She steps into the slinky black wraparound miniskirt and sheer top, which is grossly out of place for morning wear. She sees with disgust some of the evidence of last night: ticket stubs from the dance club she favors, sticky cartons of take-out Chinese food, a couple of bottles of wine and cigarette butts in the ashtray. She shovels her makeup off the bathroom counter back into her purse and leaves without waking her companion. Her eyes swimming with shame, Toni knows she has done it again: she's had another one-night stand. That's obvious. What she doesn't understand is how it happened. *I didn't want to have sex with anyone!* she thinks. *I promised myself I wouldn't. I just wanted to listen to some music and dance a little. How do I end up like this?*

Answering Toni's question requires an understanding of the cycle of addiction. Many addicts like Toni have no clue why they keep doing things they don't really want to do. As her story shows, these women may simply want some fun or companionship or conversation, yet these encounters repeatedly become sexual. They're mystified by the pattern of their behavior.

These women wonder, *how can I truly want to do one thing and end up doing the complete opposite?* One of the main reasons is a failure to understand the predictable events that Carnes terms the sexual addiction cycle. This undeniable cycle of addiction is one reason the *Just say no!* advice isn't helpful. Yes, this campaign may have helped some young people avoid initial experimentation with drugs or alcohol, but to an addict already established in her addiction, the admonition is pathetically ineffective.

Sex addicts experience a four-stage progression in each addictive episode: preoccupation, ritual, acting out and despair. Understanding and breaking this powerful, but predictable, cycle is essential for recovery. Carnes's cycle shown in figure 3 provides a visual reference.

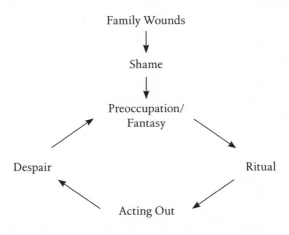

Figure 3. Carnes cycle of addiction

At the top of the cycle is family wounds and next is shame. Part two will discuss addicts' woundedness and resulting shame that is the driving force behind the addiction. The focus here is the body of the cycle of addiction, which illustrates the observable way addicts medicate their internal pain.

TRIGGERS

Let's look first, though, at the concept of being triggered, which usually gives birth to preoccupation and the acting out cycle. A trigger is
anything that serves as a stimulus that prompts a reaction or series of
reactions. The simplest example is a trigger in the present like a provocative image or person. Some kind of sexual trigger activates the
rush of brain chemicals described earlier, and we're overcome with
lust. Culture is teeming with sexual triggers and these stimuli alone
are enough to set off preoccupation.

A trigger may be a reminder of something in the past, either something that's positive or negative. Some triggers remind us of pain of
some sort whether physical, emotional or spiritual. For example, we
see a TV show or movie about abuse that's similar to what we experienced, and we're vividly put in touch with that vulnerable little girl
who was hurt. Or a friend ignores us for some reason, and we're emotionally kicked back into that wounded place of growing up in a family where we didn't feel like we mattered. Maybe someone criticizes
us, and our existing shame about our secret life pounds our con-
science. Perhaps we physically are with our families, abusers or some
other person who has hurt us and the pain is freshly awakened.
Whatever the particular pain, a trigger inflames and intensifies it in
the present moment. The awful memories and the pain associated
with them demand to be quieted.

Other triggers, though, are positive in terms of their connotations.
A song may remind us of some romantic time or a passing whiff of
cologne floods us with memories of a particular person. Sometimes a
simple neutral object like a certain model of car or just the sight of a
computer can activate the addictive process because that object has
been paired with acting out in the past. Actually, a simple memory or
thought in the privacy of our own brain can be enough of a trigger to
set the cycle in motion.

Stress can also play a huge part in the process. When we feel anxious,
lonely, pressured or exhausted because of stress of any kind, we want to
soothe that uncomfortable state. We're tense and wound up and want
to calm down. Many of us have discovered that nicotine or alcohol will

calm our mood with their depressant effect. We've also discovered that sexual activity will do the same thing—and usually better.

CYCLE OF ADDICTION

Carne's cycle of addiction outlines the predictable steps between a trigger and acting out. We'll look individually at each one.

1. Preoccupation. The first step in the cycle is preoccupation or fantasy as this step is sometimes called. As a beginning point, preoccupation is the gateway into the process of changing your mood. Whether at the moment you feel horribly rotten because of some deep pain or you just recall what it's like to feel better and want to experience that pleasure again, the first step in the process is preoccupation.

When you're triggered either into feeling emotional pain or into euphoric recall of some pleasurable experience, you begin to preoccupy in one of two ways. You either think about making the pain go away (altering a negative mood) or you think about recreating the remembered pleasure (boosting your mood). Remember, addictions are mood-altering. You start imagining what will make you feel better, which is the goal. You think and muse and stew and dream about feeling better.

As you move into playing out some scenario in your mind, you enter the stage of *fantasy*, which is varied for each individual. Maybe you picture an encounter with some special person or connecting with someone online. You mentally review images of sexual or relational activity and rehearse them again and again. You may fantasize about some encounter in the past or about some hoped-for happening in the future. The romance addict may catch someone's eye in the grocery store and fantasize about their getting married and living happily ever after. The relationship addict may fantasize that some person will fulfill all her dreams—certainly better than her husband currently does if she's married. Another woman may fantasize about a cybersex encounter or simply being able to surf the web or masturbate.

Even at this initial stage, the brain chemicals fire up with their feel-good potion. You're already beginning to feel the neurochemical hit. The addictive cycle and reactions have begun.

2. *Ritual.* Engaging in a variety of rituals is what moves the addict from the preoccupation/fantasy stage to the point of acting out. Again, rituals are as varied as individuals and their own ways of acting out. Some rituals are short such as a masturbation ritual or one that leads to looking at pornography. Those rituals simply involve securing privacy or accessing a computer or handheld device. Other rituals are much longer such as those that groom a potential partner for an affair. They may be blatant or subtle, conscious or unconscious.

Toni's illustration presented earlier provides good examples of her rituals. She chose her clothes and applied her makeup in a particular way to attract men. She went to a club and consumed alcohol. She danced, probably provocatively. She smoked cigarettes and perhaps asked a man to light them for her as a way of connecting. She flirted and used sexual humor and employed probably dozens of ways of attracting and connecting with a partner. All of these preparations and behaviors are examples of her rituals. Until she understands her rituals and takes steps to avoid them, Toni will remain perplexed by how she seemingly wakes up and finds herself in the middle of yet another sexual encounter.

Some women pursue specifically sexual rituals as Toni eventually did. These addicts are aggressive and provocative. They flaunt their sexual liberation and comfort themselves with purely sexual encounters. Other women, though, are more subtle in their rituals to the point they may not even recognize they're caught up in them.

The relationship addict (married or single) may spend many weeks, months or even years engaging in rituals that ultimately lead to an affair. She may arrange accidental-on-purpose meetings with a man she's attracted to. She may pursue increasing levels of conversation with him, first about innocent topics and then about loaded discussions like the emptiness of her life or her marriage. She may exchange e-mails or meet him for lunch or drinks. She may flirt or touch him often. She may spend increasing amounts of time with him under a variety of pretenses. Each step takes her closer to acting out.

Eventually the interactions become specifically physical and then sexual. The pair holds hands, embraces or steals a kiss. Many female relationship addicts report that the most significant line they cross isn't having intercourse; it's kissing. After the first kiss, having sex is an easy downhill slide. A romantic edge colors the relationship as the two play the verbal and emotional game of *if only*. Again, a huge element of denial is at work here as the woman tells herself, *it's not a big deal; we're not having sex or anything*. The slowly advancing nature of the exchanges may add to the denial by allowing the addict to blame her partner for initiating sexual activity, when the reality is that she clearly led him on.

For Christians, one of the most subtle and powerful rituals is to spiritualize the relationship. Because of the close connection between our spirituality and our sexuality, it's easy to confuse and entangle the two. The couple may have discussions about God's will that brought them together for some reason. They may pray together or share deeply moving spiritual music. The legitimate cover of their supposedly spiritual relationship can add both to the bond between them and also to the denial of where the relationship is heading. This tactic is one of Satan's most powerful tools to blind Christians and hook them into unholy relationships.

A different kind of relationship ritual is for a woman to act helpless or dependent or scared. This woman may present herself as less intelligent or competent as a way of attracting a man. She plays to his male ego about how wonderful he is to rescue her or solve her problems. If married, this addict may also describe how her husband falls short in taking care of her.

Women have as many rituals as they have forms of acting out. You may have a masturbation ritual, a cybersex ritual and an affair ritual and may be in various stages of each one simultaneously. Whatever your rituals, it's vital that you discover and eliminate them. Once you're engaged in your ritual, it's almost impossible to stop. You're propelled down the addictive path like a car without brakes.

3. Acting out. In this phase of the addiction cycle you act out either with yourself through masturbation or cross the flesh line to act out with another person. Often, it's only at the point of acting out that you realize you have a problem. You can identify it's wrong to masturbate to pornography or have an affair, for example. You view the specific behavior(s) as the problem, but you lack understanding about what led up to the acting out. These concrete behaviors are what you pinpoint as the trouble in your life, and you may pray repeatedly and with great sincerity for God to help you abstain from them. You once again have "fallen" into sin.

4. *Despair.* Understandably, despair is the last stop in the sexual addiction cycle. Of course you feel despair at what you've done. You've acted out again despite your best intentions. You've broken your promises to yourself and to God. Your view of yourself is again confirmed: *I am a horrible, terrible person. I'm just a whore or a slut. I'm like the woman dragged before Jesus who deserved to be stoned.* You feel overwhelming despair at continuing to do what you know you shouldn't do and really don't want to do. You're overcome with shame. Perhaps you beg God for forgiveness (again) and vow to change your ways. Part of you, however—a deeply secret and hidden part—knows you won't be successful.

It's during this phase that the Christian addict is most likely to pursue quick religious fixes such as healing or deliverance experiences or rededication. One female addict was baptized seven times as a way of dealing with her shame and imploring God's help in combating her sin. An addict may change churches or denominations as an attempt to find the magical cure. Then her shame only increases when such well-intended but misguided acts fail to deliver the help she needs to stop acting out.

Look again at the model of this cycle of addiction (figure 3). The arrow from despair leads back into preoccupation and fantasy. As crazy as it sounds, the best way to medicate the pain and shame from acting out is to lose yourself in yet another round of sexual activity. During the moments of ritual and acting out the pain can be silenced or at least ignored. It's a self-perpetuating cycle. The anesthesia of sin quickly wears off; shame resurfaces.

Often you take a side jaunt into other ways of coping before you drop back down into the sexual addiction cycle. Examples of these behaviors are illustrated in figure 4.

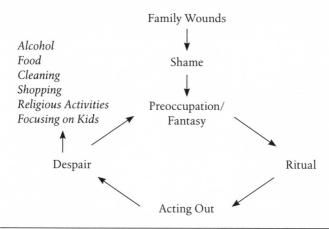

Figure 4. Carnes cycle of addiction

You may pour yourself into your children's or husband's activities or clean compulsively or shop. You may binge on food or alcohol or cigarettes or take the opposite approach and diet compulsively or totally abstain from unhealthy chemicals. You may submerge yourself in service activities and if they're within the church, you'll probably be applauded for it. You may work compulsively or exercise to excess or do any number of things to cope with your feelings of despair at having acted out again. You may sink into depression.

If you're a sex addict, however, you ultimately will return to your primary drug of choice: compulsive, unholy sexual thoughts or activities. The pattern continues; the shame escalates. To paraphrase a New Testament writer, "What a [miserable woman] I am" (Romans 7:24).

QUESTIONS FOR REFLECTION
OR SMALL GROUP DISCUSSION

1. What consequences have you experienced because of your acting out?

2. List your primary triggers.

3. What are your rituals associated with your main form of acting out?

4. What other ways do you medicate your despair besides sex or relationship addiction?

DIAGNOSIS OF

SEXUAL ADDICTION

If you've read this far, my guess is you're applying the book to yourself or to someone you care about. The patterns of your life are beginning to become clear. Some puzzle pieces are falling into place. You're engaging in some self-diagnosis. But are you really a sex addict? Or is she? Let's examine some diagnostic criteria for identifying sexual addiction in women.

Begin by taking the following self-test. This isn't a clinical, foolproof instrument, but it's a good starting point. It's adapted from two primary sources: the self-test used by the Twelve Step group Sexaholics Anonymous[1] and the Women's Sexual Addiction Screening Test,[2] which was developed by Sharon O'Hara and Patrick Carnes.

**WOMEN'S SELF-TEST FOR
SEXUAL/RELATIONSHIP ADDICTION**

1. Have you ever thought you needed help for your sexual behavior or thinking?

2. Have you tried to stop or limit what you felt was wrong in your sexual or relationship behavior?

3. Do you use sex to escape, relieve anxiety or as a coping mechanism?

4. Do you feel guilt, remorse or depression afterward?

5. Has your pursuit of sex or a particular relationship become more compulsive?

6. Does it interfere with relations with your spouse?

7. Do you have to resort to fantasies or memories during sex in order to be aroused or satisfied?

8. Do you keep going from one relationship or lover to another?

9. Do you feel the right person would help you stop lusting, masturbating or being so promiscuous?

10. Do you have a destructive need—a desperate sexual or emotional need for someone?

11. Does the pursuit of sex or a relationship make you careless for yourself or the welfare of your family or others?

12. Has your effectiveness or concentration decreased as sex or a relationship has become more compulsive?

13. Have you experienced negative consequences as a result of your sexual or relational behavior?

14. Are you depressed?

15. Were you sexually abused as a child or adolescent?

If you answered yes to even a few of questions 1-13, you likely are sexually addicted. You certainly could benefit from addressing this issue. (Additional screening tests are available, including the SAST-R, the Sexual Addiction Screening Test Revised, which is available at www.sexhelp.com. A lengthy, comprehensive Sexual Dependency Inventory is available through clinicians who are trained in its use.)

Unfortunately, no standard set of diagnostic criteria exists for sexual addiction whether in males or females. In fact, at the time of this writing sexual addiction isn't even listed in the *Diagnostic and Statis-*

tical Manual of Mental Disorders (DSM),[3] which is the catalog of recognized psychiatric and emotional problems. The *DSM* is the equivalent of the medical listing your doctor consults to find the code for strep throat, for example. This omission means that treatment for sexual addiction isn't eligible for insurance coverage, which is a significant problem for many who need help. Addictionists are conducting research and clinical trials of a diagnostic instrument that they hope will result in an agreed-upon set of objective criteria for the diagnosis of sexual addiction. Professionals are also lobbying the *DSM* revision committee to include sex addiction as a specific disorder, though unfortunately, it appears they won't succeed. In addition to the insurance benefit, inclusion in the *DSM* would add legitimacy to the problem of sexual addiction and credibility to those who treat it.

It's important to understand that omission in the *DSM* doesn't mean sex addiction isn't a bona fide disease. Almost any reader knows the reality and seriousness of this problem. A medical model is used to compile the *DSM* and frankly, most physicians are way behind when it comes to understanding the behavioral addictions. Research about the neurochemistry of addiction is in its infancy, especially when it comes to sexual behavior. Most medical doctors (including psychiatrists) aren't up-to-date enough to know that sexual activity creates the same physiological tolerance phenomena as chemical substances. Without understanding the tolerance factor, doctors have refused to include sexual compulsivity in the *DSM*.

Interestingly, gambling addiction, which is a disease quite similar to sexual addiction, is included. The liberal nature of our culture and the mindset of the decision makers may factor into some politics of what's included and what isn't. Some members of the *DSM* review group have suggested sexual addiction is nothing more than an attempt by the so-called Religious Right to pathologize sexual activity. An example is homosexuality, which at one time was listed in the *DSM* and was later removed after the American Psychiatric Association voted that homosexuality is an equally acceptable alternative to heterosexuality and shouldn't be considered a disorder.

Skeptical clinicians believe the idea of sexual addiction is the product of conservatives who want to call 99 percent of sexual behavior *sinful* and thus to squash people's fun. However, even those who don't share strict Christian values or boundaries—my respected colleagues and friends in the secular community—will agree that sex clearly can become a life-crippling problem. Sexual addiction isn't just the invention of Christians who are trying to rain on everybody else's parade. The woman whose values do allow her to engage in nonmarital sex may still find her life out of control and unmanageable because of compulsive sexual behavior. It's an addiction problem, not just a sin or values problem.

Remember, to qualify as an addiction a behavior must meet the four characteristics outlined in chapter three: preoccupation, obsession, continuation despite negative consequences and tolerance. This chapter concerns how to diagnose the patterns or behaviors that may be in question. Then these behaviors can be measured against the four characteristics of an addiction to determine the severity of the problem.

TYPICAL PRESENTATIONS OF WOMEN ADDICTED TO SEX
Few women enter counseling and announce they're sexually addicted. Again, the label is so horrible that most women run from it, not embrace it. This reluctance is understandable, but it makes identifying the core problem more of a challenge. While more women are admitting to problems with pornography and cybersex because of their extremely addictive quality, most women who seek counseling do so for other reasons.

1. Depression. Depression or dysthymia (long-standing, low-grade depression) are common issues that bring sexually addicted women into counseling. The vast majority of sex addicts are depressed according to Carnes's research.[4] Some female addicts may be on medication for depression prescribed by their gynecologists or family doctors, but it may not be proving effective. The difficulties and shame of the double life are overwhelming to most Christian women. The resulting depression can be debilitating.

Some addicts become suicidal. They can't imagine admitting their problem and can see no way out. They feel hopeless and helpless.

Sadly, some women have been on various medications, in counseling and even attempted suicide before they divulge their sexual involvements. Without addressing the underlying issue of sexual addiction, these women won't resolve their depression and suicidal thoughts.

2. Marital or relationship issues. Marital difficulties are another problem that may bring female sex addicts in for counseling. Even if an addict hides her acting out, there is still a significant impact on the marriage. Remember, *intimacy disorder* is the best conceptualization of sexual addiction. The secret of sexual sin prevents true connection and intimacy in the relationship. The marriage is strained, at best. Often the female addict is angry and blames her partner, which adds to the distance between them. The husband may engage in his own unhealthy coping behaviors, which further complicates the relationship. (I describe these in chapter seventeen.) Unless the wife is honest with the counselor about her sexual activities, the core issue escapes attention. Behavioral suggestions such as date night or exhortations from a marriage enrichment seminar are impotent to heal a relationship where there is active sexual addiction.

Sexual difficulties may be the presenting problem. Remember, many female sex addicts shut down sexually within the marriage, which causes stress and conflict in the relationship. A wife may only admit to diminished sexual desire and not disclose her sexual behavior outside the relationship, so the real problem stays hidden.

Whether an addict is married or not, difficulties with relationships in general may prompt her to seek help. She may report a pattern of unstable relationships with friends, romantic partners or coworkers. While everyone has relationship troubles at times, a sex or love addict has profound relational impairment that causes significant, chronic distress. Driven by core attachment issues, which will be described in chapter nine, an addict may have an insatiable need for attention, validation or reassurance. She may demand closeness and overreact if she thinks a partner is distancing from her. She's rightfully perceived as needy and demanding.

On the other hand, a sex and love addict may express an inability to attach to a partner romantically and express a fear about intimate relationships. She retreats when someone gets too close. She builds walls or sabotages the relationship. Partners may leave her when she's unable to be as intimate as they desire, and this loss reinforces her belief it's not safe to let down her guard. Either way, a female sex and love addict's relationship problems can feel overwhelming.

3. Substance abuse. Other women may enter therapy because they struggle with substance abuse. In fact, many female sex addicts abuse alcohol or drugs as a way of medicating their shame from their sexual behavior. (Figure 4 illustrates this pattern as part of the explanation of the cycle of addiction.) Or sometimes chemicals serve as disinhibitors to lower a woman's anxiety about acting out sexually. When she's had enough to drink, she allows herself to do things she wouldn't do sober. This seems especially true with the woman who uses cocaine. She often will trade sexual favors for drugs or act out when she's high. I've treated several women who had been sober from alcohol or drugs for a period of time, but they had realized their sexual behavior was still out of control. "I've stopped the drugs," one woman said. "What I can't stop is the men."

4. Eating disorder. Many female sex addicts also struggle with an eating disorder, either anorexia or (more often) bulimia or binge eating. Both sexual acting out and food addiction involve the same dynamics of control-release. In the control phase the woman disciplines herself (it's called "white knuckling" in recovery language) for a period of time and doesn't act out with sex or food. Then in the release phase she lets go of control and gives in to the addiction. She acts out sexually or binges on food. Many female addicts have struggled with a weight problem for years and may vacillate between their sexual and their food addictions. When they're controlling their food and maintaining a normal weight, their sexual addiction is in full swing. When they're abstinent from compulsive sexual behavior, their eating is out of control. It's easier today to admit to an eating problem than a sexual one, so again, a woman may not get the help she needs for her sexual addiction if she only addresses her food issues.

5. Anxiety disorders. Women often enter therapy to address childhood sexual abuse, which I'll discuss in detail in part two. Their clinical diagnosis may be posttraumatic stress disorder (PTSD) as a result of abuse experiences. This disorder involves a variety of symptoms such as flashbacks, nightmares, hypervigilance and so forth that are the result of unresolved trauma. A woman may spend important and beneficial time in counseling addressing the sexual abuse. However, unless she also examines her current behavior and relationships, the problem of sexual addiction may go unnoticed.

Other anxiety disorders, such as panic attacks, may bring an addict in for counseling. One woman described her experiences this way:

> I truly thought I was going crazy. One day I passed a man in the aisle at the grocery store and something about him made me feel uneasy. The next thing I knew, I was having troubling breathing. It felt like an elephant was sitting on my chest. The pain was indescribable. I broke out in a cold sweat. I couldn't speak. I just knew I had to get out of there. My two small children were with me and they were terrified.
>
> I left my basket full of groceries in the middle of the store and stumbled out to the car. It was several minutes before I stopped shaking and could drive away. I was too embarrassed to go back in to finish my shopping. I had no idea what had happened to me. After two more similar episodes, always unpredictable and without warning, I went to see my doctor. I was sure I was either dying or going insane. When he didn't find anything medically wrong, he said I was having panic attacks and referred me to counseling.

The rest of this woman's story is that she was involved in a long-term affair that was tearing her apart emotionally and spiritually. She had broken it off numerous times but always reconnected with her affair partner. At the time of this first panic attack in the grocery store, the man she passed resembled her affair partner, from whom she was apart at the moment. When the stranger looked at her, this addict knew (unconsciously) she would resume the affair yet another time, and the resultant shame triggered the panic episode. She wasn't crazy; she was a sex addict in desperate need of help.

6. Bipolar disorder. Occasionally a woman's sexual sin may be the result of another mood problem such as bipolar disorder (formerly called manic depression). One characteristic of this disorder is promiscuous sexual activity. A woman needs a thorough evaluation by a clinician experienced with assessment and differential diagnosis to determine if her sexual acting out is the result of bipolar behavior (in the manic phase). If not, she may, indeed, be sexually addicted as an independent or concurrent diagnosis. Medication is vital for the bipolar patient.

7. *Personality disorders.* Whether married or single, some women who present for therapy reporting relationship problems are diagnosed as having a personality disorder, which in simple terms, is a pervasive pattern of relating to people in a certain way. Acting out sexually is one of the diagnostic criteria of borderline personality disorder, for example. Clinging compulsively to destructive relationships may be a function of dependent personality disorder. If a woman is excessively needy or emotionally dependent on some other person for her sense of self-worth, she may use sex as a way of getting or keeping a relationship. Again, it's crucial for a woman to get help from a well-trained, discerning clinician who can make an accurate diagnosis.

TOOL FOR GETTING A CLEAR PICTURE

One of the most helpful ways to get an accurate picture of problematic patterns is to prepare a complete sexual and relationship history. In Twelve Step language, this history is part of a First Step report or a Fourth Step "searching and fearless moral inventory." Simply list every sexual encounter and every romantic relationship beginning with your earliest memory. A relationship doesn't have to be sexual to make the list. Include the boyfriend in third grade, your crush on the football captain and the coworker you flirt with. Obviously, overt sexual experiences would certainly be included. *List everything.*

If just the idea of completing this kind of a history seems overwhelming, that reaction may be diagnostic in itself, don't you think? It was for me. In some cases I had vague memories of acting out at a certain time in my life or under certain circumstances, but I couldn't recall the partner's face much less his name (even a first name). That awareness alone was painful.

After your list is as complete as you can remember, review it. Ask a trusted counselor or female friend to go over it with you. Look for any patterns. Were you often sexual even when you didn't want to be? Did you get involved with people who promised you the moon but treated you poorly? Were you usually sexual when you felt lonely or afraid? Did you use sex to feel powerful or stay in a relationship in order to feel loved? Was there always some significant romantic partner in your life (if only in your fantasies)? With prayer and support, ask God to help you see the patterns of your life.

NAMING THE DEMON

I understand the shame that may envelope from this exercise, but I challenge you to have courage. Seeing the truth is the first step of healing. We can't heal what we can't understand or describe. We must name the demon in order to be set free from it.

I believe a powerful illustration is found in Luke 8. It's the story of the demon-possessed man from Gerasenes who "for a long time . . . had not worn clothes or lived in a house, but had lived in the tombs" (Luke 8:27). I wonder how long you may have felt that your spirit was without a safe home, but instead was living in the tomb of shame and addiction. Like this man you may have felt "driven by the demon into solitary places" (verse 29). Your addiction has taken you into increasingly isolated places even if they were filled with people.

When Jesus asked this tormented man his name, he replied "Legion," because he was possessed with many demons. Although the passage doesn't say, I believe this man found a measure of healing in claiming a name and having it acknowledged by the Great Physician. There is power in stating the truth. It may feel like you're possessed by many demons: shame, guilt, despair, addiction. The problems may seem legion.

Be encouraged, dear one. There is hope! By now you've learned the truth about yourself and your problem. You are not a horrible, terrible person. You're certainly not a slut or a whore. You are a precious child of God who is suffering from a specific disease that has a name: sexual addiction. It has identifiable characteristics, presentations and cycle.

It also has roots that are deep and wide that existed and affected your life long before your first fantasy or acting out episode. Part two examines the roots of unhealthy families and abuse and abandonment. Understanding the roots that form the foundation for sexual addiction is a key step toward a life of integrity that doesn't fear being punished with stones.

QUESTIONS FOR REFLECTION
OR SMALL GROUP DISCUSSION

1. What is your score on the self-test? How do you feel about your score?

2. Have you struggled with any of the presenting problems mentioned? Which one(s)? Any others that weren't listed?

3. Complete your sexual and relationship history.

PART TWO

THE ROOT

SINS OF THE FATHERS AND MOTHERS

I am the LORD your God, who brought you out of Egypt, out of the land of slavery.

You shall have no other gods before me.

You shall not make for yourself an idol in the form of anything in heaven above or on the earth beneath or in the waters below. You shall not bow down to them or worship them; for I, the LORD your God, am a jealous God, punishing the children for the sin of the fathers to the third and fourth generation of those who hate me, but showing love to a thousand generations of those who love me and keep my commandments. (Deuteronomy 5:6-10)

UNHEALTHY FAMILIES

I remember being a little girl and spending hours perched at the top of a large tree that was near my bedroom window. It was a sugar maple and in fall it became a kaleidoscope of changing earth tones of red and burgundy, orange and deep yellow. In summer the green leaves and thick branches hid me. The gentle swaying of the wind soothed me. With incredible speed I could ascend through the limbs to my favorite spot, where I looked down on my house, the stables behind it and the driveway that led up the hill. In my tree I felt powerful and in control. There I felt that I belonged. It was my place and I was safe.

I entertained many dreams as I lounged in the top of my tree. The future promised to be bright, even perfect. I would be a writer or a teacher. I would influence lives and help others. I would be the one to board airplanes and fly to faraway places to do kingdom work as I saw my father doing. I would be rewarded with the love and admiration of many. I would be married to a strong Christian man who would adore and cherish me. He would be always at my side and would never leave our children or me. They would never know loss or loneliness.

These were pure dreams. They were positive and holy and untainted. Not once did I imagine a life of deceit or disgrace. I didn't plan a future where I would hide in fear of exposure or devastate the lives of those who mattered most to me. I didn't dream of growing up to be a sex addict.

Did you? Of course not! It's an absurd question.

Yet in our shame, most of us view our sexual addiction as a choice. As the product of somehow choosing a wrong turn in the road of life and winding up in a place we had never imagined. We wonder how we chose so poorly. We beat ourselves up for being so foolish.

The reality, I believe, is quite different. The truth is that I didn't choose sexual addiction. I didn't choose either to be a sex addict or to dedicate myself to treating it and teaching about it. Life unfolded the other way around: *Sexual addiction chose me.* Understanding that truth changes everything. My hope is that the following chapters will make this truth clear, for it is the foundation of healing.

UNDERSTANDING THE ROOTS OF SEXUAL ADDICTION

I trust I've firmly put in place the groundwork for part two. As a reminder let me state again that acting out sexually is sinful. I refuse to offer excuses for sinning. Active sexual addiction separates us from God as does all sin. We destroy our connection with him. Calling sex addiction a disease doesn't eliminate the need to pursue healing. Neither does examining the roots of the disease absolve us of responsibility to stop our sinful behavior.

My point is that understanding how we came to be sexually addicted is a huge and necessary part of recovery. This knowledge is crucial for long-term change. It allows us to take *more* responsibility for our future choices, not to shirk responsibility. It spreads salve on our shame-scraped souls and provides courage to break the cycle. It provides grace for the journey.

UNDERSTANDING IS DIFFERENT FROM BLAMING

It's important to understand also that exploring the roots of sexual addiction, which lie in the families we grew up in, is not about blame. While there may be some blame that could reasonably be assigned as will become clear in the following pages, the objective is to achieve understanding, not to blame or bash our parents. Though insight alone is not necessarily enough to prompt a change in behavior, I believe that without understanding why we do what we do and where our faulty thinking originated, it is more difficult to effect lasting change. Changing our thinking and our belief system, which obviously are rooted in what we learned in our families, lends fuel to our resolve to change our actions. A change in thinking will also help spawn a change in our feelings.

Some of you may already be struggling with this shift in direction. You're disturbed by the very thought of expressing anything negative about your parents. The old tape that commands "Honor thy father and thy mother" is playing loudly in your ear. Again, let me offer an additional foundation for this portion of our work.

First, I remind you that there is no dishonor in telling the truth. It is always honorable to state the truth. Satan is the father of lies, and one he wants you to believe at this moment is that it's wrong for you to state the truth about how you grew up and what you experienced. Remember, the truth can set you free (John 8:32). Examining the truth about the family history of most addicts is all we'll be doing in this section.

Next, we must accept the fact that there is no such thing as the perfect family. All families are flawed in some way, some more than others. No father or mother has been the perfect parent. Only our heavenly father can make that claim. You'll probably come to see that your parents did the best job they could. At least most do. Today, I understand that mine did. They were the products of their parents just as much as you and I are the offspring of ours.

HEALTHY FAMILIES AND UNHEALTHY FAMILIES

All families fall somewhere along the continuum of nearly perfect to truly awful. Most rank higher in some areas than in others. Overall, many families fall into the category of *good enough*, which means they are reasonably adequate in most crucial areas. Sadly, some are terribly dysfunctional, where children endure horrific experiences that are almost beyond belief. The majority of families are somewhere in between.

For simplicity's sake I use *dysfunctional* and *unhealthy* to describe families. Both terms are overused and at least somewhat inaccurate. They imply *functional* and *healthy* families, which are also incorrect descriptions. A family is a complex mix of positives and negatives, a blend of sweet and sour experiences. Concrete words like dysfunctional or unhealthy insinuate an either/or environment. A better picture is a family that's *less healthy* or *more healthy*, which are descriptions of relative points along a continuum. I wish I could avoid the black-and-white characterization of words like dysfunctional, but the sentence structure required is too awkward to be practical. Please keep this caveat in mind as you read.

I invite you to do an initial exercise as a starting point. Close your eyes and recall all the good things you can remember about your family. Picture the happy times and remember the positive life lessons you learned. Review the healthy role modeling you observed. Give God thanks for those wonderful experiences.

Now, in your imagination, wrap all those good memories in a beautiful package and tie a bow on top. Then set it aside. You won't need to devote any more attention to those things, because they were positive. Those things were healthy in your family. They were beneficial. They worked as God intended them. You can turn your attention to the other parts of your childhood, because the memories stored in your box need no further examination. Remember the saying, "If it ain't broke, don't fix it."

What probably do need your attention are the rest of your experiences. Life wasn't always as rosy as the gifts now stored in your box. Some things didn't result in pleasant memories or outcomes. It's to those things we must direct our scrutiny. Remember, our objective is only to tell the truth and to achieve understanding.

EXAMPLES FROM MY FAMILY

Throughout this section I'll share many examples from my own family. Today I honor my father and credit him with many positives in my life. (Since my mother died when I was a young child, I didn't know her.) From my father I learned the value of kindness and generosity. I inherited his gifts of speaking and writing, which are crucial staples of my professional work. From "Doc" (as I affectionately call him) I learned a great knowledge of the Bible, which serves as a foundation for my spiritual life. Many of the verses I memorized as a child come back to me at just the needed time. The lessons my father taught through wonderful renditions of Bible stories will remain with me always. I observed Doc as a man who prayed intensely, which was a worthy example.

I enjoy the gift of being analytical and orderly, which I also observed in my father. Doc could competently juggle many "irons in the fire," as he called them, and he taught me to do the same. I have no doubt today that my father loved his wife and his children. I'm grateful for the good things he gave and taught me.

Yet Doc was far from perfect, and our family was equally flawed. I'll share some of those examples without the intention of hurting anyone. I hope you'll remember why I choose to write with sometimes painful honesty. When we understand our baggage, we can stop being burdened by it. We can set it aside and go on with our lives unencumbered.

FAMILY SYSTEMS PERSPECTIVE

While positive family experiences can be as varied as the number of families in existence, flawed family experiences are more easily categorized. Unhealthy families share certain characteristics in common. These have been outlined by a variety of people known as family systems theorists, whose initial work began in the mid-twentieth century. The field of alcoholism recovery has built on these principles and applied them to families where addiction is present. We owe a great debt to these early pioneers of systemic thinking.

Christians, though, have a longer history of looking at less-than-healthy families. Beginning with Eve and Adam we have recorded example after painful example of the legacy of the sins of the parents. When you read the Old Testament from a family systems perspective, it's clear how the attitudes and behavior of one generation impacted the next. In some ways it's part of the legacy of original sin. Unhealthy families beget unhealthy children, who grow up to become unhealthy parents, who themselves beget unhealthy offspring. The cycle continues. In simple terms, unhealthy families are the breeding ground for later unhealthy, unholy behavior, including addiction.

GOD'S PLAN FOR THE FAMILY

God's design for the family was perfect. The family was intended to be the cornerstone of civilization and a model of God's love for his children. It was to be a place of nurture where members' needs were met and people were helped to thrive. The family was to provide a sanctuary of safety, guidance and affirmation. Parents were to supply their children with all the necessities of a healthy life: physical needs, emotional needs and spiritual needs. Family members would treat one another with dignity and respect. Individual differences and preferences would be honored. There would be a blend of togetherness and autonomy. The family would be a place to receive skills for coping with life and a safe practice ground for using them. Mistakes would be met with grace and new chances. There would be enough structure to provide security, and enough flexibility to encourage creativity. The family would model God's ways of interacting with his children.

Tragically, sin entered the world through the first family and human relationships were forever changed. God's design was perverted by Satan's deceit and the rest is history. All of us are products of our parents' fallen nature, just as our children will receive the legacy of our own. All of us were born into a family marked by sin and imperfection. All of us are replicating those problems in our own families, at least to some extent.

Our goal in part two is to discover exactly how these failings were played out in our childhood homes. To unearth and speak the truth. This chapter examines four specific problem areas in flawed families.

RULES IN UNHEALTHY FAMILIES

Dysfunctional families operate according to a variety of rules, most of which are unspoken. You only realize the rule exists when you've broken it. Some of the rules are benign. Some are even clearly stated.

In my family, which valued order and neatness, you didn't eat breakfast until your bed was made. Since breakfast involved a required appearance at the family table where Doc was usually present, this rule was simply enforced. Other clear rules involved how we spoke to each other. My traditional, Southern family greatly prized politeness, and we were expected to address others with extreme decorum. My brothers and I may have been furious with each other, but we were icily polite, at least on the surface.

Other family rules, though, are less reasonable. Four rules in particular characterize dysfunctional families.

1. Don't talk. The first is the "don't talk" rule. Obviously, most families talk, and mine did too. In fact, in some ways my family was addicted to talking. My father was a pastor and both my brothers eventually followed in his footsteps. Often there was lots of compulsive talking. (Today I'd call it *preaching*.) But we talked about the weather and about school or some church activity—or about the horrible things someone we knew was doing. We didn't really talk. Not about anything important. Not about some of the secrets that bloomed in our family. Certainly not about matters of the heart. Most dysfunctional families follow this rule.

One way it's been described is as if there's a hippopotamus pooping in the living room, but no one is going to talk about it. No one dares mention that this beast has invaded the home, that it's huge and in the way and that it stinks. Somehow the subject of soiled carpet never comes up.

There certainly are other ways that families communicate even when there's a "no talk" rule. Parents have alternative methods of delivering their messages. My father's favorite was to clear his throat. When Doc cleared his throat in a certain way, we all knew we were treading on dangerous ground. Believe me, we got the point. Other people, especially women, like to sigh. My grandmother's deep, breathy sigh spoke volumes.

Every less-than-healthy family has at least one subject that is definitely off limits. As a child I was aware we didn't talk about my mother. I was the third child of my parents and was my father's longed-for daughter after two sons. Before my second birthday, my mother was diagnosed with colon cancer. She died a few months after my third. We never talked about the fact that my mother had lived, much less that she had died. She was simply never mentioned. In fact, I had no category for "mom" or even for "mother." I only had a category for "my mother," which was one step removed from an intimate, parental connection. I had no sense of the person who was my mother, of her likes and dislikes, her hopes and fears, her dreams and disappointments. I knew only that she finally surrendered to the cancer that had ravaged her body and that she inspired many with her faith during the battle.

I don't believe there was any malice involved in our family's silence. We weren't trying to hide the fact of my mother's illness and death. I think two factors were at play. First and most obvious, it was a subject that was simply too painful. My mother died after only thirteen years of marriage, leaving an eleven-year-old, an eight-year-old and a three-year-old. In the late 1950s, single parenthood was highly unusual. A single father was nearly unheard of. No one knew what to say to describe the depth of our family's loss. It was simply too painful for words, so we all grieved alone and in silence.

The other factor and perhaps the more important one involved our religious views. We believed, of course, that my mother was in heaven with Jesus. I believe that still. But I think we also believed it was wrong to question God's will in human affairs. That theology wasn't stated, but I think it operated in our lives. If we dared to talk about my mother, the subject of her death would surely come up, and if we addressed that issue, it would be too easy to slide into a place of doubt, or fear or confusion or (worse) anger. Which brings us to the second rule of unhealthy families: don't feel.

2. Don't feel. In addition to "don't talk," an important rule in unhealthy families is "don't feel." Some feelings are acceptable, especially happiness. Others are encouraged, like guilt. (Guilt seemed like my middle name, because I was prompted to feel it regularly.) But most other feelings, especially the negative ones, are not to be entertained. It's not okay to be hurt or angry or lonely or sad.

I learned early the "don't feel" rule. Remember, I was the youngest and the only girl of three pastor's children in a motherless family. You can imagine how the church members flocked around us. Ours was a heroic story of love lost and of coping after an incredible tragedy. The church ladies (with blue-tinted hair) would pat on me after services and take my chin in their hands and cluck over me.

One Sunday morning when I was not quite five I was feeling especially out of sorts. When some good Christian sister asked what was wrong, I tearfully replied, "I just want my mama!" She looked at me for several long seconds, then firmly said, "But Marnie, your mother is in a much better place!" (That belief system again.) While I'm sure she meant well and was only trying to remind me of the right theological perspective on the death of good Christians, the message I got was loud and clear: *Don't feel what you feel!* At that point, I couldn't care less that my mother was in heaven with Jesus. I wanted her here. The woman's statement was correct theology, but it was also an awful thing to say to a child.

In a variety of other ways the "don't feel" message gets delivered. Our culture sends it to young males who are told, "Big boys don't cry." (Of course they do. And adult men cry too, or at least, they should.) We ignore or discount others' feelings of hurt or sadness or some other difficult emotion. We tell children, "You shouldn't feel that way" and shame them out of their feelings.

Anger, in particular, is one emotion many Christians are taught not to feel. Anger is viewed as inappropriate. Often certain Scriptures are used (incorrectly) as proof texts. Many Christians consider anger an especially dangerous emotion to be avoided at all costs. Unfortunately, avoiding all expressions of anger usually costs a lot: emotional shutdown, depression, codependency, or at the other end of the spectrum, explosions of rage.

3. Deny or minimize. When a family doesn't talk and doesn't feel, it usually substitutes alternate ways of coping with life: denial and blame. Denial is one of the defense mechanisms originally identified by Sigmund Freud. It's a way of dealing with life that's intended to avoid any painful realities. A person simply pretends the situation doesn't exist. It's the mental and emotional version of the child who sticks her head under the bed and believes that because she can't see anything, then no one can see her.

It's denial that allows a woman to continue to chain smoke after her doctor warns her there's a suspicious spot on her lung. The prospect of cancer is too frightening, so she chooses to believe there's been a technician error or lab error or interpretation error. Even if she has cancer, she believes she'll be the one to beat the odds.

Denial causes family members to say, "Hippopotamus? What hippopotamus? I don't see a hippopotamus!" They position its bulk in the living room so the TV is visible between its legs. They throw a tablecloth across its back and call it a piece of furniture. They deny the obvious and collude together in doing so. (The "don't talk" rule is firmly in place, remember?)

Dysfunctional families invoke denial to ignore what's evident to others. The dynamic is that if something isn't acknowledged, it doesn't exist. Sometimes denial is stated like when a mom says, "Oh, dad doesn't have a drinking problem, silly." At other times the problem is minimized. Mom might say, "Dad occasionally has one beer too many, but he goes to work and everything." Or "Uncle Tom didn't mean anything bad by offering to show you that video. He was just kidding. It's no big deal."

Children who grow up in families that operate by denial learn to doubt. When parents challenge their view of reality, children hear, "You don't see what you see or know what you know." I like to illustrate it this way: It's as if parents tell the child, "The grass is red." The child knows better, of course. But if she hears the grass is red long enough (or loudly enough), she eventually comes to doubt her perception of green. She'll look at a blade of grass and at least see it in shades of pink. It's crazy-making.

4. Blame. When flat denial doesn't work, the family increases its ammunition to blame. Parents blame someone other than the one who's responsible for the problem, and it's usually the one who breaks the "don't talk" rule. Instead of just saying, "Uncle Tom didn't mean anything," the mother adds a painful twist: "You misunderstood.

You're the one with the dirty mind." Abusive parents often blame the children with ridiculous statements like "If you hadn't provoked me, I wouldn't have hit you." As adults we see the flawed logic and the misplaced blame, but as children we have no other frame of reference, and we swallow as truth all that our parents say. Unhealthy families blame others for their problems whether those are addictions, abuse, financial difficulties, marital problems or what have you. Adults do not take responsibility for their actions or for the protection of their children.

Sometimes these parents even blame God for their troubles. Children, therefore, learn they have no protector or advocate, not even in their heavenly father.

Other rules. After these four standard rules of dysfunctional families, the possibility of others expands. Again, the varieties are endless. Some of the more common ones are:

- Dad is always right (or mom).
- Don't upset mom (or dad).
- Children are to be seen and not heard.
- It's your job to take care of everyone else.
- Boys are more valued than girls and get the best of everything.
- Our religious views are always right and are not to be questioned.
- Appearances are crucial; what people think of us governs how we behave.
- A woman is nothing without a man.
- Financial success is the measure of worth.
- Making a mistake is the worst thing you can do.

The possibilities are infinite.

ROLES IN UNHEALTHY FAMILIES

Flawed families also play roles that define the members' interactions. These roles serve to add predictability and stability to family relations. They provide a foundational system that supports the family rules. Different writers have offered a variety of roles. I'll suggest ten.

1. Hero or heroine. One of the prized roles in dysfunctional families is the heroine or hero. This person, usually the oldest child, is the superkid, the overachiever, the excellent student, the gifted one. She's the one who is the pride of the family. Members point to her and say (or at least believe), "See? We must be a wonderful family. Look at Susie! A messed up family wouldn't produce a Susie, now would it?" The heroine's accomplishments allow the family to continue in denial about any problems.

2. Saint. The saint is similar to the hero, but this role has a religious cast. The saint is the spiritual standard bearer for the family. It's his job (usually this role is given to a male, but occasionally it belongs to a female) to be the moral one. To keep the rules. Often mom or dad ordains this person for the ministry so that he's called into Christian service by a parent, instead of by God. Like a modern Samuel or John the Baptist, parents dedicate this child to God before birth, not out of sincerity or purity of motive, but to gain the affirmation of others.

3. Little princess or prince. This role is the first cousin to the hero/heroine or even the saint. This person is also outstanding, but this role has a performance component. Parents trot this little girl out to play the piano whether she wants to or not. This dancer must perform at family gatherings. This budding actress must continually be "on." Her value is measured by what she does—by her performance.

4. Scapegoat. The opposite of these first three roles is the scapegoat. Instead of doing everything right, this person does everything wrong. She's the human equivalent of the literal scapegoat in Old Testament times. The high priest symbolically placed the sins of the people onto the back of a goat, and then drove it out into the wilderness to rid the camp of the penalty of sin. The Israelites felt good about themselves because something else carried the burden of their sins.

In unhealthy families, the scapegoat serves as the target of the family's blame. The fault belongs to this person, not to whoever is actually responsible. When I began to act out as a teenager, I changed from the little princess to the scapegoat. My obvious behavior problems and bad reputation allowed the family to deny some of the internal dysfunction. The unspoken message was "We're a wonderful family, except for Marnie, of course. But that's just Marnie. What can we do? The rest of us are fine."

5. *Mascot*. Often the family favorite is the mascot. These people usually have a great sense of humor and are delightful to be around. Classmates may vote them "Most Humorous" or call them the class clown. Their role in the family, though, is to function like the thermostat on the wall. This person takes the emotional temperature of the family, and it's her job to be sure it stays within certain bounds. If the climate becomes too tense, this person cracks a joke or in some way diverts the attention from the upsetting subject. Again, the mascot helps the family avoid talking and feeling.

6. *Lost child*. Next to the family scapegoat, one of the saddest roles is the lost child. This person is literally lost within the family. She receives little attention; she's ignored. An example explains this role best. My husband David was the lost child in his family. He's three years younger than a brother who today would be diagnosed with attention deficit hyperactivity disorder. This brother was a handful, to say the least, and was constantly in trouble with their mother.

By contrast, David learned to be invisible. His mother describes him as the "perfect child," by which she means he required little attention and certainly no disciplining. After breakfast David played in his room with his army figures until he was called for lunch. During his quiet time in the early afternoon, he learned to play the recording that would read the storybook, so his mother didn't even have to read to him. Then he played with his cars and trucks or outside by himself until his father came home at suppertime. An easy child? Yes. But also a lost one who learned not to have any needs or demand any attention. It's no wonder, then, he grew up to marry a woman who totally walked all over him. Lost children are desperately lonely within their self-sufficiency.

7. *Doer*. Another valued role in many families is the doer. Usually performed by the mother or a female child, the doer's role is obviously *to do*. She's the mover and shaker. The woman of action. This is the functional one who keeps the family operating smoothly. She's dependable and efficient. She solves problems and makes things happen. She's a valuable employee who makes herself indispensable to her company. She's the rock of the family. When the going gets tough, she gets going and figures out how to cope with any crisis. Many admire her. Within Christian circles she's applauded for her servant heart. She's busy juggling many responsibilities. She's also usually exhausted and resentful.

8. Martyr. The martyr, if present in a family, is often a first cousin of the doer. She's just more obvious about her resentment. I call her a doer with an attitude. She'll sigh or roll her eyes or collapse onto the couch to alert everyone she's being the martyr. She expects to be rewarded for what she does. She wants everyone to see her service and her sacrifice. Her suffering must not go unnoticed.

9. Peacekeeper. The peacekeeper is one of the most stressful roles in the family. It's a thankless job with few rewards. The most difficult situation is where a child is the go-between for her parents. They triangle her into their relationship. Because they observe the "don't talk" rule with each other, it's the role of the peacekeeper to communicate for them. She's pulled between conflicting sides. Like the mascot, she learns to be keenly aware of the atmosphere in the home and to take action when needed. She often gets blamed when the truce fails.

10. Enabler. The last role in a dysfunctional family actually depends on a certain family configuration. The other roles may exist in any flawed family. For someone to fulfill the enabler role, some kind of active addict must be in the family. The classic picture of an enabler comes from a home where alcoholism is present. In this case, for example, the wife may make excuses for her husband's work absences. She tells the boss that he's sick when he really is drunk or hung over. She covers for him, hides his booze or threatens to leave him if he doesn't straighten up. But she doesn't take any definitive, healthy action to confront her situation.

On the other hand, she may enable by denying or minimizing the problem. She chooses to look the other way and ignore all warning signs. She resorts to her own coping strategies, which may include fulfilling some of the other roles like the doer or the peacekeeper between the addict and his children. Yet she too is strangling in the sick family system.

THE PROBLEM WITH RIGID FAMILY ROLES

It's important to understand that there's nothing wrong with being responsible or excellent at something or using a particular talent. It's okay to occasionally resolve disagreements between family members. It's nice to have a sense of humor.

The problem arises when people are rigidly locked into their roles. When they're only allowed to act or relate in a certain way, what happens when that approach doesn't work in a given circumstance?

Consider the hero in a family. One man I know was the definite hero in a family that had little else to be proud of. He was the first in his family to go to college. He became a doctor and excelled. He was well respected and liked. But he was also a sex addict. His sexual behavior clearly didn't fit into his family role. As the hero, not only in his family but now also in his profession, how was he supposed to admit his problem and ask for help? That response was outside his view of possibilities. It was unthinkable.

Or what about the mascot? Again, these people are terrific friends and acquaintances. But what happens when the mascot needs to cry? Will others allow it? One of my dear friends was the mascot in her family. She was charming and witty and the life of the party. Then her only son was killed in a tragic accident when he was only seventeen years old. As family and friends gathered at her home, their pain soon became nearly overwhelming. My friend's parents began to sob at the loss of this fine young man. This overt expression of feeling was nonexistent for this family. As the mascot, it historically was my friend's job to change the dark mood. Despite her own anguish at the death of her son, this woman began to tell funny stories about the teenager. For over an hour she recounted tales of his innocent escapades.

It wasn't that she didn't ache over the death of her child. Her pain was enormous. But at that time, her responsibility to be the family's mascot was stronger. It was how the family coped. It was how she coped. And it prevented her from receiving the comfort she desperately needed and her entire family from expressing their grief in healthy ways.

When a family operates according to rigid roles, how will the lost child ever state her needs? How can she assert herself and take responsibility for her desires and feelings? How could my husband as the lost child possibly insist that I stop acting out so flagrantly?

Consider now the effect these family rules and roles have had on your life. Do you abide by the "don't talk" and "don't feel" rules? Is there anyone who knows your dark secrets and the pain of your heart? Do you deny or minimize the addiction in your life? If you're married, do you blame your husband for not understanding you better or meeting your needs? As a little princess or a heroine, is it hard for you to admit defeat? As a doer, are you able to ask for help? As the mascot, can you collapse under the incredible pain that is tearing you apart?

In families that are more healthy, roles are flexible and shared. Someone may shoulder the main responsibilities for a time, but she's able to ask for help or to admit when she's overwhelmed. The family honors each member for her acknowledgments, and each person gets her turn in the spotlight. All can be human and make mistakes. No one is singled out as the scapegoat. No one is lost or ignored. Family members deal directly with each other to address problems and solve disputes. No one person must be the peacekeeper or the go-between. Are you beginning to see how the unhealthiness in your family contributed to your being stuck in your current situation?

As if problems with rules and roles weren't difficult enough, one more characteristic of unhealthy families needs attention. Boundary issues plague dysfunctional families, and problems in this area also form the breeding ground for later detrimental behavior.

BOUNDARIES IN UNHEALTHY FAMILIES

Boundaries are the invisible force fields that define a person's space. Boundaries define where I stop and where you begin. Boundaries provide structure, safety and security.

My colleague Dr. Mark Laaser devised one of the best illustrations of boundaries. He uses *Star Trek* to discuss the nature of boundaries and how they work.[1] Do you remember the show? It involves a starship that's exploring the galaxy. When enemies attack the ship, the captain immediately commands the crew to raise the protective shields. These shields provide safety and prevent the bad guys from overtaking the ship. After the danger is past, the captain commands the crew to lower the shields. This action allows fresh supplies to be loaded on board and waste to be removed. It's a perfect illustration of how healthy boundaries work. They are strong enough to keep the bad stuff out, while permeable enough to let the good stuff in. They can be strengthened or loosened as needed. Their purpose is to provide safety, not to constrict or to punish.

Boundary problems in dysfunctional families are of two kinds: either too loose or too rigid. We'll examine both.

Too loose boundaries. Boundaries that are too loose threaten the safety of the family. Members, especially children, are vulnerable to harm. The family environment is open to invasion either from within (by family members themselves) or from without (by people who aren't part of the family).

When boundaries are too loose several things may happen. There may be little or no privacy. I've worked with an astonishing number of women who grew up in homes where there were no doors. Their bedroom doors were literally removed from the hinges. Less extreme are the numerous women who weren't allowed to shut their doors. Others had no bathroom privacy, where people walked in on them without warning. Some families have no boundaries about nudity, and family members routinely walk around in various states of undress.

Loose boundaries provide the opportunity for unhealthy touch either physically or sexually. (I'll discuss this topic at length in the next chapter.) Frequent criticism may invade a child's spirit. Unhealthy teasing may torment. Conflict may abound, perhaps with hitting or yelling.

When boundaries are too loose, no one guides children about how to dress, speak or behave. Parents don't set curfews or guidelines about children's activities. The family doesn't teach about morality or emphasize spirituality. Having too few healthy boundaries forces children to make decisions beyond their ability.

While some children, especially teenagers, may think this kind of environment sounds like fun, where they give themselves permission to do whatever they please, the truth is that this atmosphere breeds confusion and insecurity. Children long for a capable adult to be in charge, to set standards and to provide guidance.

Too rigid boundaries. The opposite situation occurs where the boundaries are too rigid. They're too firm, too strict. Not enough "good stuff" gets in to nourish and nurture. Again, there are many examples. When boundaries are too rigid little connection exists among the family members. People keep each other at arm's length. There's no intimacy. Healthy touch may be absent. Many clients, especially males, report they don't remember their parents holding or rocking or hugging them after they were past toddler age. Fathers are particularly prone to stop touching their children in healthy ways.

Little or no affirmation warms these families. I think of the old story about the man who was celebrating his fiftieth wedding anniversary. His wife kept asking him if he loved her. Finally he said in exasperation, "I told you I loved you fifty years ago when I married you, and I'd have told you if I changed my mind." For those who grow up in the absence of affirmation, the story isn't funny. When love isn't appropriately expressed, children wonder about their importance in the family. All of us long not only to be loved but also to hear specifically that we're valued and cherished. These rigid families sometimes believe it spoils children to hear how much they're loved.

Rigid families often express harsh judgment about bad behavior— and about the people who do it. This kind of environment leads to the belief, "I'm only okay if I'm perfect. If I'm bad or make mistakes, I'm a horrible, terrible person." There's no room for creativity, for experimentation, for growth.

Avoidance characterizes rigid families. Instead of healthy conflict, silence and denial reign. The family enforces the "no talk" rule.

These families portray God as the exacting taskmaster who expects perfect performance rather than a loving father who longs for a relationship with his children. They teach God is ever vigilant in watching for mistakes and is always ready with swift condemnation. The plight of humankind is best understood in the words of the eighteenth-century preacher Jonathan Edwards: "sinners in the hands of an angry God."

Confusion of dual boundaries. Extreme confusion arises when the boundaries are both too loose and too rigid within the same family. One parent may practice a loose stance where anything goes. The other may be rigid where children are tightly controlled. Children quickly learn to pit the parents against each other and to manipulate them.

Especially damaging is the scenario where the same parent practices both boundary violations. For example, when dad doesn't touch or affirm his daughter most of the time (too rigid boundaries) yet at night he sexually fondles her (too loose boundaries), the confusion is tremendous. The harm is incalculable. Or perhaps the mother is distant and critical most of the time, but on other occasions she invades the daughter's privacy and demands to know intimate details of the young woman's relationship with her boyfriend. How is the daughter to make sense of these conflicting interactions? Which way will it be today? What about tomorrow?

I was terribly confused about boundaries when I entered recovery. Many boundaries were too loose in my home. Because I was the only female in a household of males, I easily adapted to the male environment and was viewed as simply one of the guys. It was normal for males to walk back and forth to the shower either naked or clad in only a brief towel. Doors were rarely shut and no one knocked before entering. I had few boundaries about dating and was allowed to date guys who were much older. I came and went as I pleased, even as a young child, and there was lax supervision. There were also many instances of abuse, which I'll describe in the next chapter.

On the other hand, some boundaries were too rigid. My family went to church at least three times a week or whenever the doors were open (whichever one was more frequent). It was a nonnegotiable appearance. I often went when I was too sick to be there or when it meant I'd be up all night studying for exams or finishing some school project. (And I didn't procrastinate.) I learned God was a harsh and stern being who was little concerned with my personal state. My family seemed to value people for how they appeared and what they did, not for who they were as human beings. I felt pressure to earn excellent grades and excel at anything I tried, but I rarely heard praise for doing so. Achievement was simply expected. Many times the environment felt crazy, because it *was* crazy.

Enmeshed families/disengaged families. Family systems theorists coined two other terms that describe boundary problems in families. At one extreme are *enmeshed* families. A good description of these families is that they're all tangled up like a plate of spaghetti. They insist on togetherness. One of their rules is that happy families are always together and always agree on everything. Individuality or autonomy isn't tolerated. These parents cling to their children and don't allow them to grow up and separate in healthy ways. These are the kind of folks who'll invite themselves along on a newlywed's honeymoon. Most of these families are in the loose boundary category.

At the opposite extreme are the families that are *disengaged*. They're rigid in their interaction to the point where they hardly interact at all. They don't share thoughts or feelings on an intimate level. They ignore and deny problems. They spend little time together and are more like strangers or casual acquaintances who happen to live together.

Anecdotal evidence shows that most religiously oriented unhealthy families, especially evangelical Christians, fall into the rigidly disengaged category. That means they're rigid in their boundaries and there's little intimacy among family members. The family environment is performance-based instead of relationship-based. Love feels conditional. This kind of family provides a setup for later addictive behavior. In fact, Carnes's research shows that the majority of sex addicts come from rigidly disengaged families.[2]

ADDITIONAL PROBLEMS IN UNHEALTHY FAMILIES

Sometimes further problems exist in flawed families. There may be addiction of some kind or depression or some other mental illness. Maybe there's a chronic physical condition that impairs a parent. Perhaps the mother or father suffers from posttraumatic stress disorder from her or his own childhood experiences. Maybe a parent is a rageaholic who takes out anger on a spouse and children. Often a parent may be out of the home because of divorce or abandonment.

Almost all families have some kind of family secret that affects everyone concerned, but, of course, is never discussed. I found the stash of pornography that was hidden in my home as did my brothers (I learned in adulthood). Separately, we each discovered the magazines and novels (in those days) but no one mentioned it. We simply returned to the forbidden place again and again, hiding from each other. (And from God.) We each thought we were the only one. Such is the nature of family secrets. The list of problems in unhealthy families goes on and on. So does the pain.

IMPLICATIONS OF PROBLEMS
FOUND IN UNHEALTHY FAMILIES

What difference then does it make to have grown up in a family flawed in one or more of these ways? So what if there were unhealthy rules in place or roles were rigidly enforced or boundary problems existed? How does it matter now? What does it have to do with the current sex addiction in your life? The succinct answer is that it makes a tremendous difference. These family of origin experiences influence your present life in profound ways. Understanding that influence is a key to breaking the pattern of unhealthiness.

I've already discussed some of the implications. If you grew up with the "don't talk" rule, it will be difficult for you to be honest about the ways you're struggling. If you weren't supposed to feel, how can you admit the terror that stalks your soul? If you were shackled with rigid boundaries where it was unacceptable to receive nurturing touch, how can you let down your guard and cry on a safe shoulder? If you were raised with loose boundaries, it will be nearly impossible for you to protect yourself from those who would take advantage of the sexual signals you may unwittingly send out. If your family was enmeshed, it will be tough for you to assert your independence in a healthy way and take your own stand for a different way of interacting. If you choose to break away by entering counseling, for example, your family may consider you a traitor and a betrayer of family secrets and loyalty.

Are you beginning to understand the far-reaching influence of your childhood experiences? I hope more puzzle pieces are falling into place. I pray the picture is beginning to take shape and make sense. As you delve into the roots of your addiction disease, be encouraged by the words of our Savior: "Then you will know the truth, and the truth will set you free" (John 8:32).

QUESTIONS FOR REFLECTION
OR SMALL GROUP DISCUSSION

1. What were the primary rules in your family?

2. What role(s) did you play?

3. Describe the boundaries in your family. Loose? Rigid? Combination?

4. Describe how you feel as you remember what it was like growing up in your family.

CHAPTER EIGHT

TRAUMA OF ABUSE

Perhaps the most difficult truth to admit about our childhood homes is that we may have been harmed beyond the damage that resulted from unhealthy rules or rigid roles or boundary problems. Some of us—the majority of us, in fact—also suffered specific instances of abuse. In groundbreaking research done in the early 1990s, Patrick Carnes found that astonishing numbers of adult sex addicts were overtly abused in some way.[1] Clients' stories, as shared in mine and other counseling offices across the country, verify Carnes's statistics (see table 1).

Table 1. Incidence of Trauma Among Sex Addicts

Sexual Abuse	81%
Physical Abuse	72%
Emotional Abuse	97%

It's important to understand that you don't have to be the direct victim of abuse in order to be affected by it. The power of vicarious abuse is vastly underestimated. By vicarious I mean that "only" witnessing abuse can have a profound impact.

We learned this lesson clearly from the Vietnam veterans who returned from that conflict during the 1960s and early 1970s. Even those who weren't directly injured reported psychological and emotional harm from what they saw. Men watched their buddies blown apart by hidden land mines or strafed with guerilla machine-gun fire. They saw unpredictable and pervasive violence. They were constantly threatened with harm. These veterans taught us significant lessons about posttraumatic stress disorder as they struggled to regain a sense of safety and order in the world.

Apply this principle, then, to abusive families. If as a child you saw your mother beaten by her husband or observed objects being thrown across the room in rage, you are personally affected. Even if you were never directly hit or otherwise abused, simply being in an abusive environment causes incredible damage.

One female addict who attended one of the first workshops experienced this kind of vicarious abuse. She was never harmed personally, but her father routinely beat her mother. She could hear the sounds and see the results. To keep this addict and her sisters from telling, the dad would put them in the center of a bed and then carve the air around them with a running chainsaw. He'd threaten to go after the girls if they ever told about the abuse. This precious woman was never scratched, but her soul was scarred for life.

If a family member endured any kind of abuse whether physical, emotional, sexual or spiritual and you were a witness or were aware, you personally have been harmed. Being unable to protect a loved one is traumatic. It's important to acknowledge the pain of those experiences.

This chapter explores four kinds of tragic abuse that often happen in the childhood homes of people who grow up to be sexual addicts. These types of *invasion trauma,* as Dr. Laaser calls it,[2] inflict horrible wounds on a woman's soul. Her recovery and long-term sobriety depend on her healing from these wounds. Laaser developed the chart shown as table 2, which illustrates four kinds of invasion trauma.

Physical abuse. Thankfully, significant attention has been given to the problem of physical abuse in the last twenty or thirty years. Many helpful books have been written and many courageous survivors have told their stories. It's generally accepted today that it is

Table 2. Wounds of Abuse (Boundaries Are Too Loose)

EMOTIONAL	PHYSICAL	SEXUAL	SPIRITUAL
Yelling	Hitting	Touching or penetrating genital area	Punitive and angry messages about God
Screaming	Slapping	Teasing about body	Self-righteousness
Putdowns	Pushing	Sexual humor	Negative messages about sex
Name calling	Shoving	Sexual misinformation	Modeling unhealthy lifestyle
Profanity	Spanking to the point of physical harm	Exposure to pornography	Shame-based religion
Mind rape			
Emotional incest			

never appropriate to physically harm a child. Substantial progress has been made.

Sadly, though, it hasn't always been this way. In earlier generations it was common practice to whip children into obedience. Trips to the woodshed were frequent forms of discipline. Children simply accepted such experiences as the way it was. Even today many parents ignore what they know about the harm of physically abusing children. And many adult children discount the pain of what happened to them as forms of punishment. If you were disciplined in physical ways that left marks, you were the victim of physical abuse. It is never justified to hit children with either a hand or an object in a manner that leaves streaks, cuts or bruises.

Though it may not cause a skin injury, being slapped is also a form of physical abuse. Few things are more demeaning than to be slapped across the face. It's an affront to your very personhood. To your dignity. It's disrespectful and disheartening. Yet many parents think nothing of slapping their children even in public.

Again, you can be affected even if family members themselves escape physical abuse. The abuse of a pet or some other animal harms the child. A violent environment where someone breaks or throws things in rage damages a child. She stays fearful of what will be next. Will the violence escalate? If so, who will be the target? If not fatal, even the most horrific burns or other injuries of physical abuse will ultimately heal. The damage to the spirit, however, remains.

Emotional abuse. Clinicians have yet to explore fully the trauma of emotional abuse. People often dismiss it as minor since, after all, "It's not like you were hit or anything." A children's rhyme reinforces this falsehood when it chants, "Sticks and stones can break my bones, but words can never harm me." Nothing could be further from the truth.

A parent's cruel words create enormous pain. I worked with one dear lady who was emotionally abused as badly as anyone I've ever heard of. Her mother conceived this daughter as a result of an affair, and she took the shame out on her child. (This fact, however, was a family secret, which my client didn't learn until she was grown.) This client's mother routinely told her things like, "I didn't want you before you were born, and the first time I saw you in the hospital, I knew I was right. I didn't want to take you home, but I was afraid of what the church people would think." On this woman's thirtieth birthday, her mother presented her with a beautiful card because the gifts were opened at a party a friend arranged and people were watching. But inside the card my client found a handwritten list of "30 Things I Hate About You!" This beautiful woman heard constantly that she was ugly and undesirable. Her mother purposefully bought her clothes that were several sizes too large.

As her counselor I tried to coach this woman about setting boundaries with her mother. I encouraged her to stand up for herself and to leave when her mother began to berate or criticize her. It wasn't until my client was unable to establish any boundaries that I began to understand the depths of how she had been wounded. This dear lady had been emotionally abused all her life to such a profound extent that she truly believed she was the horrible person her mother described. She felt she had no worth and no right to be treated kindly. She didn't believe she deserved to live. And because her mother "only" emotionally abused her and didn't physically harm her, she found it hard to acknowledge her deep woundedness. "I really didn't have it so bad," she said. Her obvious pain and depression spoke otherwise.

Another form of emotional abuse, perhaps a more subtle type, is what's known as *mind rape*. That's a strong term, I know. Do you remember our discussion about boundaries that are too loose or families that are enmeshed, where independent thought isn't allowed? That's the breeding ground for mind rape. Children or teens are "raped" out of their thoughts and feelings. They're told, "You shouldn't think that way. That's crazy." It's another version of the "grass is red" syndrome. You come to doubt your own thoughts and don't develop an independent sense of self.

A final kind of emotional abuse also bears a shocking name: *emotional incest*. This trauma occurs when a child is "parentified"—that is, asked to take on an adult role, usually as a surrogate spouse. The child assumes responsibilities that are way beyond what is age appropriate. It may be financial responsibility such as the case where a son or daughter goes to work at an early age to help support the family. More often, though, this trauma involves emotional responsibilities. The son becomes the "man of the house" when dad abandons the family. The daughter shoulders the household responsibilities when the mom is addicted, ill, busy or impaired. Instead of enjoying childhood with the security that a responsible adult is in charge, this child loses her youth in the face of adult responsibilities.

One daughter I know bought her family a washer and dryer when she was ten years old. Neither parent was physically or emotionally present enough to attend to the family, though they provided plenty of financial resources. Paid help lived in the home to provide an element of safety, but it was up to this ten-year-old to take care of routine household problems. When the washer quit working, the child (at the parents' request) simply hailed a cab, went to the local appliance store where her father was known and charged the set of appliances. When the parents came home, the machines were installed and, indeed, had already been put to good service.

Another common situation is where a child becomes a parent's confidant. She listens to mom's complaints about dad, for example, including mom's sexual frustrations. The relationship is inappropriately friend-to-friend, rather than parent-to-child. The child meets the adult's emotional needs, instead of the other way around. The child becomes the caretaker for either the parent or younger siblings or both.

This kind of unhealthy relationship can be extremely confusing for the child. On the one hand, she may receive praise and affirmation for being so responsible or helpful or dependable. Those compliments feel good. On the other hand, she longs to relax and enjoy the everyday pursuits of youth. She's usually tired and anxious and lonely. This dynamic also causes sexual confusion. Even if there is no overt sexual relationship or contact between the parent and the incested child, the dynamic of the relationship is still skewed. Because the child is put into a partner role, even nonsexual touch carries an undercurrent of sexuality. The basic nature of the relationship is spousal rather than parental, which taints the bond. The innocence of interaction is lost. The atmosphere is charged with expectation.

Sexual abuse. The alarming incidence of sexual abuse is tragic and growing. A widely quoted statistic estimates that one out of every three girls and one out of every six boys experiences sexual abuse by the time she or he is eighteen. Far fewer cases are actually reported and even less are substantiated according to a legal definition of abuse, but this estimate is realistic in terms of the stories heard daily by counselors, teachers and others across the country.[3] Think about it this way: Imagine that fully one-third of adult Americans suffered from one specific disease. The attention and resources that would be poured into that area would be phenomenal. Yet that's exactly the case with childhood sexual abuse. It is epidemic in our culture, but it's still largely a hidden epidemic.

To be fair, the last dozen or so years have brought good progress in breaking the silence about this travesty. Finally, professionals and survivors alike are talking about this scandalous topic. Books are available; support groups have formed; movies and TV shows address the issue. The climate is becoming safer for a woman to admit that she too is a survivor.

Still, however, there are great misconceptions about sexual abuse. I know I would never have identified myself as a victim of sexual abuse, though I was regularly molested for over fifteen years. I thought my counselor was nuts when she asked if I had been sexually abused at our first session. I denied it vehemently.

My denial wasn't because I had repressed or forgotten the experiences, though that sometimes happens. I clearly remembered. My denial was because I had a faulty conception of what it meant to have been sexually abused. My definition of sexual abuse was to be dragged off the playground by a stranger in a trench coat (always a male) and brutally raped. Since that hadn't happened to me, I never considered that I had been abused.

Sexual abuse involves many more categories than intercourse. That's only one form. A simple definition is that sexual abuse is when a child of any age (that includes adolescents, who some falsely believe are old enough to "know better") is sexually exploited by an adult for that adult's own purpose or gratification.[4] That's a pretty broad definition, isn't it? Inappropriate touching or kissing, therefore, also constitutes sexual abuse.

There are two kinds of sexual violation: overt abuse and covert abuse. *Overt* abuse involves specific physical contact. An adult either touches a child in some inappropriate way or has the child touch the adult. Overt abuse includes such things as fondling breasts or genitals, masturbation of the child or adult (either coerced self-stimulation or done by another person), sexual kinds of kissing, oral sex performed on either the adult or child, or penetration (vaginally or anally) with the hand, penis or an object. One instance of any of these kinds of behaviors can have a significant impact. Overt abuse awakens sexual responses before the child has the maturity to handle them.

Covert sexual abuse occurs without direct physical contact. Examples include inappropriate nudity, forcing a child to watch others being sexual, exposing a child to pornography or spying on a child bathing or dressing. Sexual teasing or inappropriate comments about body development or sexual activity are also abusive. These experiences, too, can be damaging. They create a sexualized environment that is harmful.

Notice that none of these activities has to be forced in the traditional sense of the word. No weapon has to be used. No threats have to be made. The perpetrator simply uses his or her status as an older, more powerful person in order to achieve the goal of personal satisfaction. This imbalance of power is one of the characteristics of sexual abuse. It's why sexual activity is still abusive even if the individual is a teenager. Adolescents simply don't have the maturity to choose to be sexual with an older and therefore more powerful person. Although the teen intellectually knows such sexual activity is wrong (as a pastor's daughter, I certainly did), she lacks the emotional maturity to understand the exploitation involved.

Note, too, that most sexual abuse occurs with someone the child knows and trusts. Most perpetrators are close to the child such as a parent, stepparent, grandparent or other relative, teacher, coach, youth leader or good family friend. The relationship provides easy access and often a (false) sense of safety. When the violator is someone the child knows, and especially if the person is someone the child likes or trusts, the experiences are especially confusing. How could it be abuse when so-and-so is a friend?

This was the main reason I didn't frame my own experiences as abuse. The violator was a trusted family friend. He came into my life when I was five and he was twenty. He was a substitute father figure, because Doc traveled extensively and was absent the majority of the time. This man spent time with me, to my great delight. He took me roller skating every Saturday morning for years. He adored and affirmed me, which I desperately craved. He was my best friend. He let me talk about how much I missed my parents, my father as well as my mother. He even let me feel what I felt. I loved him dearly, and I believed he loved me. How could he possibly have harmed me? I never told him no and he never hurt me physically. In fact, he was gentle and nurturing with his touch. So how could our activities be construed as sexual abuse? See the confusion?

Sexual exploitation doesn't require physical harm. Another hugely confusing piece is that the child's body often responds to the sexual activity. That's the way God designed our bodies. Physically speaking, the body doesn't discern unhealthy touch from healthy touch. Pleasurable sexual feelings result from sexual stimulation. There's no moral filter that governs that reaction. My perpetrator quite intentionally taught and fostered my own sexual response. The sensations felt exciting and wonderful. Many survivors' bodies react to the sexual touch in pleasurable ways, including orgasm. Again, that's terribly confusing. How could something that feels so good be so bad? How could it be abuse when the victim comes to desire those sensations? Also, there's usually a payoff of some kind involved in the abuse. The child gets special favors or treatment, for example, in exchange for the sexual activity. For me, the payoff was time and attention, which seemed well worth the shame I felt because of the sexual exchanges.

Like no other form of trauma, sexual abuse creates a wound in the soul. Remember, our sexuality is most closely akin to our spirituality, so harm in this area is especially damaging. The child and even the adult can't sort out what happened. The shame is enormous. Especially if the victim wasn't physically harmed, if she believes she consented to the abuse because of the relationship with the perpetrator, and if her body responded with pleasure, she will be exponentially ashamed. The idea that she actually is a victim of a heinous crime never occurs to her. She blames herself. She takes on the shame that belongs to the perpetrator.

And probably, she will never voluntarily tell the secret. In her self-blame, she hides the abusive activities. She's afraid of being exposed as the slut she thinks she is, especially if her adult life is marked with sexual addiction. She believes she's damaged goods, and she likely acts out that view in her adult life.

Spiritual abuse. You may be surprised at the term *spiritual abuse*, which is the final category of invasion trauma. Carnes doesn't list it, but it's real and Laaser wisely includes it. Spiritual abuse involves being "hit over the head" with the Bible. It means being motivated into right action by shame and fear of damnation instead of by a desire for a right relationship with God. It's receiving angry and punitive messages about God instead of a portrayal of a loving father who desires the best for you. As a child, I got the message that my grieving and longing for my mother showed a lack of faith since she was in a better place. That's spiritually abusive.

Perhaps more important, though, is a further definition of spiritual abuse. If you were physically, emotionally, or sexually abused by someone who represented spiritual authority in your life, you automatically are a victim of spiritual abuse. If your perpetrator was a pastor, Sunday school teacher, youth leader, church deacon, priest or any kind of spiritual guide or mentor, then you have suffered spiritual abuse. My main perpetrator was a deacon and a song leader in the church, which also qualifies me as a spiritual abuse survivor.

The implications of this truth are enormous. Because of our limited human capacity to understand spiritual things, we base our view of God largely on the early spiritual figures in our life. That is, if our earthly father is kind, loving, affirming and full of grace, it's easier for us to grasp that God interacts with us in a similar way. If our father is rigid, judgmental, harsh or distant, we similarly view God like that. It's hard to imagine we'll be accepted and loved despite our mistakes.

Think, then, about the impact of experiencing abuse at the hands of one who represents God. God is the ultimate healer, and being in right relationship with Him is key to our serenity as well as our eternity. Do you see how difficult it is to achieve that intimacy with a God we distrust because we fear he's like our earthly abusers? Healing our view of God will be a necessary part of our recovery journey, and few things are more difficult.

QUESTIONS FOR REFLECTION
OR SMALL GROUP DISCUSSION

1. Describe any emotional abuse you experienced.

2. Describe any physical abuse you experienced.

3. Describe any sexual abuse you experienced.

4. Describe any spiritual abuse you experienced.

5. Describe how you feel as you remember your abuse experiences.

CHAPTER NINE

TRAUMA OF ABANDONMENT

As painful as it may be, abuse is at least easy to recognize and understand. It's fairly obvious and clear-cut. The second kind of family of origin trauma is much more difficult to comprehend. It's the trauma of abandonment. There's this inherent problem: *How do you know you missed something when you've never had it?* If you've never tasted chocolate, for example (bless your heart) you'd have no way of knowing that delicious sensation, right? It would never even occur to you that something as wonderful as chocolate existed in the world. You'd have no frame of reference. You wouldn't miss chocolate, because you've never tasted it. Your *chocolate* category would be blank. You'd probably think that vanilla was as good as it got.

The same thing happens with abandonment trauma. How do you know you even missed out on something when you never had it in the first place? How do you know a key element may have been lacking in your life?

I distinctly remember the day I first realized—really realized, way down deep in my gut—that I had been abandoned. I was ten years old and was walking home from school with my best friend, Susan. My father was a university administrator as well as a pastor, and our path home led behind the buildings at the edge of the campus. I can see it as clearly as if it were yesterday. The library, with its slightly musty smell and hushed interior, was on our left. The massive oak trees that lined the road were on our right. It had rained earlier and wide puddles dotted the lane. I remember being worried about staining the toes of my new white tennis shoes. Neither the day nor the setting was unusual. We were just average fourth-grade girls who'd been released from school for the weekend.

As we did nearly every Friday afternoon, Susan and I were planning who would spend the night with whom. When we decided on her house Susan casually said, "I'll have to ask my mom first before you come over." It was an innocent, average statement she had probably made dozens of times before. But that day it jolted me like a lightning bolt. *Susan had to ask her mother's permission to have a friend sleep over.* For some reason, at that moment I grasped the impact of the truth that I didn't have a mother to ask. I'd always known I didn't have a mother living, of course, but my childish mind never gave it much thought. It was simply my reality. Yes, it was different from my friends, but it wasn't particularly painful. It was just the way things were. It was my life.

But that instant as my toe edged into a mud puddle and splashed brown across my shoe, it hit me: *I don't have a mother.* And nothing was going to change that fact. I would never have a mother the rest of my life, at least not a mother who had given birth to me. And if something happened to my father, I would be an orphan! Who would take care of me?

Suddenly I began to sob and took off at a hard run. I'm sure Susan wondered what happened, but I never told her. (We didn't talk about things, of course, especially not about painful feelings.) She called soon after she got home, and I just said I'd gotten choked. I remember seeing Susan's mom differently that sleepover. Her simplest actions pricked my young heart. The way she buttered toast or smoothed a child's hair. It was amazing. For the first time I became aware of a deep longing in my spirit. It was the first night I remember crying myself to sleep as Susan's mother slept down the hall.

Most of you probably didn't experience the profound loss of a parent's death. So why make such a big deal out of this abandonment stuff? Isn't the trauma of abuse the more important one? The answer is simple. While astounding numbers of sexual addicts are the victims of invasion trauma, not all addicts suffered in that way. Maybe you didn't. But I have never known a sex addict who wasn't the survivor of abandonment trauma. A full 100 percent of those who struggle with sexual addiction, both male and female, experienced some form of abandonment.[1] In many ways the effects of abandonment are more profound than the consequences of abuse. The wounds are deeper. They're more hidden. And they're more difficult to heal.

Believe me, healing from the losses in your life is the most challenging part of your recovery. Those wounds are cavernous and intense. Healing is tricky and complex. Even today, many years into this journey, it's the trauma from abandonment that still has the power to bowl me over. Abandonment, I believe, is the real slayer of the soul. We'll examine this abandonment trauma according to the same four categories developed by Laaser, as shown in table 3.

Table 3. Wounds of Abandonment (Boundaries Are Too Rigid)

EMOTIONAL	PHYSICAL	SEXUAL	SPIRITUAL
No listening	Being left alone	Intimacy unmodeled	Spirituality unmodeled
No caring or nurturing	Inadequate food, shelter or clothing	Lack of healthy information about sex	Lack of spiritual discipline
No expression of affection	No modeling of physical self-care		

Physical abandonment. Obviously, the death of a parent is a form of physical abandonment. That's clear. But there are many other forms this trauma can take. There's the abandonment of divorce, which is almost as common today as intact marriages. Even under the best of circumstances, where the parents act like responsible adults and both remain actively involved in the child's life, there is still an element of abandonment. Even when a child sees a parent several times a week or even every day, there's no comparison to living under the same roof day in, day out.

Abandonment occurs when a parent is absent for other reasons such as work-related travel or military service. Again, there isn't any blame to be placed here. Our nation's security depends on its armed forces. Sometimes for genuine financial reasons parents must work at jobs that require travel. But just because the abandonment is innocent doesn't mean it doesn't have a negative impact.

Other forms of physical abandonment, though, are less pure. Consider the dad who divorces his children along with his wife and avoids contact with them because it means having to deal with her. He may even remarry and start a new family, which is especially hurtful to his original children. "Why does he seem to care so much for them and not for me?" a daughter asks.

Or there's the abandonment of a parent's workaholism. My father was addicted in this way. Both by his nature and then because of his grief, Doc buried himself in his work. He was a full-time pastor who served a large congregation. He was available and dedicated to the members' needs. He was also a full-time administrator and teacher at a Christian university. There too he worked long hours and was accessible to both students and professors. Doc touched countless lives and brought many souls to Christ. But because of his responsibilities and his desire to be of service, he also was rarely home. We didn't take family vacations or even family outings after I was out of elementary school. I don't remember my dad watching TV or lounging with the newspaper other than on Sundays during the brief window between church and our noon-time Sunday dinner. The most consistent one-on-one time I spent with him was early Saturday mornings when he took me along to do the grocery shopping. Those were times I treasured and anticipated all week. The remainder of the days and nights I missed him terribly.

Again, the "don't talk" and "don't feel" rules came into play. I didn't believe I could ask my dad for more attention because when I said I wanted more time with him, others answered, "But, Marnie, he's out saving souls for the Lord." The answer implied Doc's kingdom work was much more important than time with me. Who was I to compete with God? (There's the spiritual abuse.) I felt abandoned by my father as well as my mother.

Emotional abandonment. It's possible, however, for a parent to be physically present in the home and for a child to still experience abandonment. That's because a parent may be emotionally absent. Mom or dad (or both) may be emotionally unavailable, even though they're physically at hand. Mom may have been the June Cleaver type who was waiting in the kitchen with milk and cookies every afternoon after school, but she still may have been emotionally gone.

Some parents lack the skills to nurture a child emotionally. They didn't learn in their own families of origin how to be intimate in relationships. They don't talk about substantive matters or share feelings. For some parents an addiction, codependency or other impairment robs them of an emotional connection with their children. Beth Moore refers to a parent's failure to nurture as "a hand withheld,"[2] which is a powerful and apt description. Regardless of the reason, children suffer, though this kind of loss is especially difficult to identify.

One sex addict challenged me when I asked about her mother. We'd spent a great deal of therapy time addressing the sexual abuse she endured from her father, but we hadn't talked much about her mother. I knew mom was trained as a nurse, but she'd left her career to stay at home full time with my client and her brother. When I suggested, "Let's talk today about your mom," this woman shrugged. "There's not much to talk about. She didn't work; she was always there. That's about it. There aren't any problems between me and my mom." When we investigated further, there were clearly some serious problems. Because of her own abuse history, this mother was afraid of men. She didn't know how to relate to men (including her own husband and son), nor did she want to. She was more comfortable with silent coexistence.

Mom was sensitive enough, though, to be aware that it wouldn't be good to treat her daughter differently than she did her son. So this mom didn't interact with her daughter either. (Call it equal opportunity benign neglect.) Finally after much probing, my client realized her mother didn't talk to her, hug her or even smile at her. This mom was totally shut down emotionally and unable to nurture her children. No wonder this female sex addict sought out partners who would stroke her and affirm her, including sexually, and no wonder many of those partners were other females. That's the power of emotional abandonment.

Sexual abandonment. Many women today experience sexual abandonment. That idea may be odd in light of our sexually saturated culture. As we discussed in chapter two, our culture devotes plenty of attention to sex. Sadly, though, most parents do not. Few churches, either, address sexuality in healthy ways.

Where did you get most of your information about sex? In my experience, female sex addicts are woefully ignorant. In terms of factual, concrete knowledge about anatomy, how the body works and normal sexual response, they often know very little. They may have had loads of sexual experiences, but they know little that's accurate about the subject.

There are several reasons for this lack of instruction. Many parents are uncomfortable talking about sex, even about the basic biology of things like menstruation. No one talked to them, and they don't know how to talk to their own children. An appalling number of my female clients report they had no idea what was happening to them when they first started their periods. "I thought I was bleeding to death," several have said. These women were left to their own devices when it came to learning about sex. They asked older sisters or friends, who probably didn't know much more than they did. That's sexual abandonment. (An extremely helpful resource in this area is Mark Laaser's book *Talking to Your Kids About Sex*.)[3]

Silence also characterizes the church when it comes to healthy teaching about sexuality. While I believe it's best for the majority of sex education to be shared by parents within the home, if parents aren't going to talk, the church needs to step in and fill the gap. Many Christians falsely believe that providing knowledge about sex somehow gives teens permission to be sexual. That's absurd. All the legitimate research indicates the opposite.[4] Those who are best informed are best able to make responsible decisions. They have less need to experiment. They have a safe place to talk about sexual temptations, which helps lessen their power.

When parents don't impart knowledge and healthy messages about sex and when the church is silent (other than preaching against sinful expressions of sexuality), children turn to culture, including to pornography, to get their information and satisfy their curiosity. As families and as communities of faith, we're abandoning our daughters to the sexual teaching of the world, including the lessons of sexual exploitation and abuse. We're abdicating our roles as teachers and protectors. We're giving our daughters over into dangerous hands.

Spiritual abandonment. The last category in the trauma of loss is spiritual abandonment. By now, you should be getting the idea of what it may mean to be spiritually abandoned. If you didn't receive religious modeling or instruction, your spiritual development was impaired. Perhaps you simply weren't taught the importance of values like honesty, integrity, generosity or service. You maybe didn't learn (or, at least, observe) that there is a higher authority that's above our self-will. You may have learned that individuals are their own god.

More subtle is the spiritual abandonment that may occur even in the religious home. Perhaps you went to church every time the doors were open, as I did. Maybe your mom taught Sunday school or your dad was a deacon or sung in the choir. You went to church camp and vacation Bible school. You had plenty of religious experiences. But if you weren't taught about a genuine relationship with God, instead of a rules-based religion, you were spiritually abandoned.

Or think again about the principle concerning spiritual abuse: If you suffered any kind of abuse at the hands of a spiritual figure in your life, you automatically were spiritually abused. The same is true for spiritual abandonment. If you were abandoned by a spiritual representative, you experienced spiritual abandonment. When my minister father was absent in my life, I was spiritually abandoned as well.

How will you believe God takes a personal, specific interest in you if your father never did? How will you believe God will provide a "balm in Gilead"[5] for your wounded spirit if your mother was unavailable? How will you trust that God will meet your needs if your pastor or youth leader failed to be there for you? When our primary caregivers are distant, preoccupied or otherwise unavailable, we project those characteristics onto our heavenly father too.

It's not that we doubt his existence. I never once questioned that God was the creator and king of the universe. I just didn't believe he cared about me. I couldn't trust a God who would take mothers of young children to be with him. I couldn't honor a God whose service required that daughters and sons be left alone. I could serve and revere God. I certainly feared him. But I couldn't open my heart to him or allow him to love me. That's the effect of spiritual abandonment.

ATTACHMENT ISSUES

The deprivations caused by emotional, physical, sexual and spiritual abandonment relate to an important psychological phenomenon called *attachment*, which was first described by psychologist John Bowlby.[6] Infants are born hard-wired for attachment, meaning we're created to bond with loving caregivers. This bonding is based on social interactions. Infants don't automatically bond with caregivers just because the adult feeds them and provides for basic needs like clothing and shelter. Attachment happens when a primary adult (usually the mother) is attuned and responsive to the child primarily through facial expression, eye contact and nurturing touch. The mother or primary caregiver provides a secure base for the child.

Consistency is key to the development of security and the ability to sustain human bonds, and experiences during the first three years of life profoundly influence attachment styles across the lifespan. The influence isn't just emotional or relational: breaches in attachment negatively affect the developing brain. Through sophisticated medical imaging technology, we're able to see the clear brain patterns that result from early childhood trauma, including loss and deprivation. A child's brain is literally affected by the stress of attachment failures, and these alterations in brain chemistry can lead to everything from depression to anxiety to a host of other mental health and relational difficulties.

Sadly, some caregivers are unable or unwilling to interact consistently with a child in a healthy, nurturing way. If your mother is herself an untreated trauma survivor, for example, she may be unable to meet your needs for emotional presence. She may feel overwhelmed by her own problems and can't properly attend to the demands of an infant and toddler. She may, in fact, expect you, the infant, to meet *her* needs. To fill her own black hole within that cries for love and acceptance. Clearly, that's an unhealthy role reversal.

Women who experience problems with attachment may grow up to compulsively either seek or avoid relationships. (Remember the discussion about sexual addiction and sexual anorexia as two ends of the same continuum.) Attachment-impaired women often sexualize their unmet needs and connect with partners they hope will make them whole. Typically, they repeat their attachment patterns in adult relationships. Theorists have described specific attachment styles that are beyond the scope of our discussion here, but the concept dovetails perfectly with our understanding of trauma and its connection to addiction. Obviously, the implications of abandonment are enormous.

ABANDONMENT

Every sex addict I've known or treated has experienced some form of abandonment. Every single one. None have escaped. In some ways, I believe the pain of abandonment is part of the human condition. It's one consequence of the original sin committed in the Garden of Eden, which forever separated humans from God. At that point the tragic flaws of sin and selfishness entered the world. Sorrow—and a deep yearning of spirit—was the result.

This side of heaven, we all will know some form of abandonment. No earthly parents can meet 100 percent of a child's needs, no matter how much they want to and try to. Since the Fall, our souls must ever long for that unbroken connection with God until we meet him face to face. No human being can fulfill that need. Our parents didn't. Our husbands can't. Our affair partners can't. It's a God-size hole that only he can fill. Our addictive behaviors and relationships are about quieting our spirits' ache for perfect connection.

QUESTIONS FOR REFLECTION
OR SMALL GROUP DISCUSSION

1. Describe any physical abandonment you experienced.

2. Describe any emotional abandonment you experienced.

3. Describe any sexual abandonment you experienced.

4. Describe any spiritual abandonment you experienced.

5. Describe how you feel as you review your abandonment experiences.

CHAPTER TEN

LONG-LASTING EFFECTS

OF TRAUMA

Abuse experiences, whether invasion or abandonment trauma, forever color the victim's world. She likely isn't even aware of how her view of people, of life and of herself is affected. One result of trauma is often the clinical condition known as posttraumatic stress disorder or PTSD. I've mentioned this condition several times, but its impact cannot be overstated. Its many symptoms are always disturbing and sometimes debilitating. Other psychiatric results include depression, anxiety, obsessive-compulsive behaviors, dissociation, emotional numbness, psychosomatic illness and a host of other troubles. As I've stated before, these problems typically prompt a female addict to seek counseling. These difficulties are what her loved ones observe. She may be able to hide her sexual addiction; she rarely can hide the results of her trauma if those around her know how to read the signs.

TRAUMA REACTIONS

Other long-lasting effects of abuse and abandonment are the trauma reactions that can result. These *betrayal bonds,* as Carnes terms them,[1] are unconscious efforts to remedy the pain of the past. They're a key way the cycle of dysfunction repeats itself generation after generation. Trauma creates unhealthy coping mechanisms, which create trauma, which creates more unhealthiness. Without intervention, the cycle goes on and on.

A complete explanation of trauma reactions is beyond the scope of this book, but they've been described clearly and comprehensively by Carnes in his classic work *The Betrayal Bond: Breaking Free of Exploitative Relationships*.[2] That book is a must-have for any trauma survivor, especially one who struggles with addiction.

Trauma reactions are the ways we respond in behavior and relationships especially when under stress. These ways are directly linked to our trauma history. They serve in some fashion to deal with the pain of the past. They provide a way to shield us from the pain of unresolved trauma or else to manage it or displace it. We'll examine each of these eight ways briefly to spur your thinking. See if you can identify which trauma reaction(s) is your primary coping technique.

Trauma blocking. Trauma blocking involves attempts to numb, block out or stuff the feelings that stem from unresolved trauma. Symptoms include using TV, music, movies or hobbies as a way to numb out; using drugs to escape; eating excessively to numb feelings; drinking excessively; having difficulty staying awake; or getting lost in work or something else to occupy your time and attention.

Trauma shame. Trauma shame is a profound sense of unworthiness and shame that has its roots in earlier trauma. Self-hatred is one manifestation of this level of shame. Symptoms include milder things like believing the trauma was your fault, trying to be perfect, feeling different from others or being unable to forgive yourself. More serious symptoms (in the physical sense) include cutting, burning, or harming yourself, engaging in self-destructive behaviors or enduring pain most people would find intolerable. Suicidal thoughts also sometimes stem from trauma shame.

Trauma repetition. Trauma repetition is repeating behaviors or seeking situations or people who recreate the trauma experience. Symptoms include being unable to stop a childhood pattern, being repeatedly in abusive relationships, repeating painful experiences, doing something destructive repeatedly or doing something to others that was done to you or to a family member. This is the classic reaction of repeating the past in an attempt to get it right.

Trauma pleasure. Trauma pleasure is seeking or finding pleasure in the presence of danger, violence, risk or shame. Symptoms include engaging in high-risk behaviors, feeling sexual when being degraded or used, being orgasmic when being hurt or beaten, getting aroused in the face of danger, needing lots of stimulation, doing sexual things that are risky or using drugs like cocaine or speed.

Trauma abstinence. Trauma abstinence involves compulsive deprivation. It includes symptoms like denying yourself basic needs like food or medical care, avoiding sexual pleasure, hoarding money or not spending it on legitimate needs, being underemployed, skipping vacations, purging to avoid gaining weight or avoiding play.

Trauma reaction. A trauma reaction is a physiological and/or a psychological alarm reaction that is the result of unresolved trauma experiences. Symptoms include most of the PTSD reactions like flashbacks, hypervigilance, excessive startle reaction, physical reactions such as cold sweats or trouble breathing, recurrent or intrusive memories of trauma or periods of sleeplessness. Outbursts of anger may also be a trauma reaction.

Trauma bond. Trauma bonds are dysfunctional attachments that occur in the presence of danger, shame or exploitation. Symptoms include helping those who have hurt you, trusting those who prove themselves untrustworthy, being unable to leave unhealthy relationships, maintaining continued contact with your abuser, obsessing about people who have been hurtful or desiring to be understood by those who are incapable or who don't care.

Trauma splitting. Trauma splitting is another way to avoid or ignore traumatic realities by splitting off the experience from current life. It may happen during the time of the initial trauma as the victim psychologically leaves her body and observes the abuse from a distance as if it were happening to another person. Examples of trauma splitting after the trauma event include feeling separate from your body, avoiding reminders of trauma, living in a fantasy world, daydreaming, procrastinating, having difficulty concentrating, living a double life and using psychedelic drugs to hallucinate.

CONNECTION BETWEEN TRAUMA AND ADDICTION

One more critical aspect of trauma is crucial for your understanding and healing. It's a unique theory postulated by Dr. Mark Laaser. Based on his own experiences, as well as those of thousands of sex addicts he treated, Laaser realized a significant connection between trauma and addiction: Abuse trauma dictates the form of acting out. Abandonment trauma provides the fuel for the addiction.[3]

A few examples are the best way to illustrate this key concept. Let's look at the first piece: Abuse trauma dictates the form of our acting out. Do you remember my story? I was sexually abused for years by a dear family friend in a very romanticized relationship. We went on dates. He told me he loved me and that one day he'd marry me. So what was the eventual form of my own sexual addiction? Intense, long-term affairs, of course. My acting out behaviors replicated the form of my abuse.

Sometimes the connection between trauma and the presentation of addiction isn't so clear. Here's another example. One young woman was brutally raped by several drunken men when she delivered a pizza to an apartment where they were partying. Her body was irreparably harmed; her spirit was shattered. Ten years later in her addiction, she became the perpetrator. The aggressive one. She determined never to be hurt again, so she was certain she was always in control. She frequented bars, but she never drank. She sought men who were inferior to her in some way. Usually they were of small physical stature or even disabled. She seduced them and initiated sexually. She was repeating the trauma experience, but with a different result. Whether it's a direct repetition or one where the outcome is opposite, abuse trauma influences the form of our acting out.

The abandonment wound, however, provides the energy for acting out. It's the fuel that drives our addiction. It's a key factor (in addition to the neurochemistry) that keeps us doing what we've decided we don't want to do. Addiction, after all, is an intimacy disorder, remember? It's not about sex; it's about a desperate search for love and connection. It's about not being abandoned.

With every acting out partner, I know today I really was looking for the father who wouldn't abandon me. I wanted a man who would prove he cherished me by spending time with me and giving me his undivided attention. Similarly, one male sex addict said, "Every time I went into a massage parlor, I was really wanting my mother's touch." The insatiable longing for intimacy and the awful ache when it is absent drives the trauma survivor ever deeper into her addiction.

ADDICTION: A COPING TECHNIQUE

Review again Carnes's cycle of addiction shown as figure 3 in chapter five. Notice that the beginning point is family wounds. Addiction is our method of medicating the pain of our family wounds. Sadly a parent's addiction is, in itself, traumatizing for his or her children. So that child must find ways to cope with her trauma, and she continues to add to her repertoire as she gets older. She eventually perhaps becomes a parent herself, whose children must themselves cope with their dysfunctional home environment. The cycle continues, generation to generation. The sins of the parents repeat to the third and fourth generations and beyond.

Addiction is one of the primary ways we cope with trauma. In the following chapter about an addict's core beliefs and emotions, I'll further explain why.

QUESTIONS FOR REFLECTION
OR SMALL GROUP DISCUSSION

1. Which trauma reaction(s) do you identify with the most?

2. Describe your current understanding of how your trauma fuels your acting out.

CHAPTER ELEVEN

ADDICTS' CORE BELIEFS,

EMOTIONS AND COPING

Perhaps you still need convincing about why your abuse or abandonment experiences are so important. Friends, family members or even Christian counselors may have told you, "That was so long ago. It's in the past. Just forgive, get over it, and get on with your life." Maybe you've given that message to yourself. After all, you survived, didn't you? You're alive. You're reasonably functional. (Yes, you have this little problem with sex or problematic relationships, but you'll get that one figured out before long, you believe.) You understand now what happened to you. So what more do you need to do?

The answer lies in recognizing some of the more hidden consequences of the trauma. Your experiences in your family of origin, especially your trauma experiences, have programmed your behavior in influential ways as the section on trauma reactions illustrated. But trauma also profoundly affects your thinking and how you cope. Again, without your conscious awareness, your thought patterns and belief systems have been shaped by your childhood experiences, especially your ones of trauma. This chapter illuminates some of those core beliefs. Hopefully it sheds light on their falseness and provides alternative viewpoints that are true.

CORE BELIEFS OF ALL ADDICTS

Credit again belongs to Dr. Patrick Carnes, who first outlined the four core beliefs of all addicts.[1] We'll examine them one by one and describe their connection to our addictive behaviors.

1. I am a bad, unworthy person. This sense of personal badness is called *shame*. It's the next part of the addiction cycle. It's the result of our family wounds. Shame is the belief that I *am* someone bad, rather than I have *done* something bad. Our feelings about our behavior are called guilt. Our negative feelings about ourselves are called shame. Guilt is about performance; shame is about personhood. It's a crucial difference.

When a child experiences abuse or abandonment, her only way of making sense of what happened is to blame herself. A child lacks the mental capacity to assign culpability to another person. Her view of the world is egocentric, which means that everything revolves around her. That's a normal developmental stage in the maturation process. And the younger she is when she's traumatized, the more pervasive the effect. That's why many theorists say that the first three years of a child's life are so crucial. That's when she comes to see the world as either safe or unsafe. Secure or savage. Friendly or frightening.

It's unthinkable for a child to believe her parents may be at fault for her abuse or abandonment. She's totally dependent on her parents to provide her every need. She's helpless to fend for herself in a hostile world. Children, I believe, are born innocent and trusting. To imagine that the ones who are supposed to care for her—the ones her very life depends on—may be harming her is simply too scary. The only alternative is that she must be to blame. It must be her fault.

I remember thinking it must have been my fault that my mother died and left me. As an adult, of course, I understand that belief is false. My mother's death was from cancer, not because of anything that had to do with me. But the egocentrism of my age as a three-year-old caused me to believe otherwise. And since my family never talked about my mother's death, no one knew I thought I was to blame and so no one could counteract my belief. Family silence, the "no talk" rule, adds to the shame.

Perpetrators often tell a child the abuse is her fault. It's one way of insuring her silence. Or if an adult discovers the abuse or the child dares to tell the secret, ignorant or cruel family members sometimes give the same message. "If you hadn't been wearing those short shorts, he wouldn't have bothered you," one woman's mother told her. Or "If you weren't so whiny, I wouldn't hit you," a parent says. When victims are blamed for their trauma, they internalize the belief *I must be a terrible person.*

If we believe we are bad, worthless and horrible, we won't think we deserve to receive healing. We won't pursue it. We may not even let others attempt to help us.

2. No one would love me as I am. Trauma creates a shameful sense of being defective. It also spawns the false belief that we are unlovable. How could anyone love a person who's so fundamentally flawed? Because of the secrets of our abuse, abandonment or other family dysfunction, we think we're unique. *Surely no one else has suffered the degradations I've known. Nobody could feel what I feel.* We believe that if people really knew us, they wouldn't like us. Worse than that, they would probably leave us.

In the language of Twelve Step recovery, we compare our insides to other people's outsides and, of course, we always come up short. Even if it's never expressed, we know what we think and feel inside. And other people appear so different. They look like they're happy or have it all together. We feel so differently from how they look.

As an adult, you know the ways you've coped with the trauma of your childhood. You know the substances and behaviors you've used to medicate your pain or to find some morsel of affirmation. These activities are your deepest secrets, and you're especially convinced that if others knew this real you, they would never love you.

Of course, then, you'll guard your hidden parts carefully. It's too dangerous to let the secret out. You'll avoid, manipulate and even lie to keep from being discovered. The risk of further abandonment is simply too great. Depending on any spiritual abuse you may have suffered, you will keep the truth from a good Christian friend or even a Christian counselor. You're too afraid they will judge or condemn you. These first two core beliefs keep you trapped within your secret life.

3. No one will meet my needs. If as a child our most basic needs for time, attention, affection and nurture aren't met—to say nothing of our physical needs for survival and safety—we fail to develop a sense of the world as a safe place. We don't learn to trust because our environment hasn't been trustworthy. When our needs are ignored or, worse, we're punished for having them, we come to believe that no one will meet our needs. We learn we can only depend on ourselves. That it's up to us to get what we need however we can get it. Often those forms of meeting our own needs are far from healthy. But they seem our only option. If there's no hope for getting our needs met, then why ask? What's the point?

Because of the "don't talk" and "don't feel" rules of our families, we usually have learned at an early age to keep our needs to ourselves. Yet not stating them doesn't ease their ache. Often, we get more resentful in our silence, because we expect others to know our needs without our having to voice them. Healthy parents are able to figure out an infant's needs even though she obviously can't communicate them through language. That pattern should continue while the parents teach the child to identify her feelings and needs and to state them. When this process fails, the child is left deeply disappointed and distrustful, as well as needy. Why should she again risk distress by asking for help?

4. Sex or a relationship is my most important need. Remember, God created us for relationship. He made us relational beings, intended for intimacy with other human beings as well as with him. Our need for connection through relationship is, I believe, our most basic nonphysical need. It's our core longing. It's the hunger in our hearts for God.

When this legitimate need isn't met (to the extent possible) by our earthly parents, it's exacerbated. It grows deeper. It becomes painful. Its importance is heightened by its unfulfillment. It becomes all-consuming.

Because of the tragedy of the sexual abuse most of us have experienced, this God-given need for relationship is often perverted into a need for sex. The two have become confused by our trauma experiences. If the only connected relationship we feel is a sexual one, sex and connection get merged in our belief system. Or if we must give sex in order to get love, the same thing happens. It's a tradeoff we're willing to make, because it's the only way to meet even partially the need for relationship.

As we mature, this unconscious belief becomes more complicated in terms of the relationship factor. It often narrows into a belief that one particular relationship is our most important need. This one person is our knight in shining armor, our rescuer, the one who will complete us and make us whole. Without him (or her), we feel we will die. Our total need for connection becomes focused on one specific individual or relationship.

The belief also becomes more entrenched through sinful sexual activity. Because of the neurochemical reaction associated with sex (in addition to the fleeting sense of connection), we find that sex is an effective medicator for our pain. It becomes our drug of choice to anesthetize our hurt. And it's remarkably effective, at least temporarily, which solidifies the belief that sex is our most important need. If this need for sex and/or a relationship seems so crucial, the thought of giving it up is especially terrifying. The prospect of being deprived of the only thing that's brought a measure of comfort, however flawed or fleeting, is overwhelming.

ADDITIONAL BELIEFS OF FEMALE SEXUAL ADDICTS

Females addicted to sex and relationships share other common beliefs. This list isn't exhaustive, and you may not identify with every one. But to some degree, most women who struggle with sex addiction must recognize and challenge these beliefs too:

- My sexuality/femininity is my most important possession. It makes me who I am.
- No person will love me unless I'm sexual with him/her.
- If he's sexual with me, that proves he loves me.

- I must be the right body size, shape or weight.
- I'm nothing without that partner. He (or she) gives my life meaning.
- If I found the right partner, I would be okay.
- My husband is to blame because he doesn't meet my needs like my affair partner does.
- If I get sexually sober, I'll have to give up my femininity.
- Being flirtatious or touchy/feely is just who I am.
- Others matter more than I do.
- It's not okay to be needy.
- It's not okay to want to be loved.
- It's not okay to want to be nurtured.
- It's not okay to consider myself and my own needs. That's selfish.
- Other women can't meet my needs, only a man.
- A woman's safe touch can't satisfy my need for nurture, only a man's.
- What I'm doing isn't hurting my husband or children as long as they don't know.
- I can keep my sinful sexual activities or relationships separate. They don't affect the rest of my life.
- My parents/perpetrators are either all-good or all-bad. It's black and white. There's no middle ground.

SPIRITUAL BELIEFS

Sexually addicted women also hold many inaccurate beliefs about God because of their spiritual abuse:

- God couldn't possibly love me after what I've done.
- God won't help me. He might love and help others, but not me.
- God has abandoned me just like all the other people in my life.
- God says it's not okay to be a feminine woman or one who enjoys sex.

- God says I must be in second place. I must be the caretaker for everyone else or the one who submits my desires to others'.

- God won't give me second chances. If I blow it, he'll condemn me.

- It's up to the female to keep men at bay. I am 100 percent responsible for the sexual purity of my relationships and if there's a problem, it must be my fault.

- I can't begin again. I can never be pure.

- The woman at the well in John 4 was instantly cured. There's no hope for me since I continue to struggle.

These false beliefs held by female sex and love addicts come from the trauma of abuse and abandonment during childhood as well as from the trauma of active addiction. Our culture and even the church cultivate some of them. To recover from inappropriate sexual behavior it's vital we understand and counteract these false beliefs.

CORE EMOTIONS

False core beliefs aren't the only handicaps that cripple a female struggling with sexual addiction. Her core emotions also add to the difficulty of healing from her disease. Though some of these emotions have already been mentioned, I want to unpack the topic more completely.

First, I think Dr. Chip Dodd best describes our emotional landscape in his book *The Voice of the Heart: A Call To Full Living.*[2] Dodd believes that we experience eight core emotions. Only eight feelings are central to the human condition. We feel *glad, sad, mad, fear, hurt, lonely, guilt and shame.* Most of what we describe as a feeling is really a state of being. (Do you remember your English grammar lessons from middle school?) If I say I'm feeling overwhelmed, I'm describing my state of being, not a core feeling. When I'm overwhelmed I'm usually feeling several different things. I'm feeling guilt because I've probably put off a task until the last minute. That prompts me to feel shame—that belief that I'm a horrible, terrible person who isn't worthy. When I'm overwhelmed, I'm feeling angry at whoever I think should be helping me in the situation. I'm afraid of what others will think of me if I don't get the task done or do it poorly. And I'm feeling incredibly lonely in that place. That no one understands me and how stressed I am. Do you see the difference between a state of being and how you feel underneath? Providing a description about your state of being offers some information and for many of us, it's a good start, but it doesn't get to the level of core emotions.

Obviously, there's a range for each feeling and varying gradations of intensity. You may be feeling mildly sad because your plans to have lunch with a friend have been postponed. Or you may be feeling unspeakably sad because someone you dearly love has just died. Those are different levels of sadness, but they're along the same continuum. The same principle applies to all the eight core feelings.

You may wonder why there are seven "bad" feelings and only one "good" one: gladness. Dr. Dodd says all our feelings are positive. All of them are "good" because all of them are important messengers. If you're feeling angry that means you value something enough to feel angry when it's awry. Anger is actually more of a top plate emotion, and underneath the mad are usually feelings of hurt or fear. If you're feeling afraid that's a signal you need to create more safety in your environment or relationships.

Perhaps surprisingly, anger is a dominant feeling for most female addicts. Most of us aren't aware of the incredible anger that consumes us, but it's there. Those snared by sexual sin are angry at the double life; we're angry with those who fail to meet our needs; we're angry at those who abused or abandoned us; we're angry at God. These feelings are largely unconscious. We (and others around us) are only aware that we're often irritable—or worse. We may overreact to minor inconveniences or infractions. Things that most people can overlook or handle with minimum fuss cause us to get furious. Spilled milk or a forgotten schoolbook becomes a major battle. We may exhibit road rage. In general, we act like a witch with a capital *B*.

Our unconscious anger impacts our mothering, which is another way the sins of addiction get handed down from generation to generation. We may be unpredictable which is confusing for our children. One moment we're patient and flexible; the next we're rigid and shaming. Because we're such wounded children ourselves, we may find the needs of our own children overwhelming. Fits of anger are often the result.

Addicts often display their anger in the language they use, at least in private. An interesting part of working with female addicts is hearing their outbursts of profanity. Even Christian women often use profanity typically associated with uncouth heathens. In the safety of a workshop setting, where women feel loved in the midst of their addiction, addicts let down their guards and use language they hide from others. (In my experience at our Bethesda Healing for Men workshops, the male addicts are no comparison.) Perhaps using salty language is another way female addicts feel powerful.

This anger, though, is only the top plate emotion. It's the first level of expression of deeper pain, for underneath the anger is enormous hurt, fear and loneliness. Along with shame, those emotions are at the core of an addict's spirit. We're afraid of discovery; we're afraid of continuing in our addiction. We're afraid no one will love or help us; we're afraid of going it alone. We're afraid of ourselves, and we're afraid of God.

Female sex and love addicts are also plagued by a desperate and pervasive loneliness. It colors our every moment. It pulses through our veins like blood. Fueled by both our trauma and our addiction, loneliness is the price we pay for our secrets. It's the manifestation of the intimacy disorder that's the true characterization of sexual addiction. It is both the cause and the result of our addiction—the fuel that drives our acting out and the price we pay for it.

Again, we've historically lived by the "don't feel" rule. Emotions like anger are especially off-limits. Loneliness isn't much better, because our genuine feelings may have been met with religious platitudes like, "God is all you need." To recover requires that we feel the total range of our emotions, the so-called bad ones as well as the good. We must feel safe enough to express our anger in all its ferocity. We must acknowledge the pain of our abandonment and our loneliness. We must admit we're afraid. We must wrestle with our shame.

God is big enough to handle all our feelings. His hands will not throw stones. Instead, "immense in mercy and with an incredible love, he [embraces] us. He [takes] our sin-dead lives and [makes] us alive in Christ" (Ephesians 2:4 *The Message*). His love and the help he provides can break the bonds of the deepest addiction.

THE THREE BEARS: AN ILLUSTRATION

Like the saying goes, sometimes a picture is worth a thousand words. I've slightly altered a concept originally found in Marilyn Murray's excellent book *Prisoner of Another War*[3] to create a visual that gives an overview of all we've covered so far. This "Three Bears and Three Chairs" illustration (as I call it) is helpful in pulling together several different pieces of the interlocking puzzle we know as life.

Original feeling child. The first piece is illustrated by a medium-sized, cuddly teddy bear. This bear represents the original feeling child God created you to be. She is the one "fearfully and wonderfully made" (Psalm 139:14). So what are some characteristics of humans who are created in the image of God? Think about infants and young children; how would you describe them?

First, children are created totally dependent on their caregivers. They willingly depend on others and ask for help. Children are trusting, forgiving and accepting of others. They're relational and seek out community. They're playful, curious, innocent and teachable. They tell the truth (sometimes to the embarrassment of the adults around them). They're vulnerable and without guile; what you see is what you get. And children are in touch with their feelings and able to express them, at least until adults show them it isn't safe to be emotional. These descriptions of young children, freshly sent from God's hand, represent *health*. God's intent is for humans to be all these things: dependent on him and others in a healthy way, truthful, vulnerable, teachable, in touch with feelings, and so forth. Mentally, place this healthy bear in the middle of three chairs.

Sobbing, hurting, wounded child. The second bear is much smaller than the first and its name perfectly describes it: the sobbing, hurting,

wounded child. This is the one who started out trusting and vulnerable and feeling, but she was wounded by life. She was crushed under the trauma of her experiences of unhealthy family dynamics, abuse and abandonment. She learned it's not okay to feel or need or ask for help. She carries within her heart the false core beliefs of wounded children: that she's inadequate, unlovable and unworthy. No matter her chronological age or her adult responsibilities, inside a part of her feels very small. Have you ever felt like you were three years old in the middle of some tough situation? You were living from your wounded place, which is difficult, indeed. Wise King Solomon asks, "who can bear a crushed spirit?" (Proverbs 18:14), and many of us know the answer is *no one, not really.* Part two has focused

on the pain and its roots for this sobbing, hurting, wounded one. In your mind's eye, place this wounded bear in a chair to one side of the healthy bear.

Coping, survivor child. The third bear represents the coping self. Actually, this Gorilla Mama isn't a bear at all, but a huge, powerful (sometimes fierce) protective part. It's her job to take care of the pain of the wounded bear, and the more wounded you are, the more coping skills you need.

That's one reason many of us are poly-addicted, which means that we struggle with alcohol and drugs or some other addictive behavior in addition to our sexual addiction. The vast majority of addicts, in fact, deal with more than one identifiable addiction. Obviously, in our context as sex, love and relationship addicts, sexual addiction is one of our primary forms of coping.

So what are some other coping mechanisms you're aware of in your life? What about food? Remember our comparison of sexual addiction with eating disorders? At the very least many of us use food as a comfort or reward. We cope through shopping and spending, excessive exercising and dieting. We manage our image through makeup and clothes and presentation. We focus on others to keep from feeling the pain within. We control and rage and manipulate and blame.

We also engage in a variety of socially acceptable coping strategies. We're perfectionists, which is our way of hiding the gnawing inadequacy inside. We over-function at work and are over-responsible. We take care of everyone and everything except ourselves, and we think that's the way we're supposed to behave. We become religious addicts and use religion to distance ourselves from our feelings and prevent us from addressing our pain. We spiritualize our trauma and assure ourselves that "all things work together for good."

Therefore, the critical thing isn't necessarily what you're doing; it's *why* you're doing it. Are you practicing spiritual disciplines like prayer and Bible study out of an authentic desire to grow closer to God, or are you unconsciously trying to appear like you're holy and doing the right things? Are you consciously making the choice to go for a brisk run to release stress and quiet your mind? Or are you driven to this behavior without awareness and do you practice it compulsively? This Gorilla Mama represents your addiction and all the other ways you (unconsciously) deal with the pain of your wounded self. Place her in a chair on the other side of the healthy bear so that your mental picture looks like this:

Healthy, feeling adult. Your goal is to live life as a healthy, feeling adult. To operate from your internal middle chair that prompts you to be in community, to be in touch with your feelings, to ask for help, to tell the truth and so on. This healthy, feeling adult can't necessarily fix the pain of the wounded one or stop unhealthy coping strategies, but she can metaphorically take those two parts of you by the hand and get them to a place where they can get help.

In reality, there's a healthy adult who stands behind all three chairs and is aware of all of them. She can talk about the bears instead of automatically acting them out. She discerns when she's triggered into her wounded self, and she can ask a safe female friend to talk with her instead of seducing a partner for the validation found in his arms. Instead of altering her mood with the high of cybersex, she recognizes her loneliness and journals about the desires of her heart. She seeks relationships with those who also live from the middle chair. In simple terms the three bears and three chairs illustrate intimacy, what robs us of health, and the intimacy disorders we practice in our attempt to regain it.

Part three describes how to achieve intimacy with self, with others and with God—the solution for the woman caught in sexual sin. The remaining chapters outline the process of healing, recovery and transformation God offers those who want to get well.

QUESTIONS FOR REFLECTION
OR SMALL GROUP DISCUSSION

1. List some of your core beliefs.

2. What are your primary emotions?

3. Describe your reaction to the Three Bears. Focus especially on your Gorilla Mama.

PART THREE

THE SOLUTION
WOMAN AT THE WELL

So Jesus left the Judean countryside and went back to Galilee. To get there, he had to pass through Samaria. He came into Sychar, a Samaritan village that bordered the field Jacob had given his son Joseph. Jacob's well was still there. Jesus, worn out by the trip, sat down at the well. It was noon.

A woman, a Samaritan, came to draw water. Jesus said, "Would you give me a drink of water?" (His disciples had gone to the village to buy food for lunch.)

The Samaritan woman, taken aback, asked, "How come you, a Jew, are asking me, a Samaritan woman, for a drink?" (Jews in those days wouldn't be caught dead talking to Samaritans.)

Jesus answered, "If you knew the generosity of God and who I am, you would be asking *me* for a drink, and I would give you fresh, living water."

The woman said, "Sir, you don't even have a bucket to draw with, and this well is deep. So how are you going to get this 'living water'? Are you a better man than our ancestor Jacob, who dug this well and drank from it, he and his sons and livestock, and passed it down to us?"

Jesus said, "Everyone who drinks this water will get thirsty again and again. Anyone who drinks the water I give will never thirst—not ever. The water I give will be an artesian spring within, gushing fountains of endless life."

The woman said, "Sir, give me this water so I won't ever get thirsty, won't ever have to come back to this well again!"

He said, "Go call your husband and then come back."

"I have no husband," she said.

"That's nicely put: 'I have no husband.' You've had five husbands, and the man you're living with now isn't even your husband. You spoke the truth there, sure enough."

"Oh, so you're a prophet! Well, tell me this: Our ancestors worshiped God at this mountain, but you Jews insist that Jerusalem is the only place for worship, right?" . . .

"It's who you are and the way you live that count before God. Your worship must engage your spirit in the pursuit of truth. That's the kind of people the Father is out looking for: those who are simply and honestly *themselves* before him in their worship. God is sheer being itself—Spirit. Those who worship him must do it out of their very being, their spirits, their true selves, in adoration." (John 4:3-20, 23-24 *The Message*)

CHAPTER TWELVE

SURRENDER AND SOBRIETY

Jesus offered grace to the woman caught in adultery and living water to the woman at the well. Similar hope and healing is available to the sexually addicted woman today. There *is* a solution! This final section of *No Stones* outlines the journey of recovery, which is a daily, intentional process. We begin first with another New Testament story that raises a crucial question.

John 5 records an interesting encounter Jesus had with a man who had been an invalid for thirty-eight years. This man daily went to the pool of Bethesda in Jerusalem, which had special healing powers. At various times an angel stirred the water in the pool, and whoever got into the water first was healed. But this man had been ill thirty-eight years without relief. When Jesus saw this paralyzed man, he asked an unusual question: *"Do you want to get well?"* (John 5:6).

The Great Physician didn't ask, "What's the matter with you?" He knows our diseases. And he didn't ask, "What can I do for you?" That question would have been premature. Instead, the Healer asks the fundamental question, "Do you want to get well?" The answer determines the rest of the journey.

For many female addicts, the answer is mixed. A part of us does want to get well. We're in so much pain and have been in that state for so long. We know our lives are unmanageable. We see the devastation our behavior brings to those around us. In Twelve Step recovery language, we've gotten "sick and tired of being sick and tired." We long for relief—genuine and lasting relief.

But other parts of us hesitate. Do we really want to be well? What would that mean? We're not sure we're ready to give up our addiction. We can't imagine life without it. (I know I couldn't.) Yes, this pain is great, but it's a known pain. It's familiar. Even predictable. We're afraid of the pain of recovery and of what recovery will cost.

I encourage you, dear one, to respond to the part of your spirit that wants to get well. She's the one who prompted you to pick up this book and read this far. She's the one who's reaching out for help. Listen to her; foster her. Nourish that healthy part of you to increase each day. When her influence grows dim beneath the power of addiction, take a timeout and be still. Search within for even the smallest glimmer of her motivating presence. Ask the help of the One who will not throw stones. Ask to be reminded of your desire for healing.

When this paralytic in John 5 was asked, "Do you want to get well?" he immediately answered with a list of excuses. He whined. He assumed the role of victim and blamed others for not being available to help him. Does this response sound familiar? How often have we excused our continuing in disease on not being able to find the right help?

I'm aware of the legitimacy of that problem. There aren't enough knowledgeable helpers, neither Christian nor secular. Too few people are aware of sexual addiction much less understand how to help women who struggle. The task of finding competent counselors and supportive friends can be tough. But the question remains: Do you want to get well? Be encouraged that it is Jesus himself who's asking it. All the resources of heaven and earth are at his command, and he is faithful to provide help to those who earnestly seek it.

I challenge all female addicts who are reading this book to keep the John 5 question foremost in mind. Perhaps you should write it out and put it on your mirror where you'll see it every morning. Note it on your calendar. Tuck it into your pocket or purse. Keep ever before you this crucial question, because it is the most important one you'll be asked as you battle the disease of sexual addiction. I cannot over-emphasize this point: Your recovery will depend on how you answer this question on a daily basis. Your *yes* will simplify many of the choices you'll have to make. Let your vision of sobriety and healing motivate and encourage you.

Without a doubt there will be many obstacles in your path of recovery. Several of them I just mentioned. A synopsis includes these realities: Few recovering female sex addicts are available to be guides for your journey because most of those seeking recovery are men. It's hard to find a sex addiction Twelve Step fellowship in many parts of the country. It's even harder to find one that has women attending. Not enough clinicians are trained in treating this disease. Even fewer churches understand this struggle and offer grace to sexual sinners. The laundry list of challenges is long, which is exactly how Satan would have it. We women who today are seeking to be well from our sexual addictions are the pioneers. We're the trailblazers. Satan would love to see us remain in bondage. He would love to see us stoned.

Yet Jesus continually calls your name and asks you specifically, "Do you want to get well?" His power is greater than both the addiction and the obstacles to healing.

THE FIRST STEP: ADMITTING POWERLESSNESS

The journey of recovery begins with an admission of powerlessness over the disease of sexual addiction. Without that acknowledgment, healing will be impossible. Like many other biblical principles, this one involves a great paradox. It's only through surrender that there can be salvation. Only through admitting defeat can victory be gained. Only through admitting we are powerless over our sexual addiction can we begin to regain any control of our thoughts and behavior. *Sexaholics Anonymous* (the "White Book") describes it this way: "The crucial change in attitude began when we admitted we were powerless, that our habit had us whipped."[1] Step One of the Twelve Steps, first formulated by Alcoholics Anonymous, emphasizes this idea: "We admitted we were powerless over alcohol and that our lives had become unmanageable." The Twelve Steps as adapted by the sex addiction fellowships say powerless over "sex" or "lust." As odd as it may sound, admitting powerlessness is wonderfully freeing. There's relief in admitting defeat in dealing with the addiction on your own.

Like all of recovery, though, this admission of powerlessness is a process, not an event. While there's almost always a single moment when the addict admits her life is unmanageable and out of control, that instance is only the beginning of a true acknowledgment of powerlessness. For most addicts, there's a process of deepening awareness. What's important today is to start that journey.

SURRENDER

The good news is that Step One is followed by Steps Two and Three, which provide the power and plan for recovery: "Came to believe that a power greater than ourselves could restore us to sanity," Step Two; and "Made a decision to turn our will and our life over to the care of God as we understood God," Step Three.

Step Two asserts that God is the source of help for overcoming addiction. For many of us, even women who consider themselves Christian, taking this step is harder than it may seem. Because of our spiritual woundedness, it's hard to trust God to meet our needs. Chapter sixteen discusses finding spiritual healing, which is a core issue of Step Two.

Step Three calls for a decision to turn your will and life over to God's care and guidance. This decision to surrender is the crucial act for all addicts. The success of our recovery program hinges on our actions of surrender. It's the demarcation line—the point where we "let go and let God."

Some of us can identify a specific time when we first surrendered our addiction and recovery to God. For me, the memory is as clear as if it happened yesterday. Although I'd been in therapy for almost five months, I wasn't sober. The instances of physical acting out were less, but they still happened. Then a variety of circumstances in my affair situation came together to a critical point. Clearly, I faced a watershed decision. Would I continue in the self-will of my affair, or would

I surrender? Without a doubt, I knew what I had to do. I also knew how strongly I didn't want to do it.

In the center of a winter night in my darkened living room, I wrestled with God. Literally, I kicked and cried and begged him not to make me choose. I desperately tried to rationalize some other option. Finally around 2 a.m., I called a wise friend in recovery. Maybe because I woke her at such an ungodly hour, Yvonne didn't mince any words. After hearing a few sentences about the situation, she interrupted me.

"Marnie, this is really pretty simple. Either you believe God's in control and you submit to that or you don't. There aren't any other choices. Now hang up and let me go back to sleep!"

Her plain words jolted me into seeing the sinfulness of my refusal to surrender. She had outlined clearly the heart of Steps Two and Three. The choice wasn't any easier, but the options were unmistakable. I got down on my knees and gave up my right to my own selfish will. It's a moment I pray I will never forget.

It's also a decision I must repeat on a daily basis. Though the experience has never been as dramatic as that first time, I discovered (much to my shock and chagrin) that surrender is an ongoing part of recovery. It's never done. Innumerable times in ways both large and small, we must admit our powerlessness, acknowledge God's power and surrender to his will for our lives. These first three steps form the foundation of a journey of healing.

SOBRIETY DEFINITION

Just as recovering alcoholics talk about becoming sober from alcohol, sexual addicts must abstain from all acting out behaviors. That state is called sexual sobriety. Without sobriety there is no recovery. It's the minimum—the foundation for deeper emotional, relational and spiritual healing.

So what does it mean to be sexually sober? Let's first define sobriety in simple, physical terms. The definition offered by Sexaholics Anonymous is the clearest and, I believe, is the one that most closely fits God's plan for healthy sexuality. The White Book says:

One might think that sexual sobriety would be a relative matter that we define for ourselves. On the surface, this might appear to be an attractive and democratic idea. We think not.

Our rationalizations are ingenious. We tried masturbation only, or having 'meaningful relationships' only, or having affairs where we 'truly cared' for the other person. Or, we resorted only to one-nighters, prostitutes, or anonymous sex 'so nobody got hurt.' Over the long haul, these forms of experimentation did not work for us. There was no real recovery. Sobriety works for us.

How can we consider ourselves sober if we are still resorting to whatever or whomever we are using addictively? With most of us . . . there was never any doubt what we had to stop doing. We knew . . .

Thus, for the married sexaholic, sexual sobriety means having no form of sex with self or with persons other than the spouse. For the unmarried sexaholic, sexual sobriety means freedom from sex of any kind.[2]

This SA standard is clear, which helps prevent confusion (and rationalization). Sobriety equals no sex of any kind other than with a married spouse. Period.

Sobriety begins when you eliminate all sexual activity. That means no masturbation or sexual involvement of any kind with any other person, including cybersex. For the addict whose acting out involves relationship or romance addiction, sobriety would include not being involved in any relationships. A total time-out from sexual and relational involvements is the beginning task of recovery. For the married addict this time-out would obviously include any extramarital relationships, even those that are "only" emotional affairs. For the single addict that objective would include no casual dating for a period of time.

If this boundary sounds radical or impossible and you feel great resistance, your reaction should be another indicator you are, indeed, an addict. The idea of being without your drug may be terrifying. Again, the White Book offers hope: "We discovered that we could stop, that not feeding the hunger didn't kill us, that sex was indeed optional."[3]

MARITAL SEXUAL ABSTINENCE

Those who are married should also commit to a minimum of a ninety-day sexual abstinence contract with their husbands. This agreement is important even if your acting out involved just masturbation or pornography, rather than actual sex with another person. It's important for a variety of reasons. First, remember our discussion about the neurochemistry of addiction. A drying out period is necessary to reset the thermostat, so to speak, of an addict's brain chemistry and sexual response cycle. The addict is hooked on her own neurochemical response, remember? Those changes occur during married sex also. Sexual activity of any kind will prevent the brain from returning to a lower tolerance threshold. Abstinence is a form of detoxification.

A sexual time-out with the spouse is also important for their coupleship. Female addicts aren't truly present when they're being sexual with their mates. Fantasy or images of former or imagined partners or activities usually take over. Sexual activity, even with her husband, falls short of the one-flesh union God intended if the woman is drunk with active addiction. Addicts need a period of time without sexual activity to allow those images or fantasies to dissipate and to learn how to be present during the encounter.

Sex for the addicted couple has usually been a loaded issue with a variety of meanings. Often sex served as a measure of the relationship. Or perhaps it was the only connection they shared. Maybe it was used manipulatively or as a way to keep the wife from being sexual outside the marriage. Taking sex out of the marital equation is an important step in creating healthy sexuality within the coupleship. Again there's the paradox: to abstain from sex will ultimately improve the sexual relationship.

Finally, sexually addicted couples are plagued by a host of unhealthy dynamics and problems besides the addiction. The relationship hasn't worked in a variety of ways, not just sexually. Removing the sexual pressure helps the couple focus on other areas of their relationship. It provides a way of starting over and of learning to interact differently.

Obviously, a couple must agree to take a sexual time-out. Ideally, it should be a joint decision. Surprisingly, many male spouses will greatly resist this plan. (I discuss this issue in chapter fourteen.) Your husband may need help to see the benefit of a sexual abstinence period. However, even if he's opposed, I believe a sexual time-out is so crucial to recovery that a married female addict should insist on it. Remember the overarching question, "Do you want to get well?" In my experience, it's extremely difficult to achieve lasting sobriety without a period of total sexual abstinence. It's almost impossible to create genuine marital intimacy without this step of starting over.

An addict/co-addict couple needs the help of a counselor who understands sexual addiction to help them navigate an abstinence period. The specific boundaries about this process are different for each couple. Some find they can continue to sleep in the same bed; others can't. Some choose to avoid seeing each other naked. Some find they can hug and exchange simple kisses; others decide to eliminate all kissing during an abstinence period. It's a challenging time and surfaces myriad emotions and issues in the coupleship that require help from a professional. Everything about early recovery, in fact, is extremely difficult for a couple and finding the right therapist is crucial.

So how do you achieve abstinence whether you're married or single? It may sound as if I'm saying, "Just stop!" In a way, actually, I am. Specific tools to help you quit acting out are discussed in chapter fifteen. They're invaluable and can make the process easier. But you still must take that first step. At some point, you have to stop acting out. It's really that simple. You don't do it by your own willpower, which, as I'm sure you've discovered, doesn't work long term. You do it by admitting your powerlessness, asking God and others for help and using the tools of recovery. But you do it. You stop. You make the decision with God's help not to act out just this one time. You focus on only this one challenge this moment.

And surprisingly, you discover you can do for one time or one hour or one day what seems impossible to do for a lifetime. That's okay. You practice some healthy denial. I call it the Scarlett technique, after the heroine Scarlett O'Hara in the movie *Gone with the Wind*. When faced with the overwhelming prospect of coping with the ravages of the Civil War, Scarlett announced, "I won't think about that today. I'll think about that tomorrow." In recovery terms, you intentionally deny the knowledge that you must make the same choice for surrender and sobriety —with all their pain and costs—tomorrow and day after day. For today, you don't think about the forever nature of recovery. You focus just on this moment, and you make this immediate choice. And when tomorrow comes, you decide again in that moment. (Chapter fifteen provides some specific tools that help.)

Recovery culture is full of quirky, sometimes cheesy sayings, and one of them is applicable here. Recovering people talk about "one day at a time," which is the only way to achieve and maintain sobriety. I discovered, as all addicts do, that just for today I could do what seemed unthinkable to consider as a lifetime choice. Just for today is good enough. That's sobriety: a string of todays.

WITHDRAWAL

When you stop acting out with sex and relationships, you enter the world of withdrawal. Beware, dear one: withdrawal is not for the faint of heart. In fact, the hardest thing I've ever done was get sober and stay sober from an addictive relationship. It's torture! I don't mean to scare you, but it's important that you don't underestimate withdrawal's power.

Many women find a few days' reprieve before they feel the harsh jaws of withdrawal clamp around them. You may still have enough neurochemicals circulating (and the early experience of withdrawal itself can generate an adrenaline rush) to protect you for a bit. Be grateful. Before long you'll be caught in a tidal wave of physical, mental, emotional and spiritual pain. Understand that this happening is normal—and that it will pass eventually.

Withdrawal is different for every woman, but it has some common experiences that many addicts endure. Some are physical. Many women report feeling nauseated or having other gastrointestinal distress. Some have headaches and other body pains. Insomnia is common. Your limbs may feel heavy and overwhelming fatigue may hamper daily functioning. Indeed, some women find it hard to accomplish routine tasks. Cooking and cleaning and childcare feel like too much. It's hard to focus at work.

Emotions that were kept at bay with addiction flood to the surface, and anger and anxiety often rule. Panic attacks may occur even for women who have never had them before. Grief may come in waves that feel like an assault. Sometimes the loneliness seems unbearable. Paralyzing. The emotional roller coaster is relentless. Core beliefs haunt you: *Who am I without a man? Am I worthy? Will anyone love me again? Maybe I deserve this pain.*

Those who are withdrawing from a specific relationship often suffer the worst. The pull toward an addictive partner can feel like an undertow that tries to suck you back into the sea of addiction. Cary describes those first terrible weeks.

> I felt like a humongous raw nerve all over. My whole being throbbed with an awareness of being without him. I saw him in every face, heard his voice in every sound, and thought of him with every breath. One day I was afraid I'd die if I didn't call him. I know it sounds silly, but at the time, I couldn't breathe. I wondered what he was doing every minute. I was on high alert in case he tried to contact me. I desperately wanted to hear from him and at the same time, I was terrified I would. I forgot things, lost things and couldn't focus. I'm lucky I didn't lose my job! I caught every bug going around because my immune system was so depleted. Almost every day reminded me of some anniversary with him or some reason I should call him. Several nights I put my phone outside in my car to keep myself from calling. It was absolute torture!

Often we pick addictive partners that somehow replicate our abuse, and we form a trauma bond that's extraordinarily difficult to break. Sometimes we return to the relationship time and time again before finally breaking free. Women addicted to this kind of partner often detach slowly over time, because it's too difficult to withdraw cold turkey before you've developed other coping tools in recovery. This process is like cutting the puppy's tail off one inch at a time: it only prolongs and repeats the pain. Yet for many women, the agony of withdrawal is simply too great to endure until they've gotten some healing from the trauma that drives the acting out and until they get connected in healthy relationships with other women.

The good news is that withdrawal does pass. In fact, your craving for sex or a particular relationship has a predictable cycle. The pull will start, gather strength and eventually peak in intensity. That top of the roller coaster is the hardest place. Take a deep breath, promise yourself you'll feel relief if you'll just hang on a bit, and engage in some kind of healthy distraction. Take a walk, call a safe friend, read some recovery literature or do whatever it takes to stay sober in that moment. If you don't feed the beast, it will shrink, I promise. Within thirty to sixty minutes at most, the majority of women report the urge subsides. Yes, it returns, unfortunately (and sometimes quickly), but each time you succeed in walking through withdrawal without acting out, it gets easier.

Getting support, establishing boundaries and practicing tender self-care are all fundamental to surviving withdrawal. Chapters fourteen and fifteen detail how to use these and other recovery tools as well as how to forge healthy relationships.

POSTPONE MAJOR DECISIONS

A recommendation routinely made to those who have lost loved ones is to avoid any major changes such as residence, employment or marital status for at least a year following the death. It's also good advice for an addict beginning recovery. If it's at all possible, don't add more stress by making a life-altering decision. The first year of recovery is a bad time to change jobs or move. It's also a bad time to make any permanent decision about a marriage (either to get out of the one you're in or to enter the one you want).

Many women who've been in affairs truly believe the addictive partner is the love of their lives. They're convinced life will be wonderful if they could just ride off into the sunset with this Mr. Perfect. If already married, they're ready to trade in their husbands for this newer model. Many may doubt they ever loved their spouse in the first place.

Such thinking is flawed and any decisions made based on it will be flawed too. Or at best, such a decision will be premature. It's impossible to make an accurate judgment about a marriage while you're actively or recently involved in another relationship. My therapist gave me an important challenge that was crucial to my recovery. She told me I needed to be fully present in my marriage for at least a year before I decided I wanted out of it. At first I wasn't exactly sure what that meant, but I agreed to try and to be teachable. As the days and months went by, I came to see how distracted and preoccupied I'd been with my affairs. I hadn't been present in my marriage at all. It took practice, hard work and commitment. But by the time the year was up, I was clear that maintaining my marriage was what I was called by God to do—and even what I wanted to do.

Female sex addicts face many decisions in the first year of recovery. Sometimes it is necessary to make a major change like to quit a job if you work closely with an affair partner. But unless there's some compelling reason, allow yourself time to benefit from the clear thinking and more stable emotions that come with sobriety before making a major, life-changing decision.

Clearly, recovery is an arduous task that takes commitment and courage. It pushes you way out of your comfort zone and tests your faith. It requires risk and self-sacrifice. Probably no challenge of recovery illustrates this point better than the prospect of disclosure, which we'll examine in the next chapter.

QUESTIONS FOR REFLECTION
OR SMALL GROUP DISCUSSION

1. What is keeping you from getting well?

2. What does sobriety specifically look like for you? (Examples: You don't look at pornography, you detach from an affair, you stop pursuing partners and so forth)

3. If married, what is your reaction to a period of marital sexual abstinence?

4. Have you experienced withdrawal? What was it like? What helped you get through it?

5. What major decision would be best postponed?

CHAPTER THIRTEEN

DISCLOSURE

Few things probably are as terrifying to you as a female addict as the possibility of being discovered in your sexual addiction. After all, you've spent a lot of time and energy hiding your secret life. So why would you voluntarily choose to disclose your acting out? The answer is another of the great paradoxes: it's because telling the secret can set you free.

As scary as it may be, disclosure about your sexual addiction is a necessary part of recovery. That's a nonnegotiable truth. There can never be healing in a relationship and true intimacy unless there's complete disclosure. No amount of fear or the hedging it produces will change that fact. It's an unequivocal bottom line: Total disclosure is absolutely necessary.

This chapter focuses on disclosure to an addict's husband and children, and so it's primarily directed to married addicts and mothers. But I urge the unmarried or childless addict to still read this section, because the principles also apply to disclosure to a future life partner or eventual children.

ARGUMENTS AGAINST DISCLOSURE

Some professionals and even pastors may offer different advice. (I know that our addict nature, which wants to avoid disclosure, preaches against it.) "What he doesn't know won't hurt him" is the reason typically given to support hiding the truth. Some who understand recovery principles only enough to be dangerous may use Step Nine as proof of their position. Step Nine is about making amends for our wrongs: "We made amends to such persons wherever possible, except when to do so would injure them or others."

This idea about injuring others by disclosing a part of our acting out is a tricky one. Initially it sounds like a noble goal. In some circumstances it is. Consider this example: say a female addict has been involved with a married man whose wife has no idea about their affair. To be sure the female addict shouldn't make direct amends to the wife, because that would mean the addict would be revealing the affair. It's the husband's responsibility to disclose his infidelity, not the other woman's. The female affair partner must be willing to make amends to the wronged wife if the opportunity presents itself after the wife is aware of the affair, but she shouldn't initiate contact with the wife before then. When it comes to already established intimate relationships though, especially a marriage, the greatest injury is to withhold the truth. Yes, there's pain involved, but the real injury is the betrayal, not its disclosure.

REASONS FOR DISCLOSURE

Intimacy within a relationship is built on two principles: honesty and vulnerability. Sexual addiction affects both. An intimate, balanced relationship is simply not possible without the basic foundation of honesty. There'll never be a deep level of intimacy if one partner is harboring secrets.

Think of it this way: do you really want to spend the rest of your life fearful that your husband would leave if he knew some particular secret? What a setup for distance and insecurity. The wall required to protect the secret also prevents an unfettered connection. A part of you remains closed off and fearful. That's not the spiritual and emotional one-flesh union God intended.

Full disclosure requires courage, but I guarantee it's the only path to the kind of relationship you've always wanted. This again is one of the paradoxes of recovery: You must be willing to risk losing the relationship as a result of telling the truth in order to have the kind of relationship you long for. You are totally powerless over your husband's reaction, and he may, indeed, decide to leave you. The flip side is that disclosure can open the door to ultimate healing in the relationship. Honesty is the only route to intimacy.

I won't kid you: Disclosure is hard for both parties. Dr. Jennifer Schneider, a leading researcher and clinician in the field of sexual co-addiction, reports that a majority of spouses threaten to leave when they learn the truth. Some actually do leave for a while. But few are gone for good. When enough time has passed, most couples report that disclosure was a crucial turning point of healing.[1]

INTIMACY DISORDER AND ITS AFFECT ON DISCLOSURE

As hard as it is to hear the truth, most spouses long to be dealt with honestly. Yet most addicts find it especially difficult to share with their husbands. An important principle is at play here. Mark Laaser points out that we are least likely to tell the truth to the person we're most afraid of losing. Despite our frustration or disappointment with our husbands, for most of us, they're the ones who fit that category. We're most afraid our husbands will leave us if they know about our secret sins.

That fear explains why we can go to a Twelve Step meeting or to a workshop for female addicts and share openly and honestly. It's the principle of intimacy disorder at work. The stakes are lower with those people. If they reject or abandon us, we know we'd survive. Those relationships don't carry the weight of a marriage. We're most likely to hide from the one who matters most. And it will be hardest to tell the truth to that person.

This fear then leads to a common mistake about disclosure. We test the waters by telling a little of the truth and waiting to see about the reaction. If it's not too bad, then eventually we may muster the courage to disclose some more. Bit by bit we let go of more of our secrets in a slow process of truth telling.

For our spouses this method is like cropping the puppy's tail one inch at a time: It prolongs and compounds the agony. Each time another piece of the story comes out, trust erodes more. The husband stays fearful and suspicious, because each time he's probably been assured, "There's nothing more to tell." Each new revelation puts him back to square one. It's far better to be totally honest and forthcoming from the beginning.

GUIDELINES FOR DISCLOSURE

The husband of a female sex addict deserves to know the full truth about her acting out. Specifically, several areas must be shared.

Nature of the acting out. The general categories of the acting out should be disclosed. Examples include whether you've used pornography, or masturbated compulsively, or had affairs, or cybersex or one-night stands. If others have been part of the activity, you should disclose whether the acting out has been heterosexual or with other women.

Extent of the acting out. Has there been one affair or several or many? A few cybersex encounters or more than you can remember? Do you masturbate several times a week or several times a day? How active has your addiction been?

Period of time of acting out. Your husband has a right to know how long you've been acting out. It makes a difference to him if it's been two months or five years or the entire time of your marriage.

Hidden consequences of acting out. You may have told your husband you lost a job because of downsizing, when the truth is you got fired for Internet sexual activity. You may have had a car accident because you were distracted talking to an affair partner on your cell phone and not because of some made-up reason. You may have become pregnant with an affair partner and had an abortion. Any of these kinds of hidden consequences must be disclosed.

Corrections to lies you've told. One of the most difficult things for addicts' spouses is the craziness they feel because of all the deceit from our double lives. Your husband has a right to hear truthful answers about situations you've lied about. For example, you may have denied anything was wrong during a particular vacation trip when you actually were agitated from being away from an affair partner and were sneaking off to call him any time you could. Your spouse deserves to know his instincts were on target.

Identity of acting out partners whom he knows. If you've been sexual with someone your husband knows, especially with someone he still has contact with, you have to share that fact. A female addict often has affairs with the husband of a friend or someone she and her husband socialize with as a couple. It's blatantly unfair to withhold that information. Your husband deserves to make his own decision about continuing a relationship with someone who's been involved with his wife. You don't get to make that decision for him.

I'm aware this disclosure is especially terrifying. Your husband will understandably be devastated that someone he knows has betrayed him in addition to you. You may fear what he'll do with that information. Will he tell the other wife? Or your circle of friends?

Yet as painful as it is, your spouse deserves to know this truth. And the marriage will never thrive if the charade continues even if the acting out has stopped. Once again there's the paradox: The only way to gain a truly intimate marriage is to surrender it to God as you risk losing the relationship by telling the truth.

What not to disclose. In simplest terms it's our responsibility as addicts to truthfully answer any question our spouses ask. The relationship can never recover or grow without this total commitment to honesty. However, some elements of our acting out aren't helpful for our husbands. I encourage spouses not to press for graphic data about the acting out like details about sexual positions or response. There's no point in knowing that kind of information and once it's disclosed, it's almost impossible for a husband to get it out of his head.

I advise female addicts not to volunteer those graphic details and to postpone telling their husbands if asked. Understand that his real desire is to know if he's sexually adequate. He wants to know if sexual activity with him will be enough. His insecurity and hurt propel him to compare himself to your acting out experiences. The questions are prompted by fear not by a desire for specific knowledge. If, however, a spouse continues to push for specific information, I believe you should answer the question—with stated reluctance.

Disclosing slips. It's critical that you disclose any slips you may have. Most couples agree to a twenty-four or forty-eight hour rule, which means that you disclose within that amount of time if you act out again. That window gives you time to talk with your sponsor or therapist about what happened and what you plan to do to strengthen your program and to prepare for a healthy disclosure.

It's important to disclose if you have even unintended contact with an affair partner. Obviously, your sobriety dictates that you don't initiate any contact. But it's possible an affair partner may contact you or you may run into him somewhere. Rebuilding trust requires that you share that information with your husband along with how you handled it. Remember the key question: *Do you want to get well?* If so, you must be willing "to go to any length" in your recovery.

Using lie detector tests. Some spouses insist (and their therapists encourage) that addicts submit to lie detector tests. I work with a couple of respected colleagues who routinely use lie detector tests, and they find them extremely helpful during the disclosure process. Addicts have zero credibility at that point, and a lie detector test offers an objective measure of whether we're telling the truth. While I don't personally favor this step as a routine practice, I don't have any serious objection to this use of a lie detector test. I'll talk about using polygraph as a trust-building tool in chapter fourteen about building healthy relationships, including with your husband.

DISCLOSURE TO CHILDREN

Most addicts are also deeply concerned about what to tell their children about their addiction and recovery. They're unsure about what's appropriate to share. They're afraid of losing authority with their children after being exposed in sexual sin. They're concerned children will tell others. They don't want to burden children with grownup problems.

The reality is that your children probably already know about your addiction. Children are much more aware than we give them credit for. One morning at breakfast, my then five-year-old son asked,

"Mommy, do you love Mr. So-and-so more than Daddy?" I was shocked and horrified. My affair partner was a family friend who was often around my children. We had never been affectionate or inappropriate in front of them, yet my son intuitively knew. In the innocence of childhood he bypassed what was "supposed to be" in terms of the relationships of the adults in his world. He was clear instead about the distance in his parents' marriage and the emotional connection between his mom and Mr. So-and-so. Children are rarely fooled.

When you're wrestling with what to tell your children about your addiction and recovery, answer this simple question: *Would it have been helpful if a parent had talked honestly with you about what was going on in your home?* I've never had one person say no. The "don't talk" rule in families is never helpful.

It's reasonable to be concerned that children will share private family matters with others. At some level they almost certainly will. Two important truths are applicable here. First children are more likely to talk to others when they can't talk to us. When we provide a safe place for dealing with difficult issues, kids are less prone to blurt out their questions or information to others. A more important truth, though, is the welfare of our children. Most of us desperately want to break the cycle of sin and dysfunction and not pass them along to our kids. Protecting our children is much more important than protecting our reputation. It becomes another spiritual issue then of self-sacrifice and surrender. We can ask God for faith and courage to do what's best for our children no matter the cost.

In my experience, children don't broadcast the family's bad news as most parents may fear. Usually the children who air the family's dirty laundry are the ones who aren't getting honest information at home. Help your children identify a few safe adults they can talk with in addition to you as their parents. Urge them to ask to talk with you more at any time.

Disclosure with children is better thought of as a process rather than as an event. It usually happens a little at a time according to what's age appropriate. It might begin with an acknowledgment that mom and dad are having difficulty in their marriage and that they're seeking help. It could include an honest statement of feeling like, "I'm sad about some bad choices I've made that have hurt your dad. That's why I'm crying a lot these days."

Many addicts are especially concerned about what to tell young children. I believe it's important to answer children's questions honestly. My own children were ages six and eight when I entered recovery, and I was appropriately open with them from the beginning. As I was breaking away from the affair partner who had been quite involved in my kids' lives, they obviously were affected by the changes. When they expressed sadness at not seeing this man, I said I understood how they felt and was sorry that my choices were hurting them. I explained that I had been involved in a "wrong" relationship with this man, and that I was sorry for that sin and was asking God to help me get my life right. Part of that process meant we'd no longer be spending time with this person.

Predictably my daughter's next question was, "What kind of a 'wrong' relationship?" I answered that it was the kind of relationship I was only supposed to have with their daddy. In a few days she asked if the wrong relationship meant I'd had an "affair." I answered yes. Then in a few hours, she wanted to know if an affair involved "that sex stuff you see on TV." Once more I said yes. I stated again that what I'd done was sinful and had hurt many people, especially their dad. I reaffirmed my commitment to getting help for myself and for the marriage. These explanations satisfied all my children wanted to know.

We often give children explanations about life that they don't understand. For example, we explain to toddlers they're going to the doctor to get a "shot" or "vaccination" or "immunization." We explain this procedure is for their ultimate protection. Toddlers don't understand this process, of course, but we share the basic information anyway. Eventually, they'll grow into a more complete understanding. The same thing is true about explanations of addiction and recovery. At age eight my daughter didn't fully understand "that sex stuff," but she knew enough to have a context for what it meant to have an affair. We may use language or describe concepts that are beyond children's ability to comprehend, but we've done something much more important: We've demonstrated it's okay to talk about these subjects, and we've laid the groundwork for them to ask questions when their curiosity is stirred by greater understanding.

The last disclosure in our family came when our daughter was in eighth grade, which was six years into my recovery. She learned in health class about sexually transmitted diseases and their connection to cervical cancer. She remembered my bout with that type of cancer when she was only four, and she put two and two together. That night she asked me about the connection and once again, I answered her honestly. It was a powerful, emotional moment as we hugged each other, cried and thanked God for his grace in healing me and our family. It was a wonderful opportunity to talk again about God's design for holy sexuality, which involves abstinence outside of marriage.

CHILDREN'S SAFETY AROUND DISCLOSURE

It's critical that parents keep the emotional health and safety of their children foremost in mind when dealing with these difficult issues. Parents should consider their motivation for sharing information with children. Is it to solicit the children's support and comfort? That's emotional incest, not healthy disclosure. Parents must use other safe adults for support. The goal of disclosure with children should be to promote healing and family intimacy, which is built on honesty.

Parents should assure children that these problems are adult problems, and that children aren't responsible for fixing them. Both parents should assure children of their commitment and love. Almost always children are concerned about the possibility of their parents divorcing. Again, answer the question honestly. If you don't know, say so. It's best to emphasize you do hope to stay married (if that's true) and that you're getting counseling toward that end. Assure children that even if you do divorce, both parents will love them and remain committed to and involved with them. Repeatedly tell children the problems are not their fault, and they can do nothing to fix them. Promise to tell them the truth and to avoid surprising them with late information. Assure them it's okay to feel whatever they feel, including anger at you.

The best method of disclosure is for both parents to talk with the children together. If your husband refuses to take part, you have no choice but to have the discussion without him. Give him some time to reconsider, and then set the time for the conversation, whether or not he chooses to participate. If your children ask say honestly that you wished their dad were there to talk with them, but that he made a different choice because he thought that was best. It's okay to admit a disagreement on this issue. It's not okay to badmouth the father about this (or any other) choice. Remember a key principle of healthy families: People take responsibility; they don't blame others. Be sure you don't give any hint that your addiction is your husband's fault.

Be certain to explain in practical terms what all this will mean for the family. For example, outline that mom and dad will each be going to support group meetings on a certain night and identify who will be taking care of them during that time. Explain about going to counseling. Ask your therapist if it would be appropriate to include the children in a family session to talk about the challenges. Be clear about any boundaries being put in place like putting the computer in a public area or no longer socializing with a particular person.

Talking honestly with children models several important life lessons. Kids see that they don't have to be perfect; that all people make mistakes; that it's okay to ask for help; that it's okay to talk about problems with safe people; that marriage is a lifetime commitment that's worth working at; and that God is faithful to see us through any difficult trial. If shared appropriately these lessons give children an invaluable foundation for life and a model for dealing with their own problems.

Just as disclosure with children is often a process, rebuilding trust with children is definitely something that requires time. As addicts, we have harmed our children. We've disappointed them. Perhaps we've embarrassed them. It takes time to rebuild a healthy relationship or to build one in the first place. As our sobriety calendar lengthens and our recovery deepens, our reputation will improve in our children's eyes.

Being open about the addiction and co-addiction in our family, as well as the sexual abuse, has been a wonderful and freeing experience for all of the Ferree family. It's given us countless opportunities to share our faith and gratitude to a God who does not throw stones. The amazing letter to the reader from my daughter at the beginning of this book is one example.

DISCLOSURE TO OTHER FAMILY MEMBERS

Disclosing to your parents, siblings or other family members is another decision you'll have to consider. These individuals usually aren't affected in the same way as a spouse or children, so there's a bit more leeway about sharing with extended family.

A general principle is that you don't have to be vulnerable with people who are unsafe. If you reasonably expect someone to be abusive in his or her response or to use the information against you, you're not obligated to disclose. Remember, having boundaries is healthy. If someone is asking for information you don't choose to share, you can respond with a simple, truthful statement like, "I am going through some hard things, and I appreciate your concern. For now, I'm not comfortable sharing any more details. Please know that I'm getting help, and I definitely ask for your prayers." I found that with some people I had to repeat a variation of this speech several times. My counselor called it *fogging*: you say the same thing several different ways.

Perhaps you're blessed with a family who will understand and support your recovery. What a gift! I still advise having boundaries about what you share with others. There's no reason to divulge details about your acting out. Ideally, as you continue your healing journey, you can be the catalyst that encourages your family of origin to build healthier relationships among family members. That process may start with your disclosure about your sexual addiction. Trust God's prompting about what to share with your family and when.

RISKS/BENEFITS OF RECOVERY

It's surely becoming clear that recovery is not for cowards. It takes tremendous courage. Achieving sobriety and telling the truth require great self-denial and maturity, but the rewards are worth every risk. God is faithful to walk with you and give you strength. "God can do anything, you know—far more than you could ever imagine or guess or request in your wildest dreams!" (Ephesians 3:20 *The Message*).

QUESTIONS FOR REFLECTION
OR SMALL GROUP DISCUSSION

1. If you're married, have you fully disclosed your addiction to your husband? What was the hardest part about that process?

2. If you haven't yet disclosed completely to your husband, what is your biggest fear?

3. If you have children, what do they know about your addiction? What's your reaction to talking with them in age-appropriate terms about what's going on in your home?

4. Have you talked with other extended family members? Why or why not?

CHAPTER FOURTEEN

HEALTHY RELATIONSHIPS

AND REBUILDING TRUST

If sexual addiction is best thought of as an intimacy disorder, then the obvious solution is to find healthy connection. One of Mark Laaser's main teaching principles is that healthy fellowship equals freedom from lust.[1] Being in safe community is the antidote for addictive behaviors. As simple as perhaps that prescription may sound, it's extremely difficult for sex addicts to do. We're intimacy disordered, after all. The very thing that will help heal us is one of our greatest fears. Being intimate means being known and if we're truly known, we risk rejection and abandonment. It's the old struggle.

As frightening as it may seem to be known in the fullness of your story, there is no other avenue to healing. Period. No one can recover in isolation. I've never known of a sex addict who has recovered by herself or even with the help of a therapist. Some may stop acting out for a time, but it's impossible to recover from an intimacy disorder without practicing intimacy. Being in healthy fellowship with safe people provides the connection all addicts need. When you risk honesty and receive acceptance, you challenge the core belief, "If you knew me, you'd leave me." When we experience enough grace from human hands, we begin to trust that God also extends his grace. Through fellowship with other recovering sisters who are farther down the road, we receive invaluable tips about how to live differently.

One of the first challenges of recovery is to find emotional safety that allows us to risk vulnerability. Ideally that kind of a safe place exists in your church. I believe Christ intended that his bride the church be a place where people support each other in their struggles. Sadly few of us are part of that kind of church environment. Most of us would find judgment and avoidance if we were honest with our Sunday school class or small group. So where can we turn for safe community?

HEALTHY COMMUNITY

A Twelve Step "anonymous" group is the best choice. A healthy Twelve Step group is probably the closest model of how the church should function.[2] Members are real with each other. They encourage and hold each other accountable. They serve each other and hold in confidence the sacred trust. They invoke God's help and seek his will on a daily basis. Twelve Step groups are simple in structure and free from power struggles. They are places where brokenness meets grace, where conviction finds pathways for lasting change.

The playing field is level in a Twelve Step fellowship. It's a group of women and men who all have experienced powerlessness over their sexual behavior and are seeking a different way of life. That's the only requirement for membership. This common denominator of sexual sin creates an automatic cushion of acceptance. All are in the same boat. No one is any better or worse than any other. This presupposition allows the female addict to enter with relative assurance of being understood and accepted. Indeed, most addicts report, "I finally felt like I was home."

MAIN TWELVE STEP GROUPS FOR SEX ADDICTION

Three primary Twelve Step groups exist for sex addiction recovery. The first is Sexaholics Anonymous (SA), which is most closely patterned after Alcoholics Anonymous. As quoted earlier in chapter twelve, SA has the strictest sobriety definition, which prohibits any sexual activity, including masturbation, other than sex with a spouse. SA is more prevalent in the southern United States and on the west coast.

The second major fellowship is Sex Addicts Anonymous, which is primarily active in the Midwest. SAA also holds to many of the traditions of AA. It differs from Sexaholics Anonymous in that members of SAA decide their own bottom-line sobriety definition. You could attend a SAA group and use the SA sobriety definition if you choose.

The third fellowship is Sex and Love Addicts Anonymous. Again members decide their own definitions of sobriety. In my opinion, SLAA is the weakest of the Twelve Step groups. It's not unusual for a woman in SLAA to consider herself sober because she's only being sexual with one man at a time or only with a man she really "cares about." For those of us who are relationship addicts that sounds like our disease. A benefit of SLAA, though, is that it usually has more women attending meetings than the other groups.

As important as it is to connect with a sex addiction recovery group, finding one is often difficult. Though some geographic areas have Twelve Step meetings, many others do not. (Information about contacting Twelve Step groups is provided on the Bethesda Workshops website, www.bethesdaworkshops.org.) One of the greatest needs in the field is for more Twelve Step groups for sex addiction. A further complication is that even fewer groups have women attending. It's not unusual for a woman to be the only one of her gender in a roomful of men. That scenario is uncomfortable at best. For women whose addiction is more of the relationship or love varieties, it's hard to stay present in that environment. Some of the male addicts may also be uneasy with a female in a meeting, which is often obvious to the female attendee and may add to her fear. In time, though, the men usually become more comfortable, just like women get used to attending mixed meetings. Don't let discomfort—yours or theirs—keep you away from meetings.

ALTERNATIVES TO A SEX ADDICTION TWELVE STEP GROUP

When it's not possible to attend a sex addiction Twelve Step group either because one isn't available or because the male environment is too distracting at first, it's still important to find regular support. The best alternative is to attend Alcoholics Anonymous, which is almost universally available. In many ways addiction is addiction is addiction, which means that although AA focuses on the problem of alcohol instead of sex, relationships or lust, the principles of recovery are the same. Alcoholics Anonymous meetings typically have a number of women present, which may feel emotionally safer.

A word of caution, though, is important. AA meetings are not nearly as safe for the recovering female sex addict as meetings specifically for sexual recovery. In fact, many AA meetings are full of unrecovered sex addicts. It's not unusual for a person to be in recovery from alcohol addiction but still to be active in a sexual addiction. It's important that a female sex addict practice strict boundaries if she attends AA. Take care to connect only with other women. Don't exchange phone numbers or socialize with male alcoholics especially outside of meetings. Attending a women-only AA group is best.

It's also prudent to only identify yourself as a recovering addict and not specifically as a sex addict. Avoid telling your story too freely in an AA setting. Refer simply to your "drug of choice" instead of to acting out sexually. After you've connected with a woman who seems solid in her recovery, ask if you can privately tell her your full story. She likely will be able to offer support and understanding. A recovering female alcoholic may also be willing to be a sponsor and guide you through the Twelve Steps.

Another option for Twelve Step recovery is to attend Overeaters Anonymous. OA is geared for those who struggle with an eating disorder, whether it's overeating or anorexia. Because many female sex addicts also suffer from some level of an eating problem, OA may be a viable option.

FAITH-BASED SUPPORT GROUP

Many Christians long to work on their recovery within the context of their faith. It's a wonderful marriage; indeed, spirituality is central to recovery. Faith-based support groups for sexual addiction are now offered by a number of ministries, though they aren't as prevalent as a regular Twelve Step group. Celebrate Recovery is the best known and the one most widely available. Unfortunately, while CR often conducts a breakout group for sex addicts (it also deals with other "hurts, habits and hang-ups") they are almost always closed to women. With the exception of a few scattered locations throughout the United States, only men struggling with sex addiction can attend a breakout group. It's a huge oversight.

L.I.F.E. Ministries ("Living in Freedom Everyday") does offer specific groups and material for women. I've written their L.I.F.E. Guide for Women, which is Twelve Step based and designed for use in a support group setting. (Information about L.I.F.E. Ministries and the workbook is also available on the Bethesda website.) This fellowship is spreading and one may be available in your area.

Even if you're blessed with a faith-based local group, I still insist you also attend a regular Twelve Step fellowship for a few reasons. First, you need more than one meeting a week and most faith-based groups only meet once. (In fact, you need all the meetings you can get.) Because they are fairly new, many faith-based groups lack members with long-term sobriety. The regular Twelve Step fellowships have been around a long time and are more likely to have people attending who have stronger recovery. Unfortunately, many faith-based support groups also tend to be fairly rigid. Some are even shame-based, where members chastise each other for lapses in sobriety. The focus is on performance and on getting it right instead of on the process of healing. Most addicts are already full of shame, and you'll feel worse if you try a Christian-based group and are rejected for your failures. Just be aware that any group is only as healthy as the individuals who are generally present. No group is perfect. If one doesn't work for you, try another.

Unfortunately, finding an appropriate Twelve Step or faith-based group is harder for most female sex addicts than it is for males. No matter which group you try, commit to attending at least six meetings before you decide it isn't for you. It may take several times before you hear a story that's familiar or find someone to identify with. Don't give up. Keep pushing yourself outside your comfort zone. We're intimacy disordered, remember? We don't like groups and prefer to isolate. We believe we can handle our recovery by ourselves. Don't be fooled. The difference between those women who recover successfully and those who don't is simple: it's the ones who regularly attend a support group. Again, the John 5 question is important: *Do you want to get well?* You must be willing "to go to any lengths" in your recovery including driving a great distance or trying several groups before you find the right one.

RELATIONSHIP WITH A SPONSOR

Being part of a support group provides global relationships, but you need to develop more specific healthy connections. One of the most important is with a sponsor. Look for a woman whose recovery you admire. (Don't pick a man, for sure, which is probably who you're drawn to first.) It's not necessarily important that her story be similar to yours. What matters more is that her sobriety is strong. Her life should also show evidence of growth beyond sobriety—of genuine recovery at a deeper level.

This affiliation offers the best practice field for doing a relationship differently. Your sponsor is your primary guide for recovery. You'll interact with her more than anyone else (every day!) on a consistent basis. If you dare to present yourself without pretense, your relationship with your sponsor can become your first healthy connection. Because she's been through her own recovery, she can be patient with your intimacy disorder. A sponsor will definitely trigger your issues of attachment, but it also provides the first real opportunity for healing them in a peer-to-peer relationship.

FEMALE FRIENDSHIPS

Connecting with women is a tough challenge for most female sex addicts. Part of our problem is that most of us naturally relate more easily to men than we do to women. We don't know how to interact except in sexual ways, which doesn't work in healthy friendships with women. Because of jealousy, many addicts strongly dislike other women. (I always thought women were the enemy because they're the competition for men.) Yet building healthy friendships with women is an important part of recovery. With other women we can practice new relationship skills without the complication of romantic involvement. We can risk being honest and sharing our feelings.

Forging healthy relationships with women is one of the most important tasks of recovery—and one of the hardest. The problem? You bring *yourself* into the relationship. You still struggle with the baggage of attachment issues and abandonment. You're trying to build a different kind of relationship, a healthy intimate connection, while shackled with your woundedness and your impaired coping mechanisms. Do you remember the three bears and the three chairs illustration from chapter eleven? In a healthy relationship you live out of the middle chair in your created, authentic self, but you don't know yet how to do that or even what it looks like.

You're used to reacting out of your wounded bear and living from the false core beliefs. You're still a sobbing little girl inside who's afraid no one will meet her needs. You've practiced a lifetime coping with unhealthy techniques, and sex and relationships are only one way your survival skills have failed. You sometimes overcompensate or blame or use food or shopping to soothe yourself. You focus on other people and desperately seek to please them. You stuff your feelings and ignore your needs. You put on the perfect front or you throw temper tantrums to manipulate. In a myriad of ways you do what you've always done with the exception of acting out sexually and relationally. Sobriety is a great start (indeed, nothing good happens without sobriety) but it's not enough to create automatically the healthy relationship skills you've lacked all your life.

It's so important to seek healthy women with whom to practice a different kind of relating! Again, this is why a healthy sponsor who has worked on her stuff is critical. But other women in your inner circle also need to be aware of their own woundedness and unhealthy coping, and they need to be much farther down the road in the journey of healing. Then even when you do whatever you do that's unhealthy, they can respond rather than react based on their own issues. They can step back, see what's happening and speak from their middle chair in their authentic selves about the situation. They can model intimacy and guide you in its practice. A therapy group is an ideal place to practice building intimate relationships, because you have the help of a professional to coach you (and referee or resolve issues when necessary).

RELATIONSHIP WITH A COUNSELOR

It's vitally important to work with a healthy counselor. We'll talk in chapter fifteen about finding a counselor trained in treating sexual addiction and trauma. My point in this section is to find a *healthy* clinician. You'll bring your wounded, coping self into counseling, and you'll play out your intimacy disorder in the therapeutic relationship. Your counselor needs to be healthy enough to respond appropriately. That means she (or he) needs to have done her own work around woundedness, coping and authenticity. She must be connected in healthy personal relationships where she gets intimacy and support. Your healing is the focus of your time together, not whatever is going on in the therapist's life. She must be free from the messiah complex that plagues many in the helping professions. Her self-worth can't depend on making you better. She has to be willing to say the hard things you may need to hear. She needs clear boundaries that she enforces without apology. She must practice good self-care.

These attributes aren't necessarily something she'll overtly share with you. Many professionals who work in this field have some kind of personal experience with addiction and co-addiction. Some choose to self-disclose and others do not. That's okay; each person makes an individual choice that's right for her. You don't have to demand that your counselor share her story; that may not be how she works. Simply observe your interactions with your therapist and trust your gut. Listen to any warning bells that alarm in your spirit. Talk with your sponsor or another healthy woman about any concerns. Talk with your therapist, too, and see how she reacts. A healthy clinician welcomes interaction about any challenges in the relationship.

PARENT FIGURES

Another important solution to sexual addiction is to find a healthy "family of choice" to nurture you in your recovery. All of us had parents who were flawed in some way, and no matter if we're age twenty-four, forty or seventy-four, we can benefit from some reparenting. Psalm 27:10 promises, "Though my father and mother forsake me, the LORD will receive me." A later psalm assures God will be a "father to the fatherless" (Psalm 68:5). While our Father God is the only perfect parent, we can seek a spiritual family to further our growth. Ask a mature woman to share in some of the activities you may have missed with your mom. Pray with her. Cry with her. Ask her to hold you. The chronological age of the person doesn't matter. The emotional and spiritual maturity level does.

Ideally the best "parents of choice" are a married couple who are also in recovery and aware of the needs of the wounded little girl inside the female addict. If it's not possible to find a couple, be especially careful in your choice of a father figure. He should be a godly man who's familiar with abuse and addiction. He must be conscientious in observing appropriate boundaries, which should include contact only in public places with reasonable accountability. A trusted pastor or teacher may be a good choice. Look to him for guidance you may have missed from your father. This relationship should be less emotionally intimate than with a surrogate mother figure, especially early in your recovery. It can be helpful, though, as one tool in the process of building healthy relationships.

MALE FRIENDSHIPS

Establishing safe friendships with men should be postponed in the early period of recovery. For the first two or three years, I found it necessary to avoid any one-on-one conversation with a man whenever possible. It was too easy to flirt or get lost later in fantasy, and I certainly wanted to stay as far away from any old rituals as possible. Being in the company of men in Twelve Step meetings, though, was ultimately helpful. I came to see men as simply other hurting souls rather than as sex objects or potential partners. Eventually a handful of recovering Christian men came to be brothers in my family of choice. For the female addict, any male relationship must be subject to rigorous accountability and strict boundaries no matter how long she's been sexually sober.

MARRIAGE RELATIONSHIP

Being healthy in your marriage is your hardest relationship task. The coupleship has been wounded more than any other relationship by your addiction, and this painful history takes a long time to overcome. This arduous process starts with telling the truth and disclosing your acting out, which we discussed in the last chapter. That step, though, is only the beginning. Your next task is to rebuild trust with your spouse.

Rebuilding trust. Please understand that it's your responsibility to become trustworthy. As an addict you should make it your job to prove you're sober and committed to recovery. Don't make your husband ask. Volunteer by word and action that you're serious about living differently. Don't make a big speech about being sober and what you're going to do to stay that way. Your husband doesn't trust what you say. In fact, the old joke is "How do you know when an addict is lying? When her lips are moving!" Forget about talking the talk and just walk the walk.

Several specific actions are important to the process of becoming trustworthy. These aren't rocket science—just common sense. As a recovering addict you must be where you say you are and do what you say you're doing. Let your husband know if your plans change and you're going to be late. Avoid circumstances that might be suspicious. Ask for and accept accountability for your actions. Specifically invite your husband to review your cell phone calls or your email account or computer history. Call from a land line when possible to verify you're where you say you are. Be considerate, especially about situations that you know are triggers for your husband.

If there are specific things that have enabled your acting out, be willing to change them. For example you may need to change your cell phone number if that's how an affair partner contacted you. You may need to eliminate or curtail travel. You must take responsibility for your own emotions, rather than blame your husband.

A number of clinicians use a lie detector test as a way of rebuilding trust within the coupleship. I am totally opposed to that idea. In fact, I believe using lie detector tests is actually detrimental to a couple's journey of establishing trust. First, such tests are notoriously unreliable even when administered by so-called professional examiners. Most of us addicts have lied so long and so well that the results of a polygraph test are suspect at best (whether we either pass or fail). On the other hand, telling the truth may be such a new experience that we show physical signs of stress which skew the test results even if (for once) we're not lying.

More importantly, though, using a lie detector test makes the trust-building process dependent on the results of some artificial, external gauge rather than by the obvious signs of a transformed life and increased intimacy. When we addicts are consistent in walking our walk, our spouses will eventually believe us when we talk the talk (provided they're doing their own recovery work). If a partner is doing his own work on himself, whatever he needs to know about the addict and any possible slips will eventually be revealed. I've seen it time and time again. Without playing detective a husband will receive the information he needs. If he is out of denial and tuned in to reality, he'll know. A lie detector test won't be necessary. He'll see what he needs to see and he'll trust his own judgment.

Understand that rebuilding trust is a process and usually a long one. Don't expect your husband to trust you just because you've been sober a few weeks or months. Especially if you've acted out for a long time and have done a good job of hiding your secret life, accept that it will be a long time before your husband trusts you again. So how long will it take? The answer is both simple and complex: It will take much longer than you would like, and much less time than you deserve.

Coupleship recovery. One partner, however, can't heal a troubled relationship no matter how much individual work she or he does. Two healthy spouses are required to build a healthy marriage. One can't do it alone. But when both wife and husband in a sexually addicted couple are willing to address their own issues and when both are willing to work on their halves of the coupleship, amazing things can happen.

A first leg of a couple's healing journey begins with a period of sexual abstinence. It's ironic isn't it, that a key recovery task removes the sexual focus from the relationship? Yet this prescription makes sense when the couple remembers that sexual addiction is an intimacy disorder, not a sexual one. A planned time-out from all sexual activity allows the couple to concentrate on creating other kinds of connections.

As I described in the section on abstinence for addicts (chapter twelve), the intentional decision to abstain from sex for a time counteracts the false core beliefs held by addicts and co-addicts alike. It goes a long way toward rebuilding trust within the relationship, because each spouse discovers the other is willing to work on the marriage without any expectation of sexual reward.

Husbands, though, often resist an abstinence contract (as do female co-addicts). Couples' counseling is especially helpful in those cases, as well as perhaps individual counseling for the husband to explore his reaction. I urge couples not to bypass this important step and miss the powerful growth they can gain.

It's also critical that couples find other recovering couples to mentor them in their journey. Just as addicts and co-addicts need support and fellowship, couples do as well. Twelve Step support groups for couples are slowly spreading across the country. One husband had the following comments:

> In the beginning it wasn't my idea of a fun Saturday night, but it was good to be with other couples in recovery. My wife and I found out we weren't the only ones who had problems. We saw other couples working on their relationships and learned from them. We could get feedback and found friends to ask for help.

It *is* possible for marriages to be saved. Indeed, it's possible for them to be better than either spouse ever dreamed. The couple who with God's help journeys the road of recovery from sexual addiction and co-addiction is blessed with the kind of intimate marriage each has always longed for. It's a road that at times winds through the pit of hell, but it's also one that leads to green pastures and still waters.

**QUESTIONS FOR REFLECTION
OR SMALL GROUP DISCUSSION**

1. If you're not part of a Twelve Step group, what's keeping you from attending?

2. What will be hardest about connecting with a sponsor and other women in recovery?

3. Can you identify anyone who can become a healthy parental figure?

4. What trust-building steps are you willing to practice regularly?

CHAPTER FIFTEEN

TOOLS OF RECOVERY

Healthy relationships are part of who you are in recovery. Using the tools of recovery is what you do. Both are vital. *Being* and *doing* equal successful transformation. One of my colleagues, Ken Graham, says that the tools of recovery don't heal you, but they put you in a place where God can work with you. I like that perspective. Following are a number of specific tools for cooperating with God in his good work within you. These are the steps necessary for "working a good program," as the Twelve Step fellowships describe it.

PRAY DAILY

Step Eleven encourages the maintenance of "conscious contact with God, asking only for knowledge of God's will and the power to carry that out." Daily prayer is one good way to stay connected to God. This isn't just the rote prayer of our earlier days. It's the intentional, real cries of the soul. Converse with God like you would with your best friend. Just talk to him.

One wizened recovering addict shared an observation that first prompted this practice for me. This man had talked with some friends who each had relapsed after several years of sobriety. He asked them what happened and looked for common denominators in their answers. He discovered not one of them had specifically prayed on the morning he relapsed. All had begun to slip in their conscious contact with God. That story had a huge effect on me. I determined I would place a hedge of prayer around my day. With few exceptions, I've taken that step every morning since. Most days I end my prayer time by reciting the Third Step prayer from the Big Book of Alcoholics Anonymous:

> God, I offer myself to Thee, to build with me and do with me as Thou will. Relieve me of the bondage of self, that I may better do Thy will. Take away my difficulties, that victory over them will bear witness to Thy power, Thy love, and Thy way of life. May I do Thy will always.[1]

I've found also that the posture of prayer is important. I make it a habit to physically get down on my knees before God every morning. That literal act of submission reminds me of the daily surrender I choose to make to God. That position challenges my pride, which remains my most stubborn character defect.

ATTEND TWELVE STEP MEETINGS

Please allow me to illustrate the importance of connecting with a Twelve Step group by telling a little more of my own recovery history. I spent a hellacious first year trying to get sober and stay sober. (I certainly don't recommend that approach.) I was doing some of the right things. I went to my counselor weekly, read lots of books and journaled profusely. But I couldn't maintain lasting sobriety. One of the biggest reasons was my steadfast refusal to attend Twelve Step meetings and make healthy connections outside my affair partner. I totally rejected the suggestion.

Then one morning I was drinking coffee and idly looking through the newspaper. Suddenly every sense jolted wide awake, because I saw an item that chilled my soul: the obituary of a former affair partner who had died of AIDS. I had run into him about a year before and been hurt when he refused my sexual advances. I wondered what the problem was since we'd been lovers many years before when I was in my first marriage.

That early summer morning I knew. This partner surely was already aware of his infected status, and he made the honorable choice to avoid exposing me. Immediately, I thought of the recovery slogan "There but for the grace of God go I." And that day shaken to the core, I went to my first Twelve Step meeting. Through the help of the support and accountability I found in the fellowship of recovering addicts, I finally achieved lasting sobriety. I wish I'd been willing to go to Twelve Step meetings sooner.

WORK THE TWELVE STEPS

Merely attending a Twelve Step support group isn't enough. In my experience, lasting recovery requires actually working through the Twelve Steps. Many who're new in recovery fail to grasp what that means. It's an enormous undertaking. One woman naively thought she could work the Twelve Steps in a matter of a few weeks. "After all," she said, "there're only twelve of them. How long could that take?" Most women find it takes a minimum of a year to work through the Steps—and that's only the first time. Revisiting the Steps regularly is an ongoing part of recovery.

Many excellent resources are available to guide you through working the Steps. (Several are listed on the Bethesda Workshops website.) My main point here is to emphasize the importance of working all the Steps. It's not enough to simply read them. It's not enough even to think about them a great deal or talk about them with a therapist or recovering friend. Actually writing out the lists and inventories is critical.

The first three Steps are comparatively easy to work for most Christians. They most directly concern our relationship to God—and the fact that we're not him. Eventually the first three Steps become incorporated into daily life. They're part of an ongoing process of continual surrender. Too many women, though, stop after Step Three. They wonder then why sobriety and serenity elude them. Some long-timers in the program refer to this error as the "One-Two-Three dance." It's a good starting point, but it doesn't get you anywhere. If you're going to deal with the core woundedness and character defects that form the basis of addiction, you have to look deeper than powerlessness and surrender. The remaining Steps are about repentance, confession, restitution and finding true connection with others and with God. Some recovering people have given this broad outline of the Steps, and thoroughly addressing each one is crucial:

Steps 1-3	Making peace with God
Steps 4-7	Making peace with ourselves
Steps 8-9	Making peace with others
Steps 10-12	Maintaining the peace and giving it away

USE THE CHIP SYSTEM

Most Twelve Step groups make use of a chip system to mark different progressions in an addict's recovery. The chips are usually molded plastic discs about the size of a quarter. (They're similar to poker chips, which I always find ironic.) Different colors designate different lengths of sobriety. A white chip is usually the marker of surrender. It's offered at the end of every meeting to anyone "who wants to try a new way of life for twenty-four hours." A recovering person picks up a chip to mark thirty days of sobriety, then two months, six months, nine months, a year and multiples of years. It's a public ritual celebrated during a meeting as a way of providing affirmation and accountability for the addict's progress. (The sex addiction fellowships vary somewhat in how they use the chips, but this is the basic idea.)

Use the chip system to your advantage. Take a deep breath, get up from your seat and ask for a surrender chip in the beginning of your recovery. Grip it firmly in your hand and don't let it go. I mean literally: keep it with you at all times. Put it in your pocket or your purse where you'll become aware of it often. Let it be a constant reminder of your surrender and your commitment to recovery. Be intentional about picking it up every morning when you get dressed. Even today, I'm rarely without the first white chip I picked up many years ago. In fact my surrender chip is a big factor in my clothing choices. If an outfit doesn't have a pocket for my chip, it usually stays in the closet.

READ RECOVERY LITERATURE

One of the most helpful tools is recovery literature. A book, article or daily meditation reader is constantly available. You can find enormous insight and encouragement at your fingertips. Reading is like attending a mini-meeting of one. Gradually, more material is being written for female sex addicts. *Ready to Heal* by Kelly Mc-Daniel is a terrific book targeted for both female sex addicts and co-sex addicts. Sue William Silverman's memoir *Love Sick* is a powerful story of her experience in treatment. *The Woman Within* is a nice daily devotional book for women in recovery. *Serenity: A Companion for Twelve Step Recovery* is a marvelous Bible that combines Scripture with Twelve Step principles. Make it a priority to read something recovery related every day. (Find these and other reading suggestions on the Bethesda website.)

JOURNAL

My therapist suggested that I journal at our first meeting, and I was struck with the rightness of the recommendation. It felt like a clear God-moment, where a loving Father prescribed just the right approach for me. As a writer I had journaled for years, and now a mental health professional was suggesting that approach. I felt affirmed in my first step into recovery. Many women, of course, aren't writers and may naturally resist journaling. Give the practice a chance. Don't worry about your sentence structure, your spelling or punctuation. Just get your thoughts on paper. That simple act often brings clarity. It's a great way to quiet the screaming voices inside. To soothe yourself and release your emotions. It's also encouraging to go back later and see how God resolved whatever was troubling you.

ESTABLISH ACCOUNTABILITY

If you're like me (and most addicts) the idea of submitting to accountability is less than appealing. We're often rebellious types and we're not very interested in someone telling us what to do. Accountability, though, is one of the key foundation blocks of a strong recovery. Without some external factor, it's too easy to give in to the temptation of the moment.

Effective accountability is something you invite into your life. Others may try to impose it on you, and it's definitely true that you must be accountable to a husband or sometimes other key people like a boss. But the most valuable accountability is the forms you establish voluntarily. If you don't choose it, you'll ultimately defy it.

With a sponsor. The best way to build accountability into your life is to get a sponsor in a Twelve Step program. As mentioned before this should be a mature woman whose recovery and spirituality you admire. Share your specific history with your sponsor: your triggers, rituals and acting out behaviors. Detail your boundaries and invite her to challenge you anytime she sees a violation. Ask her to guide you through a specific working of the Twelve Steps and to hold you accountable for completing them. Obviously, she should have worked through them herself.

With a recovery network. Adequate accountability, though, requires more than one person. One of the biggest mistakes recovering women make is to have only one accountability partner. Many of us believe that if we're totally honest with our therapist, for example, that's all we need to do. Or maybe we have one friend who knows our story but no one else. True accountability requires that several people are privy to our history and commit to walk a recovery path with us. We addicts are crafty and we can easily fool one person. We need a variety of women in various categories of our lives (people who know us at work, church, in social contexts and so forth) to hold us accountable. Please allow me to emphasize again: Being part of a group is vital for long-term recovery. No one can be successful in this journey alone.

Through daily contact. The most effective accountability is practiced daily. It's not enough to commit to calling your sponsor when you're tempted to act out. At that point, you're likely to adopt an "I don't care" attitude. Especially in the early stages of recovery, it's critical to commit to calling your sponsor every day. Just a brief check in is fine as long as it's done every day. Simply report about your sobriety, any temptations or triggers you face and how you're feeling.

Making a daily phone call is more difficult than it seems. Addicts talk about how tough it is to pick up "that 100-pound phone." Most of us resist that kind of connection either out of rebellion or out of fear. (Sex addiction is an intimacy disorder, remember?) But if you're in the habit of making a call every day no matter what, you're more likely to talk about your struggles during that call than if you had to make a specific effort when you're in trouble.

Your accountability network needs to be well informed about you. Share your story, including your experiences of abuse and abandonment, as well as your acting out history. Articulate your triggers. State your bottom line behaviors along with the rituals that lead up to them. Work together on developing boundaries, which are key components of a recovery program.

BOUNDARIES

Boundaries are the protective hedges that safeguard your sobriety. Instead of thinking of boundaries as arbitrary rules to squelch your fun, view them as benevolent guards that keep you safe. Without boundaries your best intentions to stay sober will fail. Operating within appropriate boundaries actually provides the freedom to enjoy a different kind of life.

Because most of us didn't grow up with healthy boundaries, we find it hard to set them. Boundaries are a totally foreign concept. (When I entered recovery, I wouldn't have known a boundary if it bit me. I had no clue how to put boundaries in place.) Again, a variety of excellent books have been devoted to the subject. A brief explanation of boundaries, divided into four key areas, follows.

Physical boundaries. The most obvious boundaries are physical ones and the most obvious example in this category is avoiding sexual activity. That boundary is the bare minimum—just a small starting point. One recovering woman believed all she needed to do was avoid having sex with her affair partner. She thought it would still be okay to talk with him and have him over for coffee as long as they didn't sleep together. Of course, it wasn't long before they were sexual again.

Physical boundaries should include no contact with acting out partners. Don't drive past his house or work. Avoid places you went together. Stay away from gatherings where he's likely to be present.

Don't call him, even just to listen to his voicemail message.

If Internet acting out has been part of your pattern, you need to establish boundaries around your computer use. If you're going to keep using the computer, put it in a main room of the house where it's visible to others. Use the computer only when others are at home. (If you live alone, you may have to disconnect the Internet totally for a while.) Install a filtering program that prevents access to pornographic sites. Several filtering options are available for downloading online, and others you can buy through a computer store or Christian bookstore. Be ruthless about cleaning up your computer. Remove all inappropriate e-mails from your saved folder and the addresses of those who sent them. Delete any problematic sites from your list of favorites. Then put some accountability in place: ask your sponsor to periodically review your computer's history file without warning.

More drastic boundaries are sometimes called for. Some of these were outlined in the section on rebuilding trust. If you work closely with an affair partner and aren't able to stay sober from that relationship or limit contact, you will need to find another job. If you've socialized with someone you've acted out with, those interactions must be stopped. Sometimes these boundaries affect others too, and it's tempting to maintain some level of relationship with an affair partner to lessen the effect on innocent parties.

An example is my own children, who were distressed to lose contact with a man they considered a dear family friend. But because I had acted out with him, it wasn't right to continue having him in our home. I felt guilty and ashamed to see my children's pain as they grieved the loss of that relationship, but the greater good of my sobriety and a restored marriage outweighed their grief.

Resist the belief it's possible to stay friends with a former affair partner. It's not. *No exceptions.* That hope of salvaging a healthy friendship from the train wreck of a long affair kept me trapped in sexual sin for many months. Never lose sight of the overriding question: do you want to get well? If so, healing often requires tough decisions and painful consequences.

Many times we also have to set boundaries with people besides

affair partners like those who have joined us or enabled our acting
out. Alcoholics Anonymous talks about the necessity to "change
playgrounds and playmates." If your best running around cohort is
someone who's covered for you or has her own struggle with acting
out, you'll have to set strict boundaries in that relationship.

In general, every aspect of your life should be reviewed in terms of
the boundaries that may be needed. Do you need to change your
wardrobe? Your drinking habits? Where you go for entertainment?
Who you hang out with? Leave no stone unturned.

Mental and emotional boundaries. The next two boundary categories are less concrete and overlap in many ways. If sexual addiction
is really about a search for intimacy instead of about physical release,
then the need for mental and emotional boundaries becomes clear.
As women, our drive for connection is especially strong. When we're
loose with our thoughts and emotions, we're more vulnerable to sexual sin.

The Bible refers to the practice of mental and emotional boundaries as "guarding your heart" (Proverbs 4:23). These boundaries are
most applicable for those in recovery from relationship and romance
addictions. Don't entertain thoughts of an affair partner. Stop playing out the *what if?* scenarios. Avoid books or movies that may be
triggers. Throw away the mementoes. (If that seems too drastic, at
least box them up and give them to your sponsor. Commit to leave
the box untouched for a year. If you're serious about working your
recovery program, I predict you'll be ready for your sponsor to dis-
pose of them when the year is up.)

Be careful about the music you listen to. Music seems to touch us in
deep ways like few other things. One song may send you reeling for
days. Don't torture yourself. Turn off the radio. Listen only to recorded
music where you have control over what you hear. In a proactive way
fill your thoughts with positive messages from Christian music.

Spiritual boundaries. Spiritually, it's important for the recovering
woman to guard against shame. Since shame is at the core of our addiction, we can quickly relapse if we let shame get the best of us. Be
thoughtful about the spiritual communities you associate with. Is

your church a place of judgment or a place of grace? If you feel beaten up in your church and condemned for having problems, that's not a safe place to support your recovery. Set a boundary to protect yourself from those who would throw stones.

ENFORCING BOUNDARIES

I remember the excitement I felt when I first started setting healthy boundaries. I finally understood their importance and was proud to be taking such a positive step in my recovery. I told my affair partner I couldn't see him anymore and asked him not to call me or come over. Smugly, I thought that would end our contact. So I was shocked when he called repeatedly the next day and when I didn't answer, then showed up at my front door. How dare he? I had set a boundary!

Of course, I opened the door and invited him in to explain again my boundary of not seeing him. (Crazy, huh? Some of us are slow learners.) Then I blamed him when we once more violated my pledge to stay abstinent. After a few experiences like that I finally talked about it with my therapist. She quickly reminded me of the obvious: it was my responsibility to enforce my boundaries. (What a novel concept.) I couldn't depend on my acting out partner, who was just as addicted and unhealthy as I was, to do that for me. Holding the boundaries was up to me no matter what others might choose.

Fortunately, my counselor also gave me some practical suggestions. I learned to screen my calls with my answering machine, instead of automatically picking up the phone. (This was in the days before caller ID.) I didn't go to the door when I heard a knock. And hardest of all, I asked for my house key back to keep the affair partner from letting himself in when I didn't come to the door. In every setting you must think through specifically how you'll enforce your boundaries. You can't depend on others to abide by them.

CONTINUING RECOVERY

Recovery is a new way of life. Creating safe, intimate relationships is both a challenge and a joy. Using the tools of recovery like going to Twelve Step meetings, using a sponsor, working the Steps, being ac-

countable and maintaining boundaries makes it possible to live so-
berly. The results can be astounding. As the Promises of Recovery
assure, "We will know a new freedom and a new happiness."[2]

Yet behavioral sobriety is only the beginning. It's the tip of the
iceberg of the transformation God desires for us. And it's also quite
fragile. Without going deeper into our recovery, lasting sobriety will
elude us. Serenity will be fleeting, if not impossible. We'll remain at
high risk for relapse.

So what's the solution? The next chapter describes the core healing
that's necessary for a woman's true release from the intimacy disorder of sexual addiction.

QUESTIONS FOR REFLECTION
OR SMALL GROUP DISCUSSION

1. List the tools of recovery that you use regularly and describe the
   effect they have on your recovery.

2. What boundaries do you need to put in place? To tighten up?

CHAPTER SIXTEEN

HEALING FROM TRAUMA

The advertisements were already beginning to play as Savannah balanced her popcorn and eased into her seat. She'd been looking forward to seeing a movie all week. As a single mom who juggled work and children along with her recovery program, she didn't get out to the movies very often. But a friend had recommended this one and suggested they see it together. They were going out for dessert afterward to celebrate Savannah's first year of sobriety. She felt happy and proud of how far she'd come.

Two hours later though Savannah was reeling. Her stomach churned and her hands were clammy. She couldn't stop the images that flew through her head or the sickening memories they evoked. Worse, she was overwhelmed with a desperate desire to act out, which was something she hadn't felt for months. Surprised and confused, she cancelled the plans for the celebration outing and started for home.

Instead, she found herself steering aimlessly through the dark streets. She felt disconnected and driven. Before long she realized she'd turned onto a once-familiar road and was idling outside a once-frequented dwelling. With a start she quickly hurried away and was relieved when she pulled into her own drive.

Once inside, though, Savannah turned on her computer. Intending only to check her e-mail, her fingers automatically began to type. One by one the letters of an off-limits site appeared. Horrified, she turned off the machine and reached for the phone. *I don't care if it is almost midnight,* Savannah thought. *I'm obviously in trouble. Something weird is going on here. I haven't been this close to a slip in months.*

If Savannah's experience seems unusual, be assured it's not. Far from weird, it's a near universal occurrence of recovering addicts. It's even fairly predictable. Despite a year of sobriety, Savannah found herself flirting with acting out because she'd been triggered into her trauma. In her case unexpected scenes from the movie had resurrected the pain of childhood abuse. Though sometimes we're able to anticipate triggers, they are usually unexpected. They differ as much as individuals and their particular traumas. What's universal is the damaging power of unhealed woundedness. As Mark Laaser teaches, our unresolved trauma equals our risk for relapse.[1]

HEALING FROM TRAUMA

This truth about the power of trauma underscores why it's so necessary to move beyond sobriety into the healing of deeply-rooted issues. Like subterranean caverns, these hidden pockets of pain wait to swallow the unsuspecting woman who ignores their presence. The journey of recovery is best viewed as a dual track endeavor. One rail is achieving and maintaining sobriety; the parallel rail is healing from family of origin and other wounds. Resolving the traumas of abuse and abandonment and healing the shame they create are the ultimate tasks of recovery.

Each woman must walk her own path of healing and no two will be alike. We can identify, though, some predictable stages in the journey. The order and the timing may vary, but the steps to healing are similar for all. One of the fundamental elements of the recovery process is grieving.

GRIEVING

Several models of grieving have been outlined by theorists over the years. Most of them relate to grieving associated with the death of someone significant. Many people think of grieving only in that context. But it's not necessary to have experienced a death in order to have pain worth grieving. Don't overlook the appropriateness of grieving your wounds from trauma. A model of grief that's especially appropriate to recovery is one outlined by Jonathan Bowlby.[2] He identifies four stages: numbness, yearning and searching, disorganization, and reorganization.

Numbness. The initial response to a death is to go numb. It's a survival mechanism. The shock of the event, even an expected death after a long illness, causes us to shut down. We turn off our emotions and mechanically go about doing what has to be done. Friends may comment, "She seems to be doing so well" when they see us at the funeral home. The truth is that we're doing neither "well" nor "badly." We're simply functioning on autopilot in a state of shock.

The trauma of childhood wounds causes a similar numbing response. The pain is too overwhelming to process, and we shut down because we have no other way to deal with it. Addicts are well acquainted with the *land of numb*, as Mark Laaser calls it. In fact, much of our acting out behavior is an attempt to stay in that numbed out zone—to keep the painful feelings from rising to the surface. Sobriety encroaches on our state of numbness. When we're not using our medication of choice, long-buried feelings emerge. As painful as it is, this experience is a signpost of recovery.

Yearning and searching. In the next stage we deeply miss what was lost. We yearn for the person or thing. We search for it. Mark Laaser tells one woman's story that well illustrates this phase. Her only son had been killed in a car wreck during his senior year in college. Because his body had been burned beyond recognition, this grieving mother became convinced that her son wasn't really dead. Instead she chose to believe he had arranged an elaborate plan to disappear so that he could take part in some super secret mission for the CIA, which had been his lifelong dream. She looked for him in every crowd and explored the Internet for word of covert operations he might be part of. She yearned and searched for her lost child.

In not too dissimilar ways, we who have been wounded in our

families of origin yearn and search for the childhood we lost. We long for a return to innocence and safety. We search for security in the arms of partners. We seek affirmation through cybersex with strangers. We wish for the life we didn't have.

When we enter recovery, we also yearn for the addiction we're in the process of giving up, especially if our acting out has involved people who have become significant in our lives. We grieve for the loss of the affair or relationship. The sinful nature of the behavior doesn't eliminate the need to grieve it. Give yourself permission and time to grieve for the addiction you're now willing to surrender. God understands.

The primary emotion of this stage is sadness. Depression. It's an emotional wilderness-wandering that's part of recovery.

Disorganization. Next is a period Bowlby terms disorganization. Life as we knew it is over and will never be the same. The griever faces unsettling questions: Who am I now that this loved one is gone? What sense can I make of the world after this has happened? How am I supposed to go on? What's expected of me?

In similar ways the recovering woman goes through a period of disorganization as she grieves over her trauma. Her spirit screams clearly she was harmed, but how does she make sense of that knowledge in light of the myths she's been taught? How does she mesh the "red grass" message with the green grass she clearly sees? What does it mean about her family or those who harmed her? The world seems jumbled and beyond comprehension. Disorganization is characterized primarily by feelings of anger. Life wasn't supposed to be this way. It isn't fair!

Reorganization. The final stage of grief is reorganization, where the griever comes to terms with the loss. She's able to experience her pain without being overwhelmed. Although scarred, she believes life can go on and that she can find joy in it. She has somehow found an element of meaning in her suffering and made peace with it. So it is with grieving our childhood wounds. We ultimately accept the reality of what was (and wasn't), we allow ourselves to feel the depth of our pain, we work through our anger and sadness, and we choose to go on. In recovery terms, this is the serenity that comes with sobriety and healing.

These stages of grief aren't clear-cut. They may overlap or we may leapfrog among them, but in general they provide a framework of the process of healing. The process takes as long as it takes and may be repeated numerous times. But eventually if we're courageous and persevere, healing happens. But just how exactly does it happen? How do we move through these stages and come out safely on the other side? A variety of methods and tools can help you move from hurting to healing.

COUNSELING

Almost always the recovering addict needs a skilled therapist to fully heal from her trauma. It's another example of one of the core principles of recovery: No one can adequately heal alone. We need safe community and fellowship. We also need a guide who can lead us through the journey. Although a sponsor is invaluable, she rarely is equipped to address deep trauma issues. Most addicts need a counselor clinically trained in trauma resolution.

Finding a therapist who's knowledgeable about trauma and sexual addiction is critical. I believe those criteria are more important than whether or not the person is a Christian counselor. It's easier to find help for your spiritual needs than it is for your addiction and trauma. No ethical therapist will denigrate or discount your faith. But a professional who doesn't understand trauma recovery and sexual addiction may do more harm than good.

Because of the relative newness of the sex addiction field, locating an informed counselor may be difficult. The best way is to ask other recovering people for recommendations. Ask your doctor or mental health professionals for counselors trained in addiction. Contact your local drug and alcohol council for referrals. (If you can't find a sex addiction specialist, a counselor familiar with eating disorders or chemical addiction is better than one who doesn't work in this area at all.) Be sure the person is adequately trained to deal with trauma. Check the Resources section of the Bethesda Workshops website for organizations that list specific therapists.

It's wise to interview the therapist to see if she/he seems to be an appropriate choice. Ask if she is trained in treating addiction in general and sex addiction in particular. Ask if she's familiar with Patrick Carnes and if she recommends the Twelve Step program of recovery. Ask if she goes beyond treating the addiction to look at the family of origin and trauma issues underneath. Ask if she works from a family systems perspective.

TELL YOUR STORY

Possibly the most helpful experience in healing from trauma is simply to tell your story. To be heard and validated in your pain is incredibly healing. It's amazing the burden that feels lifted when you share your pain with a safe person. Patrick Carnes calls this person a "fair witness."[3] She's someone who has no agenda other than to be a supportive witness to your pain. Scripture affirms this process when it instructs us to bear each other's burdens (see Galatians 6:2).

Trauma survivors need repeatedly to tell their story. Two or three times is far from enough. Telling only one person like your therapist isn't enough. I'll never forget how frightened I was when my therapist asked my permission to invite my pastor to meet with us for spiritual support when I was just beginning my sexual abuse recovery. I agreed and she reached for the phone to call him. Immediately I was seized with a fierce panic attack. I was terrified the pastor either wouldn't believe I had been abused or else he would think it was my fault. To experience his validation and comfort was powerfully affirming.

Yet within two hours of leaving his office, I was overwhelmed again with fear and doubt. Thoughts gnawed at my heart like *I was a teenager before my perpetrator had intercourse with me. I knew better! Surely it was my fault!* The lies I had believed all my life were stronger than the words of my therapist and minister.

Again and again I needed to tell my story and be assured of the truth about my abuse. I had to be reminded that I was five, not fifteen, when my molester began to seduce me. Many times I was sure my fair witnesses were tired of listening, but the ache inside for validation felt insatiable.

Healing from trauma requires that you tell the story . . . and tell the story . . . and tell the story. There are a variety of ways to tell the story. You can write it out in a narrative. Assemble a memory book of pictures of yourself at different ages and describe the pain of each one. Create a collage of pictures that illustrate your feelings because of your abuse or abandonment. Verbally share with safe people. With each repetition part of the shame falls away and God's voice of truth becomes louder.

CHALLENGE FALSE BELIEFS

Do you remember the discussion from chapter eleven about the ways that trauma experiences affect your thinking? The shame generated by trauma creates powerful false beliefs, which must be identified and changed for deep healing to take place. In clinical language this process is called *cognitive restructuring.* And once again it's something you can't do alone. After all, your own best thinking got you here, right? A recovery slogan refers to the "stinking thinking" of addicts and abuse survivors. You can only see things from your own perspective and that viewpoint is skewed. Other people like your counselor, sponsor and support group must help you identify the lies you believe because of your trauma. Each one must be brought into the light of truth.

Reading and meditating on Scripture is a wonderful way to attack these lies of woundedness. Write out some paragraphs about how God views you. List his promises to love and sustain you. Read psalms of encouragement and guidance. If you don't know where to look in the Bible for these kinds of passages, visit a Christian bookstore and ask for a recommendation of several good devotional or inspirational books. Ask other women what's been encouraging for them.

ANGER WORK

Telling the story and challenging false beliefs help your cognitive healing, but they don't necessarily address the emotions. Some kind of experiential work is the best medicine for the chronic emotional pain caused by trauma. Experiential exercises provide a physiological, kinesthetic release of emotions, which can be powerfully healing at a deep level. Doing anger work is one way to unleash stuffed feelings and reclaim your power as a person worthy of safety and respect. Examples of anger work include:

- Screaming at the top of your lungs and saying everything the powerless child couldn't voice

- Beating a bed, pillows or some other safe surface with your fists or a plastic or foam bat. (This exercise is called "bataca" work after the name of the bat that therapists use.)

- Throwing ice or cheap dishes (get them at a garage sale) against some hard surface to hear them break

- Writing a letter you don't mail to those who harmed you and saying anything you want to say. (Share the letter with your therapist, sponsor, or a safe friend.)

The specific technique doesn't matter. The point is to do something physical where you are clearly in control and powerful. Yelling while doing any of these activities is helpful. Like lancing a boil, anger work releases the poison of trauma. It cleanses the spirit of shame. It moves you from the position of victim to survivor.

MEDICATION

Sometimes no amount of grieving, counseling, trauma work or any other nonbiological intervention is enough. For some women medication is necessary. Clinical depression is one condition that usually requires prescription medication. Many cases of PTSD or anxiety attacks also benefit from drug therapy.

The Christian community is sometimes suspicious of using psychotropic medications. We think that praying more or having more faith or surrendering more or talking more will solve the problem. Such thinking is ignorant. Scientists understand more about neurochemistry every day, and it's clear that many psychological conditions (including bipolar disorder and many instances of depression) require medical treatment.

The recovering female addict may need the boost of an antidepressant for a period of time, especially early in recovery or when she's working though trauma. Medication was extremely helpful to me at different times during my own journey. Often it's possible to discontinue the antidepressant eventually after emotional stability and healing is well under way. The use of an antidepressant can prime the pump of the brain so that it eventually can resume manufacturing and using the right amounts of neurochemicals on its own.

Don't think you can just pop a pill and avoid the painful work of emotional healing. That's false. There's no way through the pain but through it. But often the right medication can give you the energy and focus to do the hard work of healing. Take advantage of it as one tool if your physician recommends it. Counselors are usually the first to suspect a medical evaluation for depression or some other psychological problem is in order. If your therapist suggests you see a doctor, take her advice. Never borrow medication from someone else.

INNER CHILD WORK

The deepest work of recovering from trauma involves healing the wounded little girl inside who still is hurting. Her pain must be acknowledged; her broken heart must be comforted. She must be provided a place of safety to cry, grieve and explore her pain. She needs time and attention and nurturing. You, as the adult woman in recovery, are the one who must take responsibility for giving her what she needs. With God's help you must embrace the task of "healing the child within."[4]

Providing safety is the foundation of inner child work. No healing can take place in the face of ongoing danger. That's why sobriety and boundaries are crucial to this process. You can't address the deep pockets of pain if you're in survival mode. And you can't stay sober during this healing process unless you're well grounded in fellowship and support. Without community, the pain of addressing your trauma will trigger you back into your addiction.

Once your recovery is stable, turn your attention to your inner child. Remember the way Marilyn Murray refers to her: the sobbing, hurting, wounded child, which is an apt description.[5] Take time specifically to acknowledge her presence. Be proactive in connecting with her and comforting her.

Many female addicts who failed to get the nurturing they needed as children have no clue how to nurture this sobbing, hurting child within. One way to get in touch with her needs is to spend some time around young children. Observe what they say and how they behave. Little girls need lots of hugs and verbal affirmations. They need a companion in their play and a listener to their dreams. Listen to your heart as you ask your little girl within what she needs. Begin an intentional, daily process of providing for yourself the nurturing you missed as a child.

The language of nurturance is different for different people. Many of the following suggestions will seem silly or embarrassing like the anger work activities probably did. Quash the judging voice inside. Step out of your comfort zone, trust the process, and see what happens.

Here are some ways to heal your inner child.

Begin by connecting with your pain at a specific age. Start with your earliest memories of being hurt or disappointed. How old were you? Find a picture of yourself at that age and display it where you'll see it often. Take time daily to hold that picture, to call yourself by name (yes, out loud) and to assure yourself of your unique worth. Promise that child you'll never leave her again—that you're committed to helping her heal.

It doesn't matter if you doubt what you're saying. You probably will. Say the words anyway. One of the principles of recovery is that when we take action, our thoughts and feelings will ultimately follow. Over time, substitute pictures of yourself at older ages and repeat the process.

Practice daily affirmations. Write out what you wish you had heard as a child and put these reminders in several places where you'll see them throughout the day. Tape one to your bathroom mirror, one to your steering wheel, put one in your purse, another in your desk drawer and lay one on your pillow. Take a deep breath and read each affirmation slowly, out loud if possible.

Again you may not believe the words at first. That's okay. Keep saying them. Remember, you've heard and believed the lies all your life. After several hundred times of hearing a different message, the automatic negative thoughts will slowly begin to change.

Buy yourself a comfort friend like a stuffed animal. Tailor your choice to your most pressing need. Is it for safety and protection? Then buy a firm-bodied friend that feels strong when you hold it. Is your need for comfort? Then get a soft, cushy friend that will melt into your arms.

Sleep with this friend every night. (Yes, really.) Create a ritual about getting her settled in a special place before you leave for the day. As corny as it sounds, holding a stuffed animal or doll can be enormously nurturing. For months when I began sleeping with a teddy bear my arms ached when I woke up from holding it so tightly. I felt comforted and reassured to have something literally to hold onto during the dark stretches of the night.

Take your little girl out to play. For those who were robbed of a childhood because of abuse or abandonment, play is a foreign concept. It seems frivolous or wasteful. Yet few things are as healing as laughter. It's an elixir of the soul.

Invite recovering sisters over to play. Have a slumber party and play children's games like Twister. Listen to music from the 1950s and dance. Go to the park and swing or ride the merry-go-round. Make snow angels or go sledding. Blow bubbles or draw chalk pictures on the sidewalk. Give yourself permission to play.

Buy yourself simple presents. Look for ways to reward yourself for the hard work of recovery. Buy a silly refrigerator magnet or coffee mug. Keep fresh flowers on your table. Treat yourself to a cafe latte. Take a bubble bath. You're worth it!

Solicit healthy touch. Despite our involvement in acts of sex, most addicts are horribly touch deprived dating back to our childhood. We long for safe, nonsexual touch. One of the benefits of being part of a Twelve Step or support group is that we can get healthy hugs from other recovering people. Join hands while saying the Serenity Prayer. Give and receive hugs with women in recovery.

With appropriate boundaries and accountability, ask your surrogate parents to hug you.

Engage in the activities you missed. If you always wanted to go to the zoo or take piano lessons or see *Fantasia*, it's not too late. Many community centers offer classes or activities for adults at a reasonable cost. Try your hand at pottery or study French. Ride a Ferris wheel at the county fair. You're not too old to be a kid. I saw a bumper sticker once that said, "It's never too late to have a happy childhood." In some ways that's true. These suggestions are based on the principle that we can reexperience some of the things we missed. That's healing the child within.

FORGIVENESS

As surprising as it may seem, forgiving those who have harmed you is a necessary and crucial part of healing from trauma. As long as we harbor unforgiveness, I believe we stay shackled to our past. We are just as tied to those whom we hate as we are to those we love. Only forgiveness can set us free.

An adequate discussion of forgiveness is a book in itself. But a few keys points are basic to our understanding of the connection between forgiveness and healing. First it's important to be aware of what forgiveness is *not*. To forgive doesn't mean to ignore the offense or refuse to deal with it. True forgiveness means recognizing the depth of the wound. That's why this section on forgiveness comes after the ones on grieving and anger work. I'm not talking here about stuffing it or bypassing the hard struggle of working through the trauma.

Forgiveness also doesn't mean that you say the trauma wasn't sinful or that you weren't harmed by it. To forgive isn't to agree that the trauma was okay. Neither is forgiveness letting the perpetrator off the hook. The offender is still accountable for his or her actions, and it's still appropriate that he or she experience consequences for those actions. Forgiveness doesn't mean the offender has asked for forgiveness or deserves it. Nor does it necessarily mean a restoration of the relationship. You can forgive someone and still choose not to have contact with that person.

Forgiveness is a gift you give yourself. It shows that you value yourself and believe you merit respect. It affirms your worth as an innocent child of God who deserved protection. It means you're willing to stand up for yourself, take responsibility for your healing and embrace a life of freedom. Forgiveness is fundamentally about you, not about the one who harmed you.

Forgiveness is an intellectual decision not an emotional one. That means you make a conscious choice no matter how you feel. You may still be angry, yet you forgive. You may still be in pain, but you forgive. You may still be wearing the scars of the abuse, but you forgive. You make the choice to put your energy elsewhere. And the choice is to embrace life and growth and joy rather than to focus on the darkness and pain. Forgiveness is not for the benefit of the perpetrator; it's for your own well-being.

Forgiveness, I believe, is one of the most mature forms of surrender. You surrender your right to be a victim and assume the identity of a survivor. You put down your burden of trauma and take on the task of moving forward. Without forgiveness, I don't think it's possible to experience serenity.

However, also like surrender, forgiveness isn't a one-time thing. It's a choice you must make repeatedly even about the same abuser and the same instance of abuse. For example, I had to forgive my perpetrator again when my own daughter turned fifteen. That's the age I was when he violated me fully, and when I saw her innocence at that birthday, I cycled back through the stages of grief and once again had to choose to forgive. Forgiveness doesn't exempt you from the pain of the trauma, but it keeps you from clinging to that pain in a sadistic dance. Forgiveness is the key that allows us to open the door to the joy of the moment instead of wallowing in the horror of the past.

Our perpetrators, though, aren't the only ones we must forgive: We must also forgive ourselves. For those of us enveloped in shame, this process can be the harder of the two. Our core belief that we are horrible, terrible people hamstrings our ability to extend grace to ourselves. It's easier to beat ourselves up than it is to walk in newness of life. Living in shame, after all, is one of the results from our trauma.

Core healing means that we exchange our identity of refuse for one of redemption. We become women redeemed from sexual shame by the power of God's forgiveness toward us and by our forgiveness of ourselves and others.

LEARN FROM YOUR FANTASIES

One tool of practicing self-forgiveness is to learn from our fantasies, because they give us a picture of our deep woundedness, which helps us be merciful toward ourselves. A great deal of misunderstanding prevails among recovering people about fantasy. Some Twelve Step programs and clinicians insist that one goal of recovery is to stop fantasizing, and they outline a variety of ways to do that. One of the more extreme behavioral ways suggested for interrupting fantasy is to snap a rubber band against your wrist every time you catch yourself fantasizing. The pain is supposed to punish you out of your fantasy. I think that's crazy. I don't believe it's possible to punish or shame ourselves out of our fantasies. If we could, we probably would have stopped long ago.

I advise a totally opposite approach based on an innovative theory conceived by Mark Laaser. I believe it's a unique and powerful way of understanding the connection between trauma and addiction—and breaking that cycle. While fantasy can be a form of acting out for women, it can also be a powerful teacher in recovery. As Laaser explains fantasy can actually be your friend, because fantasy provides a window into your trauma, and ultimately into what you need to heal. Fantasy is, in fact, an attempt at trauma resolution.[6] As such it provides a picture of your woundedness of abandonment and the shame of abuse.

Our fantasies are our various attempts to resolve trauma. We seek to overcome our experiences of loneliness by imagining touch or nurture or connection. Or we rewrite the script of our abuse by providing images of safety or escape. Or fantasy sometimes re-creates the pleasurable parts (sexually) of our trauma experiences. Understanding your fantasy is a key to understanding your trauma. The objective isn't to figure out a way to stop fantasizing. Rather the goal is to find healthier ways to resolve your trauma. Ultimately healthy relationships and healthy trauma resolution will free you from obsessive fantasy.

Laaser outlines a variety of elements that provide important clues about the fantasy's deeper meaning. Three main characteristics are part of all fantasies.

People. Who shows up in the fantasy? What does the person look like? Male or female? One person or more than one? Tall or short? Rugged features or smooth? The list goes on. Also, what does the person act like? What's his or her personality? Charming or distant? Sensitive or macho? Again, the list goes on.

Ambience or setting. Where does the fantasy take place? In a mountain chalet by the fire? On the seashore? Is it a safe place or a frightening one?

Activity. What's the nature of the activity? Is it overtly sexual? Is it more romantically oriented? Is it merely talking or doing something together? Is it violent? If so, are you the perpetrator or the victim?

Often one characteristic is more important than the others. It may not matter, for example, where the fantasy takes place or what happens as long as a certain person is there. Or it may not matter who shows up as long as a specific activity occurs. Maybe it's the setting that's most important. One factor usually dominates.

Fantasy exercise. I invite you to try an exercise aimed at helping you understand your fantasies. Stop reading and get paper and a pen. Take a few minutes and recall your most frequent fantasy. Many women have more than one favorite fantasy, but try to figure out the one that's most common. At least narrow it down to two. Next, write down the fantasy or fantasies. (A word of caution, here. Avoid graphic descriptions. The point isn't to write the great American porno novel. Just the outline is all that's needed. If you find you're triggered and tempted to act out, call your sponsor or another safe friend and talk about what you're feeling.)

Fantasy interpretation. Now take a deep breath and consider your fantasy. No matter how perverted or debased the fantasy may seem, be assured it has a meaning. There's a reason why you fantasize the way you do. Remember, understanding your fantasy is key to understanding your trauma and what you need to heal. Following are some guidelines for interpreting your fantasy as Laaser outlines:[7]

People. The main character in the fantasy (other than yourself) often represents the person who most abandoned you. This person may look or act like the one who wounded you most deeply through abandonment. It's this person's love and nurture you're seeking in your acting out behavior. Thus it can be either a man or a woman, and the gender you fantasize about doesn't necessarily indicate anything about your sexual preferences. The person represents instead the character of your greatest abandonment wound.

For example, I have two primary sexual fantasies. In the one that's more romantic than sexual the main character is tall, dark and handsome like my father and my perpetrator. In the more sexual fantasy the key figure is a woman, which obviously represents my mother who died when I was very young. All three people abandoned me in significant ways.

Ambience or setting. The atmosphere or setting of the fantasy is most closely tied to the environment where your trauma took place whether that trauma is abuse or abandonment or both. It could be a replication of that environment, which is usually the case if the fantasy is violent. Or it could be the opposite of your trauma scene: a place where you're safe instead of in danger. It could be somewhere that you imagine you'll be protected and nurtured. The setting could represent a place of excitement or pleasure.

Activity. The nature of what happens sexually in the fantasy correlates with your invasion trauma (abuse). Either the fantasy is a duplication of the trauma or it's the opposite of the trauma. In either case it's an attempt at trauma resolution. You may still be the victim or passive player in the fantasy, which is a reenactment similar to the trauma pleasure reaction discussed earlier in chapter ten. If you were the victim of brutal sexual abuse, you may be the perpetrator in the fantasy, which resolves the original trauma by giving you the power you didn't have as a child. You may fantasize about activities (either that happened or that you imagine) which promise comfort or pleasure. Interpreting your fantasies isn't rocket science. There's no great skill or mystery here. Simply compare your fantasies to your trauma experiences, and look both for similarities and opposites.

Determine the need behind the fantasy. The final step is to look beneath the specifics of the fantasy to the message it conveys. The key question is, *what do I need in this situation?* If the fantasy is about romance and hearts and flowers, you're most likely needing companionship and nurturing. If the fantasy is about being hurt, you're obviously needing safety. If the key element is a particular setting, you probably need whatever was lacking in that original atmosphere of your childhood experience. Is that to be heard? Or noticed? Or protected?

The solution to the problem of intrusive fantasy is to get the underlying need met in a healthy way. Is your deeper desire for safe touch? Or for affirmation? Attention from a nurturing woman or man? Approval? Safety? Then how can you satisfy that longing in a wholesome way?

I predict you'll be surprised at how simple it is to supply most of your core needs without ever resorting to unholy relationships or activity. I've learned I can ask a safe female friend for a generous hug and my fantasies about same-sex relationships disappear. I can state my need for validation to a trusted male colleague, and I'm no longer plagued by thoughts of pursuing him sexually to get his approval. Remember, recovery is a dual track process of healing from past trauma wounds and making healthy choices in the present. Our fantasies both describe those wounds and define those choices.

HANDLING TRIGGERS

This chapter opened with a description of one recovering woman's experience of being unexpectedly triggered. It's realistic to assume we'll be triggered the rest of our lives. It's part of the ongoing nature of human experience. There will always be reminders of both our addiction history and our trauma history. It's impossible to escape or avoid this universal happening. It's one of the challenges of the human condition.

The difference recovery makes is what happens after we're triggered. The benefit of recovery is that a trigger's impact is less, it doesn't last as long and we're able to handle it without acting out.

Our boundaries protect us. Our healthy relationships give us safe people with whom to process. Our work around trauma resolution allows us to identify the trigger in the first place, instead of automatically falling into our old trauma reaction patterns.

Rachel explains it this way:

> Recently I stepped into an elevator with another male passenger. As the doors closed I became aware of his cologne, which was the kind my stepdad always wore. I was immediately uneasy and got off at the next floor. When I couldn't shake the memory of my stepdad's abuse, I called a recovering friend who knew my story. She reminded me that I was an adult now and no longer controlled by an angry, abusive man. I talked about it at a meeting the next day too and felt the power of the memory fade away. A few years ago I would have had a major panic attack and been shaky for days. Or I would have tried to pick up some guy to prove I was the one in control. This time the memory bothered me for a few hours, but it wasn't that big of a deal.

Genny's experience of being triggered is similar:

> I was Christmas shopping and suddenly realized my former affair partner was browsing one aisle away. I only saw him from the back, but from the way my stomach clutched, I knew I wasn't mistaken. My first thought was to speak to him, just to say hi and ask how he's doing. Then my mind clicked in and I turned away. I know today that's not what I need. Instead, I connected with a safe friend.

Sometimes we can accept that we get triggered into our trauma, but we find it harder to admit that we're triggered into temptation to act out. Be gentle with yourself. There's no shame in being triggered even if it's the temptation kind. Temptation does not equal sin. Simply accept the happening as part of the ongoing journey of recovery and handle the trigger by using the healthy tools you've learned.

SPIRITUAL HEALING

Finally healing from trauma requires that we heal spiritually as well as behaviorally, cognitively and emotionally. Spiritual healing for female addicts involves some unique challenges. Scripture portrays God as a male entity, a father. When we've been wounded by our relationships with males, especially by our fathers, it's hard to trust a masculine God. Maleness is associated with objectification, sexuality and often pain. It's tough to picture healing at the hands of a male authority figure.

The first task of spiritual healing is to heal our view of God. One recovering woman describes firing her old God and finding a new one. It's not that God has changed, of course, but that he's become new in terms of our understanding. This process is the assignment of Step Two: "Came to believe that a power greater than ourselves could restore us to sanity." That Higher Power is God the Father, Jesus Christ the Son and the Holy Spirit.

Healing spiritually requires first that we renounce our faulty thinking about God. We explore Scripture to learn about God's true nature. We study his names such as Wonderful Counselor and Everlasting Father and Prince of Peace. We repent of our vending-machine view of God, which demands that he immediately give us what we want. We pray for help in learning to trust him. We increase our faith by practicing submission and obedience. We connect with a healthy group of believers who are on a similar spiritual journey.

Gradually we discover the "God of our understanding" referred to in Twelve Step language is the Holy Father who loves us enough to send his only Son for our salvation. He becomes our Abba Father, which is a term that denotes the kind of relationship a loving daddy has with his cherished daughter.[8] God is no longer a distant and stern watchdog who's removed from our daily lives. Our connection with him becomes increasingly intimate until we firmly believe *God is my beloved daddy and I am his darling.*

The New Testament story of the prodigal son illustrates this kind of father (Luke 15:11-32). It's the story of a rebellious child who was probably a good deal like us. What mattered to him most was satisfying himself, and he was willing to do anything it took to achieve that end. He demanded his father advance his inheritance, which was outrageously disrespectful in that culture. Then the son squandered the gift in wild living. He descended into the depths of depravity and only thought of his father when he'd come to the end of himself and truly had no other option for survival. (Is this sad tale sounding familiar?) Then, surely also like us, the son was overwhelmed with remorse. He realized how sinful his behavior had been and he repented. But under the black cloud of his shame, the prodigal couldn't imagine his father would ever forgive him. He hoped only to be allowed to be a servant in his father's house—perhaps to earn his way back into some tiny shred of paternal acceptance.

But the father had a different relationship in mind. He didn't want a slave or a servant or a friend or even a relative. The father longed for a son. The father knew his boy's sinfulness and he loved him anyway. He knew the perversions of the son's heart and he loved him anyway. He knew the shame in the young man's spirit, and the father went running gladly to meet him and welcomed him with open arms. The son anticipated severity; the father lavished his favor. The son expected to grovel like an outcast; instead the father granted radical grace.

Our heavenly father similarly welcomes the prodigal today. Our eternal daddy watches and waits for us to come home. He is ready with redemption and free with forgiveness. We don't deserve grace and we certainly can't earn it, but God gives it without hesitation because of the blood of his Son. And our response is to make daily choices to live in surrender within the father's house. His will becomes the desire of our hearts. A relationship with him becomes our all-consuming passion. An intimate connection with our Father God provides the ultimate healing from our trauma as wounded children.

QUESTIONS FOR REFLECTION
OR SMALL GROUP DISCUSSION

1. Describe your process of grieving. What stage is strongest for you at the moment?

2. What anger work feels right for you now?

3. Which steps will you begin taking to heal your inner child?

4. What can you learn from your fantasies? What do you really need?

5. Where are you in your spiritual journey?

CHAPTER SEVENTEEN

FOR HUSBANDS AND OTHERS

(INCLUDING CLINICIANS)

The sex addict herself isn't the only one who's affected by her sinful behavior or relationships. Those closest to her, her family and friends, are also affected. Their pain can be enormous and their fears crippling. Their lives too are usually in disarray. They also are in need of hope and healing. Our focus here will be primarily on husbands of female addicts, though many of the principles could apply to others in significant relationship with an addict.

CAUTION FOR FEMALE SEX ADDICT READERS

I'm compelled to issue a strong warning to married women reading this book for their own personal recovery from sexual addiction. *This chapter isn't for you!* In fact, it's important that you refrain from personally sharing this material with your husband. You're not the best one to deliver the messages conveyed in these next pages. You don't have the credibility to be heard concerning these matters. Your husband needs to learn these truths from some objective third party, not from you. Trust me on this one. Read on if you'd like, but remember: Keep your mouth closed. You may suggest your husband read this book, but no dog-earing pages, okay?

MALE SPOUSES OF FEMALE ADDICTS

There's a particular shame associated with being the husband of a
sexually addicted woman. Our culture has clear messages about what
it means to be male. A real man is strong, virile and in control. His
wife is adoring, faithful and pure. Having a wife who's sexually addicted is totally the opposite of this he-man picture. What does this
say about his manhood? About his Christian leadership in his home?
As hard as it is for a female spouse to admit she's married to a sex addict, it's doubly hard for a husband to share this truth about his sexually addicted wife. The comments of my own husband, David, illustrate this fact.

> I felt so alone in my situation. We looked like such a perfect couple.
> Marnie was all involved in church and her writing. We had these two
> beautiful kids. We lived in a nice house. I couldn't believe this was
> happening to me. I didn't talk to anyone. Part of it was I didn't want
> to hurt Marnie's reputation, but mostly I wasn't comfortable talking
> about this. No other guy ever talked to me about this kind of thing.
> I'm very private. I couldn't say how much I was hurting.

Take courage, husbands, and know that you are not alone. Tens of
thousands of other people are faced with the sexual addiction of a
family member or loved one. Other men, even Christian men, are in
your situation. They're just too embarrassed to talk about it, much as
you've probably been hesitant to tell the secret. Because sex addiction
is typically thought of as a male problem, most husbands of female
addicts are reluctant to ask for help. Men who seek recovery because
of their wives' sex addiction are truly pioneers.

SPECIAL FACTORS

Society takes a different view of men whose wives act out sexually
than when the roles are reversed and the man is the sexual sinner.
Wives of unfaithful or addicted husbands are often encouraged to
forgive their partners and save their marriages. The wife is sometimes
even blamed for her husband's problem (which is a totally false understanding of addictive behavior). When the wife is the offending

spouse, though, she's almost always blamed in that case for the troubled marriage. The husband is often encouraged to divorce her. He's viewed as the victim of an especially egregious offense. If he chooses to stay with her, he's considered either saintly or spineless. He may even be called by other unflattering terms.

MALE SPOUSES AS VICTIMS

In any relationship where one spouse struggles with an addiction, the addict is almost always seen as the bad guy. He or she becomes the identified patient who needs to be cured. The addict is the one who needs treatment. When the addiction is sex and the addict is female, that view is especially the case. As described in the beginning of this book, female sex addicts are subject to a unique shame. Acting out sexually is particularly unacceptable for women.

It's easy then for the husband to assume the white hat role of the victim of his wife's addiction. Husbands see themselves as blameless for the deteriorated state of the marriage, which is an opinion typically reinforced by society and the church. People believe if the wife would just get fixed and stop sinning sexually, everything in the relationship would be fine.

If the sex addict wife is unwilling or unable to straighten out her problems, the husband is thought to be better off if he cuts his losses and moves on. According to Jennifer Schneider, a leading researcher and writer about those in relationship with sex addicts, men whose wives are sexually addicted are more likely to divorce them than are women whose husbands are the sex addicts.[1]

If the addicted wife does stop her sinful behavior and both spouses are willing to remain in the marriage, the husband and others often believe no further work is needed as long as the wife stays sexually and relationally faithful. The crisis is supposedly over, the problem is solved and the ugly chapter is best closed forever. It's easy (and understandable) for husbands of recovering wives to fail to explore the part they play in the dynamics of the relationship. According to Schneider, husbands of female sex addicts are less likely to consider their own co-addiction—their own attitudes, emotions and behav-

iors that have been less-than-healthy for the marriage. One of my
goals for this chapter is to challenge that failure.

Consider again David's comments.

> For years I hoped Marnie would come to her senses and stop. I knew
> I couldn't make her, but I didn't think beyond that. I was getting to
> the point where I would have left if she'd kept on, and I'm sure people
> would have understood. But I didn't want to be apart from my chil-
> dren. I didn't see that I had anything to do with our problems. It was
> all about her. I was the one who took care of the kids and kept the
> house running. I wasn't out there doing all this stuff. Compared to
> Marnie, I looked great.

I pray David's comments will connect with husbands of sexually
addicted wives. As a recovering female addict, I'm keenly aware of
my risk of being stoned by men who're reading this section. I accept
that I too may not be the best messenger. (I urge you to read some of
the excellent books about co-addiction recommended in the Bethesda
Workshops website. They have more credibility because they're not
written from an addict's perspective, and yet they validate my position.) I'm willing, however, to take the risk of sharing truths that may
be hard for husbands to hear, because I feel a deep burden to help
men who've been damaged by their wives' sexual addiction. And I
know the only worthwhile help is that which points husbands to the
reality of their own situation. So take a deep breath, men, and ask
God for an open mind as you learn about sexual co-addiction.

SEXUAL CO-ADDICTION

First, a sexual co-addict is simply someone who's married to a sex
addict. *Co-addict* is a term that describes the nature of a relationship
much as *aunt* or *father-in-law* describes a particular family constellation. It's a definition of the affiliation between two people.

Much of our understanding about sexual co-addiction again comes
from the field of alcoholism recovery. Initially professionals thought
the alcoholic was the only one in need of recovery. Experience, however, showed that spouses of alcoholics also needed healing for their
own issues and behavior. Addiction is truly a family disease.[2]

In no way should these statements be taken to imply that sexual co-addicts are responsible for their partner's behavior. They're not. The addict is 100 percent responsible for maintaining sexual integrity and avoiding sexual sin. Period! The spouse of an addict, however, has his own issues. Again, think of an alcoholic family. Frequently, the alcoholic's spouse either enables the drinking by making excuses for the behavior, or else the spouse ignores the problem even to the point of denying anything is wrong. A similar dynamic is present in sexual addiction.

COMMON CHARACTERISTICS OF MALE CO-ADDICTS

An adequate treatment of the characteristics of a male sexual co-addict and the issues he faces would require a book in itself. Unfortunately, most books about co-addiction focus on women who're married to sexually addicted men. To my knowledge, no book yet exists that specifically addresses male sexual co-addiction.

Less research has been done about male co-addicts than even about female sex addicts. Dr. Schneider, though, has outlined some initial common denominators among men whose wives are sexually addicted.[3] First, a majority of male co-addicts struggle themselves with some kind of an addiction. In a small study Dr. Schneider conducted, 71 percent of these husbands were personally sexually addicted or chemically dependent. It is easier then for these spouses to understand their wives' addiction. They have experienced powerlessness themselves, and so they can relate to their wives' experience. They are generally more supportive of the need to attend Twelve Step meetings or therapy.

My clinical experience is that co-addicted husbands who aren't themselves addicts fall into two distinct groups. The first group of men is extremely angry. While men react more with anger to the revelation of their wives' acting out (as opposed to sadness, which is how women usually react), these men seem to stay stuck in their anger. Some are even rageful. In general, these men are controlling in their marriages in a variety of ways. They exert their authority and operate from a one-up position. They're more blaming and rarely are willing to look at themselves in terms of the relationship dynamics. If they're Christian, these men are prone to misusing Scripture to insist their wives must "submit."

Husbands in the second group are more passive. They're likely to shut down emotionally and deny, ignore or excuse their wives' sexual addiction. They'll tolerate behavior most spouses would find totally unacceptable rather than confront the problem. They avoid dealing with their wives and instead pour their energies into their jobs, children or hobbies. They frequently believe that their patience, kindness and love will win their wives back and cause them to stop straying. These men hope if they're nice enough, the women will eventually come around. They are quicker to forgive and forget, especially if their wives embrace recovery.[4] David says:

> I understand today that I dealt with Marnie's affairs by shutting down. I pretended like it wasn't happening. I just wrote her off and didn't think about it. I focused on the kids and was super involved with their activities. They were my life. I wasn't outwardly angry or hateful toward Marnie. I just didn't deal with her or our marriage. That was simpler.

These passive men are easier to live with than their rageful brothers, but they're not any healthier in an emotional sense. These calm husbands also fail to consider their own behavior and issues. All three groups of husbands—the also-addicted, the angry and the avoidant—are contributors to the relationship problems that are causing them so much pain. While they are not responsible for their wives' sexual addiction, they are responsible for their own co-addictive disease of codependency.

CODEPENDENCY

In brief, the word that best describes the co-addict personally is *co-dependent*. In some way almost all co-addicts (male and female both) who aren't in recovery are codependent. While this is a very broad term which is often overused, there are some typical characteristics of codependency.

Most of those who are codependent struggle with unhealthy relationships and live unbalanced lives. They have difficulty identifying feelings. They tend to lose themselves in relationships and usually put others' welfare before their own. Codependents suffer from low self-esteem and believe they never quite measure up. Their self-worth comes from the validation of others. They compromise their own values and integrity to avoid conflict or rejection. They attempt to influence and control others' thoughts, feelings and actions. Codependents, like addicts themselves, believe sex or a relationship is equal to love. They often will use sex to gain approval or acceptance or to keep a relationship. In essence, codependents are as unhealthy as addicts, they just appear quite different. The truth is that addicts and co-addicts are two sides of the same diseased coin.

CO-ADDICTIVE BEHAVIOR

Spouses of sex addicts engage in a variety of behaviors that comprise their own version of "acting out," though it's often socially and religiously acceptable acting out. These behaviors are mood-altering just as an addict's behaviors alter her mood. They ease the husband's anxiety or emotional pain at least temporarily. These actions also are attempts to change or control the addict, but they fail to get the desired result. Instead they only add depth to the addictive system in the relationship.

Sexual co-addiction actually involves the same cycle that was described in chapter five for sexual addiction. Husbands of sex addicts began by obsessing and preoccupying about their wives' behavior. They ruminate and stew and wonder and worry. They then engage in a variety of unhealthy rituals. One of the most common is to practice "search and seizure." They look for evidence of their wives' acting out in her purse, car, clothing, office, phone records, anywhere. They monitor her or spy on her. Based on the information discovered, the husbands react. Some explode in anger. They accuse and blame and threaten. Others act out by becoming hypersexual in an attempt to entice the addict to stay at home. Still other men become emotionally distant and shut down, preferring to ignore their wives' behavior. Another group engage in their own addictions either chemical or behavioral. All eventually feel shame and despair. Sooner or later, some trigger sets the cycle in motion again. History repeats itself and the feelings of insanity follow. No healthy changes happen in the relationship.

> I didn't confront Marnie about her behavior because I was afraid she'd leave. I was okay with not having her, because we hadn't been close for a long time. But I couldn't imagine being without my children. So I acted out by shutting down. I totally ignored some pretty outrageous things. Thinking about what she was doing made me crazy, so I didn't think about her at all. I pretended she wasn't out with him, even when I knew she was. But I felt worse and worse inside. I was angry with her and angry with myself for putting up with it. But I just withdrew more and more into my shell. It was the only way I could deal with the pain.

SPECIAL CHALLENGES FOR MALE CO-SEX ADDICTS

I believe male co-addicts are up against special challenges. As mentioned previously there are even fewer male sexual co-addicts seeking recovery than there are female addicts. In support group meetings a male co-addict is usually alone among a larger number of female co-addicts. It's especially hard to find a male sponsor in a Twelve Step group for addicts' partners. David says:

> I was the only man in my S-Anon meeting most of the time. For sure I was the only man who was there consistently. In the beginning it made me feel even more alone. But eventually I got to know the other spouses and I saw those wives were in the same boat. We were more alike than we were different, and I felt accepted. It was still hard to be the only guy, but it helped to have a group and to talk about the addiction and co-addiction.

A more subtle challenge concerns the children of a female addict/ male co-addict marriage. I described the effect on children in chapter five as part of the discussion about the consequences of a female's sexual addiction, but the point is so vital I'll mention it again here. Most fathers are poorly equipped to handle the parenting responsibilities alone when their wives are physically and emotionally absent because of sexual addiction. Many dads feel overwhelmed with their marital problems and their own codependency, and they simply lack the energy to help children deal with their difficult home environment. One preschool boy cried, "Why doesn't daddy ever play with me anymore? What did I do to make him mad at me?" Children are the true victims in an addicted family system.

Another special characteristic of male co-addicts is their high rate of depression. This feature applies to female co-addicts too but health care professionals are more likely to overlook depression in men. Because it presents differently in men than it does in women, many husbands aren't diagnosed with depression and so fail to get the treatment they need. Both the anger and the emotional numbness felt by many male co-addicts can be signs of hidden depression. David describes his struggle with depression:

> As time went on I got more and more depressed. I was almost totally zoned out. Like the books say, my depression was my anger turned in on myself. I was too avoidant to be angry at Marnie, so I stuffed it all inside. By the time she started recovery and then I went for help, I was really in bad shape. But I didn't realize it and no one else seemed to have a clue either. Marnie's therapist is the one who actually recognized it when I met with her.

CO-ADDICTS ARE WOUNDED TOO

Not surprisingly husbands of sex addicts also grew up in less-than-healthy families. They come from families that practiced dysfunctional rules, roles and boundary violations. They also have suffered abuse and abandonment. In fact in the landmark study about trauma experienced by sex addicts, Patrick Carnes found that the rates of abuse among addicts and co-addicts were nearly identical.[5]

Table 4. Comparison of Incidence of Trauma Between Sex Addicts and Co-Sex Addicts

Type of Trauma	Sex Addicts	Co-Sex Addicts
Sexual Abuse	81%	81%
Physical Abuse	72%	71%
Emotional Abuse	97%	91%

Co-addicts then come by their codependency honestly just as addicts learned their own unhealthy coping tactics in their families of origin. David shares:

> I came from a good family with good Christian parents who loved me. I didn't have any of the abuse like Marnie did. But we didn't really talk about things either or share our feelings. And I understand now that I was a lost child because I was so easygoing and nondemanding. My dad also struggled with depression most of his life, and my mother had her hands full at times trying to help him. I just learned not to draw any attention to myself or rock the boat. So it was normal for me to do the same thing in my relationship with Marnie.

Is it becoming any clearer that the diseases of addiction and codependency are really flip sides of the same coin? They are simply different but equally impairing diseases. Figure 5 illustrates this point.

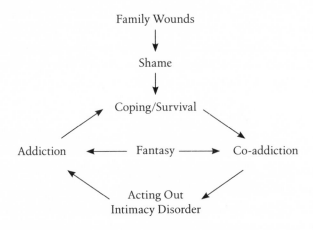

Figure 5. Development of disease

The woundedness of co-addicts is the fuel for their codependency just as addicts' trauma is the driving force behind their addiction. Both addicts and co-addicts are simply trying to cope with life. To survive as best they can. Both spouses are crippled in terms of skills necessary for a healthy bond. Neither one knows how to be truly intimate in a relationship. Both suffer from an intimacy disorder that prevents genuine connection. David shares:

> I wished we had a better marriage and daydreamed about how nice that would be, but I didn't have any idea how to make it happen. I didn't know what to do, so basically I didn't do anything. I was afraid I'd do something wrong. Today I'm aware it wasn't a healthy way to react, but at the time it was all I knew how to do. I guess I was definitely a good co-addict.

A HUSBAND'S PERSONAL RECOVERY

This reality underscores why a husband should take his own journey of recovery no matter what choices his wife may make. He also is in need of healing from his own experiences of abuse and abandonment. In fact, it's that woundedness that caused him to hook up with an addict in the first place. Like "heat-seeking missiles" as Laaser describes it, addicts and co-addicts are drawn to each other.[6] Each (unconsciously) seeks to connect with a partner who can heal core wounds. Rather than being codependent because he's in relationship with an addict, the truth is that a partner was suffering from codependency *before* he married a sex addict. David's story illustrates this point well.

> Because of my dad's depression as well as his personality, my father was a quiet, passive man. My mother was the dominant one in our family. I learned early to go along with whatever she said. I took for granted women were the driving force in relationships. So it's understandable I was drawn to someone like Marnie, who's very outgoing and strong willed. In fact that's what first attracted me to her. Plus she was sweet and caring like my mother. Marnie handled all the talking, feeling and relationship stuff between us, and that was fine with me. I'd never done those things in my first marriage or earlier relationships, and with her I didn't have to start. It was familiar.

The reality of a partner's preexisting codependency emphasizes the importance of a husband's own recovery journey. Without working on his own issues, a husband is at high risk to enter a relationship with another addict if he divorces his addicted wife. It's another example of the multigenerational pattern of addiction, only this time applied to the codependency side of the diseased coin. (Men who doubt that prediction might benefit from exploring their own relationship history. In all likelihood, their romantic partners had some kind of significant problem.) Trading one addicted partner for another is certainly no improvement.

For his own sake as well as potentially for the sake of his marriage, a male co-addict can begin his own journey by admitting that he needs help too. The first step is to realize he is totally powerless over his wife's sexual addiction. He didn't cause it, but neither can he control or cure it. Those are the "Three C's" of codependency recovery: "I didn't cause it; I can't control it; and I can't cure it." The only person a co-addict can change is himself.

A husband can learn to set appropriate boundaries against inappropriate and sinful behavior. He can choose to take actions that will be helpful for himself and his marriage. He can avoid his own flavor of harmful codependent acting out.

For emphasis, please allow me to repeat the main point of this section (and kindly put down the stones). It is crucial that the husband of a sex addict become involved in his own journey, regardless of whether his addicted wife makes a similar choice. He can pursue healing and reap wonderful benefits, no matter the final outcome of the crisis addiction has caused the marriage. The process of recovery for a co-addict husband is the same as outlined for the addicted wife: participation in a Twelve Step fellowship, counseling, trauma work, cultivating spirituality, perhaps medication and so forth. David describes his healing process:

> Things definitely improved when Marnie stopped acting out. It was such a relief when she stayed sober, and for a good while that was enough. But then we got to a certain point and stopped making progress. I realized I had work to do too. I needed to learn how to stand up for myself and not shut down. I needed to talk more and share my feelings. I started my own therapy, got on an antidepressant and went to my own group. Our marriage has gotten better and better the more

we both grow and step out of our comfort zone. Intimacy is still hard for me sometimes, but we're so much closer than we were before. I'm glad we've stayed married and our relationship is really good today. But I'm also glad I've gotten into recovery for myself. I needed recovery just as much as Marnie did.

CHILDREN OF FEMALE SEX ADDICTS

I feel a deep burden for a child whose mom is (or was) a sexual addict. I think of my own children as I write, and I remember their pain. If you're the child of a female sex addict, please allow me to address yours. Let me assure you of some truths about your mother's addiction.

First, your mom did the things she did because she's an addict, not because she wasn't concerned about you. It wasn't her intention to hurt you, though she surely did. As hard as it may be to accept, your mom also probably didn't intend to hurt your dad. Her initial sinful choices escalated into an addiction, which became the all-consuming force in her life. It's not that she didn't love or care for you. It's just that she was ruled by her addiction more. It's not your fault. You could have done nothing to win her attention or command her recovery. I pray that you're reading this book because your mom now is embracing a changed life, and she asked you to read it.

Perhaps at this moment you're full of anger and bitterness. That's okay. You feel what you feel, and your feelings are certainly justified if you've been parented by an addicted mother. You wonder if you can forgive her. If you can trust her to meet your needs. If you can ever share an intimate connection where you can be honest about what it was like to grow up in your home tainted by her sexual sin. You long for her to fulfill the role she should have assumed when you were conceived: to be your mother. No matter how old you are, there's a deep desire in your heart for true mothering.

Be comforted, dear one: It's definitely possible for you to have the kind of relationship you've always longed for with your mother. If she accepts the challenge of recovery, your relationship can improve as she gets healthier. Trust between mother and child can rebuild just as it can between husband and wife. Healthy communication can replace secrecy and lies. Intimacy can flower instead of isolation.

But a healthy relationship takes two healthy people, even between parent and adult child. If your mom is a sex addict, you also are powerfully affected by her disease. If you've read this far, even if you're only trying to understand your mother, by now you surely see your own pain. You've experienced the trauma of growing up in an addicted family. You know the burden of secrecy and the loneliness of abandonment. Perhaps you feel the pain of abuse. Whether you're fourteen or forty-five, it's vital that you too take your own journey of healing. (And if you're old enough to be reading this book, you're old enough to take responsibility for your own well-being.)

Are you shackled by the unhealthy patterns you learned from your mom? To not talk or not feel or to practice avoidance or blame? What pain, sin or unhealthy coping strategy is present in your life? Without recovery, children of sex addicts are at high risk of either addiction or codependency. Look at your own relationship and sexual history. Which coping strategy do you favor? Do you have addictive tendencies? Do you medicate with acting out behaviors of your own? Or perhaps you fall into the camp of codependency. Was it your role to take care of your mom? Or at least did you wish you could take care of her in terms of changing her behavior? And are you repeating that dynamic in other relationships? Are you a rescuer or caretaker? The same steps of recovery outlined for the addict and her spouse apply to an addict's children.

Outside of the blessing of a restored relationship with my husband, one of the greatest gifts of my journey has been to watch our daughter embrace her own recovery. At age sixteen she started attending a Twelve Step group for sexual co-addiction when she realized some of the characteristics of her own relationships. Today she shares openly about our family's journey and her own. Our son is also in recovery from addiction and codependency, and his courage in facing his own issues inspires me.

FAMILIES OF FEMALE SEX ADDICTS

A daughter's struggle with sexual addiction also affects her family of origin, if only because of their concern and love. Her problem may be baffling and embarrassing. As she pursues recovery and learns about healthy and unhealthy families, she may share information that's painful for parents or siblings to hear. If talking honestly hasn't been a part of the family's pattern, it's especially challenging to break the silence about a difficult topic like sexual sin.

It's easy to be reactive and defensive. It helps if the addicted daughter is far enough along in her recovery to understand the difference between blaming her family and understanding them, but she may not be. In any case, it's not helpful when the family, in turn, blames the sex addict and refuses to take an honest look at any problems that existed within the family.

Parents of addicts. Parents, allow your daughter to think what she thinks and feel what she feels, even if your perspective is different. It's fine to express your own opinions and emotions, but accept the fact that the addict's view of her family may be different. The most important thing is that you are beginning to talk about tough issues.

A recovering female addict may be extremely angry about any abuse and abandonment she experienced growing up. And she may be quite fierce in expressing that anger. She may set some strong boundaries about contact with her family, at least for a time while she works through her pain or establishes a healthy sense of separate identity. Again this part of the recovery process is surely painful for you as her parent. The best response is to honor your daughter's boundaries while assuring her of your continued love. The quickest resolution to difficult family issues comes when both parents and adult children are respectful of each other and are willing to look at their own contributions to the problems. Often, it's best for a family to tackle painful topics with the help of a therapist. If you're invited to attend one of your daughter's counseling sessions, be grateful she's willing to broach deep issues and go with an open mind and loving heart.

There's no point in parents beating themselves up over any failures in their parenting. Most Christian parents do the best they can with the understanding that's available to them. All adults are wounded from their own families to some extent, and loving parents are no exception. (And you qualify as a loving parent or you wouldn't be reading this book.) Adults bring baggage from their own upbringing into their jobs as parents. Without intentional intervention based on understanding of family systems and woundedness, unhealthy patterns are repeated.

If today you wish you'd done some things differently in raising your children, say so. Express your regret about specific mistakes. Ask for forgiveness. Be sure your own life and current interactions with your daughter are healthy. Few things are as healing as when parents are honest with their adult children about what happened in the family in earlier years—and when parents make any changes that need to be made. You and your daughter can grieve together for the pain you've all experienced. It's never too late for you to have a different relationship.

Perhaps, though, your daughter isn't yet addressing her sexual addiction. You're reading this book for yourself, hoping for answers in how to deal with her. As I encouraged husbands and children of female sex addicts, it's important that you take your own journey of recovery. Reach out for help. Participate in a Twelve Step fellowship for family members of addicts. Understand the ways you may be enabling or excusing your daughter's behavior. Learn how to detach with love. Set appropriate boundaries. Participate in your own therapy.

Equally important, if your daughter is married, resist the temptation to view her marriage relationship through a rigid, black and white lens. There's not a good spouse and a bad spouse. Both the addict and her husband are struggling and both are in need of recovery. His behavior may seem less sinful, but it probably isn't any more productive for their relationship. And if he's involved in self-righteous judgment of his wife, he's caught in sin just as much as she is. Allow the addicted couple the space to deal with their situation without imposing your timetable and solutions.

Brothers and sisters of addicts. Siblings of female sex addicts face challenges in dealing with their sister's addiction similar to those their parents face. However, they have an additional factor that poses a unique difficulty. As other children in the family, siblings' view of parents and the home environment may be radically different from their sister's. As a sibling of a sex addict, you may be baffled by her perception of your home life. You may wonder if you grew up in the same family and had the same parents.

In reality, you didn't. No two children, even identical twins, have the same family experience. Each parent-child relationship is a complex constellation of factors that is influenced (among other things) by the child's personality, development and behavior. Mothers and fathers parent each child differently because each child is different and because parents themselves are different with each child. Parents are different because they're older with successive children, or because they're more (or less) mature or because of an infinite variety of circumstances. For example, parents who practice strict, rigid boundaries with their firstborn may mellow into more balanced interactions with subsequent children. Parents who are absent, addicted or impaired in some way with one child may be significantly healthier or more available with other children.

As a sibling who's concerned with a sister's sex addiction, you must recognize she may have had different family experiences that shaped her thinking and behavior. Accept her reality as what it is: her reality. It's not necessarily right or wrong, it's just hers. Avoid arguing about your different memories or perception. Like parents, feel free to share your own opinion but don't try to convince your sister she's mistaken in her viewpoint.

Just as I encourage an addict's husband and parents, I urge siblings to seek recovery for themselves. Three possible benefits may result. If you disagree with your sister's view of your family, you may understand her better through discussing the situation and family history with an objective third party like a counselor. You also may be enlightened about some of the family dynamics and come to revise your own assessment and so begin your own healing work. And if you already recognize some painful reality about your family of origin experiences, you, too, are in need of help if you haven't yet taken your own recovery journey.

Perhaps your sister has some specific issues with you either from when you were children or from your adult relationship. Again, I encourage you to view any discussion with her about those problems as an opportunity for deeper intimacy. If you're in agreement about any trauma history in your family, it's high time you and your sister shared your pain. You are uniquely able to support each other.

Kay, a recovering female addict, found incredible healing through her relationship with her brother:

> When we were kids, I looked up to my oldest brother. I adored him and felt a special connection with him. But as adults we drifted apart. Things became strained between us. When I had been in counseling just a few months, I called him out of the blue. Carefully, I asked some general questions about his view of our family. He was wary and changed the subject, and I got extremely frustrated. Something snapped inside me and I let him have it! I told him that was one problem with our sick family: We wouldn't talk about the secrets.
>
> Then I dumped out all my garbage. Boom, just like that, I told my brother about my sexual abuse as a kid and about my addiction. I just didn't care anymore about protecting my perfect family. To my amazement, my brother reacted by doing the same thing! He told me about his own molestation and his own struggle with pornography and addiction. He too had recently entered sexual recovery. He apologized for putting me off and admitted he was still too afraid to talk about our family stuff without knowing where I was coming from.
>
> It was a huge turning point in our relationship and in our individual journeys of healing. We both found validation when we shared our memories. We understood and supported each other like no one else could. We grieved and prayed and laughed together. We even jointly confronted our parents about their abusive behavior when we were children and their own addictions.
>
> Having a brother to share the pain of recovery and the joy of healing is one of the greatest blessings in my life. There's finally someone in my family who's willing to be real.

FRIENDS OF FEMALE SEX ADDICTS

Friends are in a great position to be helpful to the woman struggling with sexual addiction. Without the family ties, friends can be more objective. They can listen without taking comments personally. It's probably easier for friends to detach and set healthy boundaries than it is for family members.

The best gift friends can give a woman caught in sexual sin is to provide a safe place for her to share her struggle. Believe her when she confides she has a problem. Because of their own discomfort, friends occasionally dismiss a woman's concerns. They may tell her, "You're a Christian—you surely can stop if you really try"; or they minimize her problem by saying, "Oh, we all fantasize sometimes. It's not that big of a deal." If you have a friend who finds the courage to tell you she's struggling with her sexual behavior, accept her confession.

Encourage her to get specific help. Offer to go with her if necessary. One of my clients was so fearful of telling her story even to a therapist that she couldn't bring herself to drive to the appointment. Her friend came with her for the first several visits and sat in the waiting room during our sessions. That specific support boosted my client's courage and commitment to recovery. Offer to provide your friend assistance and accountability.

The recovering woman may also need practical help with everyday matters. There were frequent times early in my recovery when I was so overwhelmed with my abuse and addiction I could barely function. Several nights I poured cereal for my children's supper, because it was all I could muster. Friends can provide tangible help like an occasional meal or an afternoon of running errands. Christians do that for each other when there's a death or serious illness, why not when a woman battles a powerful disease like addiction?

Friends can help with childcare while a woman attends Twelve Step meetings or counseling sessions. Or maybe what the recovering addict needs is a quiet place to do some taxing emotional work. Yvonne, one of my dear friends, allowed me to stay in her guest room for several days while I journaled out the horrible details of my abuse. She gave me a time-out from the responsibilities of the real world and a comforting place to process my pain. Both were incredible gifts.

CLINICIANS WHO TREAT FEMALE SEX ADDICTS

Therapists who work with sexually addicted women can literally be lifesavers. You may be the one who stands in the gap and offers grace and hope to a desperate soul. What a privilege and responsibility. Details about the treatment of female sex addicts are beyond the scope of this book which is written for strugglers themselves, but I would be remiss not to point out a few key points. (See the handbook *Clinical Management of Sex Addiction*[7] for comprehensive information on treating sexual addiction.)

On a personal level the most important thing is for you to be a healthy individual as well as a trained clinician. Review the paragraphs in chapter fourteen about a recovering woman's relationship with her counselor. Have you done your own work before you try to work with others? The sexually addicted woman will trigger your own issues, and you'll need to be aware of your countertransference vulnerabilities. Her possible personality disorders or traits are challenging, and if they push against your own unhealthiness, it's a dangerous mix.

Clinically speaking, you may have already realized that the presentations and underlying issues for female sex addicts aren't very different from their male sex addict counterparts. There are some nuances, to be sure, but by and large there aren't significant differences in these populations. What is different is how you *treat* sexually addicted women. This population requires a different approach from male addicts. The therapeutic relationship is even more critical because of the shame female sex addicts carry. You need to go slower and use a gentler approach. Patrick Carnes's task-centered treatment modality[8] isn't as effective as it is with males, and sometimes it's even counterproductive. Female sex addicts are more fragile and need more therapeutic nurturing. You must take care to create a safe container for their healing. They need to trust your commitment to them over time in order to be vulnerable enough to heal. You must endure their countertransference with patience and grace.

Female sex addicts are desperate, wounded and often without hope. They are one of the more challenging clinical populations because they gather into one package many difficult issues such as untreated sexual abuse, depressive and anxiety disorders, attachment issues and personality impairments. However, the clinician who partners with God in treating sexually addicted women has the rewarding experience of making a radical, even eternal difference in the lives of hurting sisters.

HOW CHURCHES CAN RESPOND TO FEMALE SEX ADDICTS

A hugely important task for churches is to be a safe place for hurting people. I've used this quote before, but I love its vivid description: Churches must refuse to "shoot their wounded"[9] and instead must offer help and hope. In the body of Christ (of all places) women should be free to be real about their wounds and their struggles. It should be okay to be who you are with the problems you face. Christ's church should be a place where it's acceptable to talk about tough issues. For too long certain topics have been taboo. My own minister (the one who was so comforting when I told him about my abuse) declares, "Silence is the great sin of the church."[10] In a healthy church, addiction and recovery are mentioned from the pulpit. Abuse is openly acknowledged as one of life's more difficult sorrows. Those struggling with addiction are welcome and even encouraged to attend.

Jesus rebuked the religious leaders of his day for shunning sinners. He said to the scribes and the Pharisees, "It is not those who are healthy who need a physician, but those who are sick; I did not come to call the righteous, but sinners" (Mark 2:17 NASB). The Great Physician clearly understood that those who are sick need a place of healing. I'm privileged to belong to a Christian church family that cultivates an identity as a "hospital church." A safe church is a place of grace, where sinners are pointed to a Savior who loves them and longs for their transformation.

As Cloud and Townsend's excellent book *Safe People* describes in a section on healthy churches, leadership must embrace this kind of ministering spirit.[11] Healthy leaders model vulnerability and brokenness instead of projecting the image they have it all together. Leaders provide examples of Christians who admit their problems and address them. They're open about past struggles, and this vulnerability offers hope to those facing similar challenges. Leaders are accountable about every aspect of their lives instead of operating in isolation.

A healthy church refuses to sidestep sexual sin even among its own leadership. While many churches prefer to quietly send away a pastor who falls into sexual acting out, which leaves future congregations open for similar problems, the healthy church confronts the issue and assists the minister in getting help. He or she is held accountable but not shamed or ostracized. It may be appropriate for the person to step down from leadership until treatment is completed and a lengthy track record of solid recovery is visible, but decisions are made with the goal of the leader's restoration, not condemnation. (See Mark Laaser's *Restoring the Soul of a Church* [12] for a comprehensive discussion of how churches should respond to a leader found in sexual sin.)

Finally, churches can help women battling sexual addiction by providing specific resources. The church can serve as a clearinghouse of information about books, counselors, treatment programs and recovering people who can be helpful to the female addict. The church can sponsor seminars that educate about healthy families and healthy sexuality, as well as about the problems of abuse and addiction. The church can certainly open its doors to Twelve Step or other recovery groups that address sexual addiction. It's shameful that most churches sit empty the majority of the week.

HOW ALL CAN HELP

Anyone who's concerned about a woman who's battling sexual addiction—whether that person is a husband, family member, friend, church member or in any other category of relationship—can help by doing one simple thing: spread the word about the disease of sexual addiction and the assistance that's available. Break the silence about this problem and share what you've learned about its solution. Correct those who foolishly believe sex addiction is a laughable condition. Speak out about pornography and other sexual exploitations. Be a crusader for sexual wholeness and sexual health.

If you need further encouragement that it's possible to recover from sexual addiction and live in integrity and intimacy, I pray the final chapter of *No Stones* provides that hope.

QUESTIONS FOR REFLECTION
OR SMALL GROUP DISCUSSION

(For *husbands*, not for the female addict)

1. What is your reaction to the concept of co-addiction and codependency?

2. What co-addictive behaviors have you engaged in?

3. What wounds do you bring into this relationship?

4. If you're not yet involved in your own recovery journey, what's stopping you?

CHAPTER EIGHTEEN

LIVING HAPPILY EVER AFTER

No matter how painful her past and how problematic her present, it is possible for the sexually addicted woman to live happily ever after. Through surrender, she can achieve sobriety. With the tools of recovery, she can maintain integrity. By the power of the Great Physician, she can heal from trauma. By accepting responsibility and walking in faithfulness, she can reearn trust. In honesty and vulnerability, she can build intimate relationships. Through grace, she can even come to see meaning in her suffering and sin as she embraces opportunities to reach out to those women who are still struggling.

"EVER AFTER"—A LIFELONG ENDEAVOR

People who've never battled an addiction often don't understand why an addict continues to go to meetings and work her program years after she first entered recovery. They may question her dependence on those "crazy groups." They may push her to relax her boundaries and "lighten up with all that stuff."

It's not that these family members or friends aren't proud of the woman's changed lifestyle. It's not even that they're unsupportive. They're simply uninformed about what all recovering people learn: Ultimately, recovery is about practicing a new way of living, not simply about avoiding the practice of an addiction. Recovery is a commitment to a different life, forever and ever. To stop recovery because you've been doing it a long time is like deciding to stop breathing—ludicrous. (And life-threatening.) Walking in recovery is a "forever" journey.

That's why I continue to refer to myself as a *grateful recovering sex addict*, and I will do so for life. I don't ever plan to stop claiming membership in that category of sinners. I dare not, because that designation keeps me grounded. It keeps my choices in line with my vision. It keeps my feet on the ground and my eyes on the Savior. It keeps me reminded of the grace offered through no stones, for which I can never be sufficiently grateful. It's an identity I didn't choose, but it's one I view today as a positive, not as a negative. It's simply a description of who I am as much as *woman* or *therapist* or *writer*.

Be encouraged, dear sister, that the road won't always be as difficult as it is in the beginning. The process definitely gets easier. The comparison to breathing is a good one, because eventually recovery will also become automatic. It will be just an everyday necessity of life. Part of the simple basics of healthy living. You may even come to take it for granted at times. It's no longer specifically "recovery"; it's just living.

To be sure, sometimes the challenge of a steep mountain in life will labor your breathing. A pneumonia of the soul may require focused attention. You may even need the occasional respirator of a return to therapy or treatment. Such is the unpredictable nature of the journey. You need not fear or shrink from these challenges, for you have the tools to deal with them.

But for the most part the intensity of the passage from active addict to a recovering one is short-lived. After a period of months or years, the way is clearer and more easily navigated. You'll know the rough spots and you'll be prepared. Keep putting one foot in front of the other, and your steps will become more sure.

LAASER CYCLE OF RECOVERY

Referred to frequently in this book, Carnes's cycle of addiction (shown in chapter five) depicts the story of the sexually addicted woman.

This graphic illustrates the family wounds that leads to shame, that lead to acting out, which leads to despair. (I hardly need to remind you of this progression.) In place of this cycle of pain and sin, a life lived "happily ever after" is characterized by a different graphic: a cycle of recovery. Mark Laaser created this illustration,[1] which is shown in figure 6. Instead of the diagram of degeneration, Laaser's cycle visualizes the progression of transformation available to the woman who truly wants to get well.

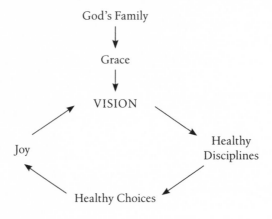

Figure 6. Laaser cycle of recovery

This healthy cycle is the perfect representation of the new life available in Christ to the woman in recovery. As a beginning, she can connect with the family of God, first by understanding her adoption by the ideal Father as a holy and perfectly loved child welcomed into his family. In an earthly sense, she can create a family of choice that's made up of spiritual sisters, brothers and parents in the family of God.

The legacy of God's family is the incredible gift of grace, which replaces the shame generated in unhealthy relationships. Grace then inspires vision, which will be explored at length in later paragraphs. The female addict practices healthy disciplines such as going to meetings, working the Steps, using a sponsor and maintaining conscious contact with God. These healthy rituals lead to healthy choices, where the addict "walks her talk" of recovery. Her insides match the outside she presents to the world. She no longer lives in fear of discovery but moves in the light of openness and transparency. And finally she reaps the reward of recovery: the paradoxical joy that can only be found on the other side of pain.

What woman facing the stones of sin doesn't hope for this deliverance? God, the loving Father, promises it:

> "For I know the plans I have for you," declares the LORD, "plans to prosper you and not to harm you, plans to give you hope and a future. Then you will call upon me and come and pray to me, and I will listen to you. You will seek me and find me when you seek me with all your heart." (Jeremiah 29:11-14)

The recovering female addict discovers that the experience of joy doesn't have to wait until she reaches heaven. It's possible in this life. There's joy in the journey, not just in its destination. This joy isn't the giddy adrenaline rush of addiction, but it's something far better and much deeper: the sweet serenity of transformation.

And this isn't just an abstract joy. It's a tangible experience of the redemption from sexual abuse, sin and addiction. It can be felt by the recovering woman and observed by others. It has concrete symptoms and specific characteristics. It's marked by unambiguous signs of renewal.

SIGNPOSTS OF THE JOURNEY

The first marker is the "peace . . . which transcends all understanding," which is described in Philippians 4:7. This peace doesn't necessarily mean the freedom from pain. The wounds of trauma and the remorse of addiction still occasionally throb. Consequences of earlier sins may be ongoing. But in the midst of the difficulties, a recovering woman can say along with the hymnist, "It is well with my soul,"[2] because she's living a different kind of life prompted by the grace of a Savior who refuses to throw stones.

For some women this peace has physical manifestations. One addict had suffered with gastrointestinal problems for years, which doctors couldn't link to any specific physical condition. After the first year of sobriety, she was delighted to find her symptoms had disappeared. Her body had been shouting with the disease she had denied, and when she dealt with her addiction the physical distress went away. After longer in recovery, this woman identified any stomach churning as a sign she needed to be more attentive to the healthy disciplines of working her program.

Practicing honesty is another signpost of healthy recovery. Without any secrets to hide and without the false belief that only perfection deserves acceptance, the recovering addict tells the truth. There's such freedom in honesty. It's wonderful to be where you say you are, doing what you say you're doing in the company of who you say you're with. Life is much simpler when you don't have to keep your stories straight.

Honesty also encompasses truthfulness about thoughts and emotions. Female sex addicts are also codependent, as are all addicts. (We get the double dose of disease.) Ongoing recovery involves addressing this additional aspect of an addictive illness. A key sign that a woman's recovery has moved beyond sobriety into this deeper layer of healing is that she can be honest about her opinions and feelings. She no longer depends on others for her identity and validation, so she's confident to share her mind and heart freely.

Another signpost along the journey of recovery is appropriate vulnerability. A woman becomes willing to ask for help from safe people. She admits her needs, her hopes, her anger and her fears. Without pretense or embarrassment she shows her authentic self. She allows herself to be known.

Her honesty and vulnerability create intimacy in her relationships. Unlike her earlier attempts at intimacy, these relationships are marked by integrity. According to strong boundaries and with accountability, a woman enjoys close friendships with healthy women and men. Characterized by sexual and emotional integrity, she conducts these relationships in honor. The love, acceptance and affirmation the female addict once sought in sexual sin she now finds through holy fellowship.

The recovering woman is also intimately connected with God.

She's committed to her relationship with him above any other thing. The promise of Psalm 37:4 has come true: "Delight yourself in the LORD and he will give you the desires of your heart." The promise has come true because her heart's desire has been transformed. No longer does she value sex or a relationship or freedom from loneliness as her life's goal. Above all else she desires an intimate relationship with a God who will not throw stones.

A VISION FOR LIFE

This new desire becomes the vision that gives her life purpose and direction. It is the foundation and the goal, the base and the summit simultaneously. All choices are examined in light of this vision. All options are subject to its molding. Alternatives are measured against its standard. The vision of a life lived in holy relationship with God and others guides her days.

One hallmark of a woman's recovery vision is that she develops a new view of herself. She reclaims the gift of her sexuality through "spiritual virginity." By that I mean she allows God to cleanse her from the stains of her past. She sees herself as a new creation in Christ, beautiful and wholly pure. She guards her body as the temple of God and the bride of Christ. In purity, she practices surrender and selflessness. She seeks to be a living sacrifice to the Father who has redeemed her from sin and shame.

A radical shift in her thinking and behavior happens as she embraces God's plan for healthy sexuality. She understands that the greatest fulfillment comes from the pleasure of one woman and one man who are married for life. She accepts God's boundaries for sexual expression as evidence of his desire of the best for his children. She expands her view of what it means to be a woman created in the image of God.

HEALTHY SEXUALITY

A helpful model for healthy sexuality was designed by therapist Ginger Manley, who is another pioneer in the field of sexual addiction recovery. She outlines five core dimensions of healthy sexuality:[3]

Behavioral. The behavioral aspect has been the primary focus of this book, because it concerns the area of addiction. If a woman is addicted to pornography or other forms of compulsive sexual behavior, she must address that problem before she can experience healthy sexuality. The joyous one-flesh union between a wife and husband will be impossible if she's consumed with outside sexual activity or images. Even if she's single, her sexual self will be perverted if she's active in addictive behavior.

Personal. The personal portion of healthy sexuality involves healing from trauma. If a woman's thoughts and behavior are still driven by any wounds of abuse or abandonment, she won't be able to enjoy healthy relationship much less healthy sexuality. Without healing she'll run from intimacy. When triggered she'll be overcome by trauma reactions. More specifically, in order to experience (or anticipate) healthy sexual relations, a woman must have healed from any sexual violation. She must be able to be present and vulnerable during a sexual encounter.

Physical. The physical dimension first concerns the mechanics of a couple's sexual functioning. They must address any physical problems (such as pain during intercourse or a husband's impotence) that might impair their sex life. This physical area also applies to a woman individually. She must have a healthy body image free from feelings of unattractiveness or inadequacy. She must believe her Maker's declaration that she is "fearfully and wonderfully made" (Psalm 139:14).

Relational. Healthy sexuality is much more about an intimate relationship than it is about body parts or techniques. This area underscores why a woman must move far beyond sobriety in her recovery journey. She must stop reacting out of fear of abandonment. She must relearn how to do relationships: how to have healthy communication and conflict, how to give and receive, how to forgive and ask for forgiveness, how to play and grieve and partner and love. In the sexual area, a recovering woman must be married to a man who's also on a journey of transformation if they're going to enjoy the fullness of healthy sexuality.

Spiritual. The spiritual component is at the center of the other dimensions. It's the core of healthy sexuality. The recovering addict follows her vision of holy sexuality, which is the higher calling of recovery. She knows she's been redeemed by holy Love, and she accepts no substitute that cheapens her deliverance.

INTIMACY WITH GOD

The spiritual component of healthy sexuality returns us full circle to the theme of this book: our desire for intimate connection with God as well as with people. Part three, this final section about the solution for sex addiction, opened with the gospel story about the woman at the well who encountered Jesus. You remember she was probably sexually addicted—at least her history of five husbands plus a sixth live-in is good indication. Jesus knew her secret sins, yet he asked for her help. (No one is beyond usefulness in God's kingdom.) She was amazed he would even speak to her for she was both a woman and a Samaritan. On both counts she was beneath a Jewish man. It was considered improper for them to have any contact. Jesus asked her for a drink from the well, and the Savior and the sinner began a fascinating discussion about living water.

Jesus offered a promise to the woman at the well and to all who thirst for healing: "Whoever drinks the water I give [her] will never thirst. Indeed, the water I give [her] will become in [her] a spring of water welling up to eternal life" (John 4:14). They went on to discuss the true nature of worship, which Jesus made clear was more about *how* than it was about where—about attitude rather than place. The connection between water and worship may be lost on some readers.

The living water Jesus pours is found through worship. Not just the specific times of joining other Christians for corporate praise. That's the issue the woman debated with Jesus: Where's the right place to gather? In answer, he defines worship in much broader terms:

> It's who you are and the way you live that count before God. Your worship must engage your spirit in the pursuit of truth. That's the kind of people the Father is out looking for: those who are simply and honestly *themselves* before him in their worship. God is sheer being

itself—Spirit. Those who worship him must do it out of their very being, their spirits, their true selves, in adoration. (John 4:23-24 *The
Message*)

I believe this description applies to our relationship with God as
well as to the parameters of worship. Our spirit must be engaged with
God. We must pursue truth as God himself is pursuing us. He's seeking worshippers who are vulnerable before him—those who are
"honestly themselves." There is no willful disconnect between the
life of the spirit and the life of the flesh. Instead an adoring child
praises God with her very being, her spirit, her true self. Into this
kind of integrated, worshipful life God pours his presence. He supplies the thirst for pure relationship. He gives the living water of intimate connection with himself. And this relationship with God forms
the basis for eternal life.

The application for the modern recovering woman is simple: God
alone can fill the aching hole in her soul. The desperate attempts to
still the longings through addictive partners or compulsive activity
will never satisfy. Only God will be enough.

Intimacy with him is the goal of all of recovery. The surrender, the
meetings, the boundaries, the accountability, the fellowship—all are
vehicles to closer communion with God. And this redemption of the
once-broken relationship with the Father doesn't happen because the
addict is more deserving after recovery. It's not that she's more worthy when she's sober. Not at all. It happens because she's more recep-
tive and responsive to the love God has lavished on her all along. It is
she who's more available for intimate relationship, not God. Her recovery from the intimacy disorder called sexual addiction allows her
to connect intimately with God.

SHARE THE NEWS OF REDEMPTION

Before I end this examination of a sex addict's transformation, I want to
point out one final lesson in the story of the woman at the well. She
shared the news about her encounter with Jesus. She hurried into the
nearby town and told all who would listen about what she had experienced. She was way ahead of any language about recovery, but she natu-

rally was practicing the last of the Twelve Steps: "Having had a spiritual awakening as a result of these Steps, we tried to carry the message to all who still suffer and to practice these principles in all our affairs."

Her decision to broadcast her story was probably not as easy as it might first appear. It was quite outside the norm as well as likely outside her comfort zone. As a Samaritan woman in the first century, she was supposed to be silent. Invisible. She certainly wasn't allowed to go around preaching to the men of the village. That was unheard of. It was beyond improper; it was vulgar. But she shared anyway.

This Samaritan woman also had to be vulnerable about her past in order to explain why the conversation with Jesus was so spectacular. She had to admit her sins and her failed relationships. She had to identify what Jesus had known about her. Like the other woman caught in adultery, this woman at the well faced possible judgment. Yet she went to the townspeople. She told her story. And she brought others to see the One who had taught her about living water. She refused to let her fear or shame keep her from sharing the good news.

Recovering women must also spread the amazing message about the gift of redemption from sexual abuse, sin and addiction. Thousands of addicted females need to hear about the hope of recovery. They need to understand their disease and the process of healing. They need to witness the transformation of women once active in their addiction.

I suspect the woman at the well discovered the best way to quench her own thirst was to share living water with others. The same is true for the recovering woman in the twenty-first century. The best way to keep her vision fresh is to give it away. It's another wonderful paradox of recovery: Shared gifts quickly multiply. Other sisters join those on the journey. More women reach out in loving support. The fellowship of intimacy broadens. The circle expands. And woman by woman the cycle is broken. One by one daughters redeemed from sexual shame walk in the grace of no stones.

The end of a matter is better than its beginning.

(Ecclesiastes 7:8)

**QUESTIONS FOR REFLECTION
OR SMALL GROUP DISCUSSION**

1. What's your reaction to the cycle of recovery? Does this transformation seem possible for you personally?

2. Which component of healthy sexuality provides the most challenges (behavioral, personal, physical, relational or spiritual)?

3. Where are you in terms of your intimacy with God? Are you drinking from a spiritual source of living water?

4. Can you envision one day sharing your story beyond the setting of recovery groups?

TWELVE STEPS OF SEXAHOLICS ANONYMOUS

1. We admitted that we were powerless over lust – that our lives had become unmanageable.*

2. Came to believe that a Power greater than ourselves could restore us to sanity.

3. Made a decision to turn our will and our lives over to the care of God as we understood Him.

4. Made a searching and fearless moral inventory of ourselves.

5. Admitted to God, to ourselves, and to another human being the exact nature of our wrongs.

6. Were entirely ready to have God remove all these defects of character.

7. Humbly asked Him to remove our shortcomings.

8. Made a list of all persons we had harmed and became willing to make amends to them all.

9. Made direct amends to such people wherever possible, except when to do so would injure them or others.

10. Continued to take personal inventory and when we were wrong promptly admitted it.

11. Sought through prayer and meditation to improve our conscious contact with God as we understood Him, praying only for knowledge of His will for us and the power to carry that out.

12. Having had a spiritual awakening as the result of these Steps, we tried to carry this message to sexaholics, and to practice these principles in all our affairs.

CHARACTERISTICS OF A SEX AND LOVE ADDICT

The following are some characteristics of sex and love addiction that we have used to hide the progressive loss of self, which is the heart of the disease:*

1. Having few healthy boundaries, we become emotionally and sexually involved with people without knowing them.

2. Out of fear of abandonment or loneliness, we stay in or return to painful, destructive relationships, always struggling to conceal our dependency. Real intimacy is rare, if it has ever existed.

3. Fearing emotional or sexual deprivation, we compulsively pursue and involve ourselves with one relationship after another, sometimes having more than one sexual or emotional affair at a time.

4. We confuse love with such things as neediness, intensity, pity, sexual or physical attraction, being a victim or being a rescuer.

5. We feel empty or incomplete when we are alone. Though we fear both intimacy and commitment, we continually search for relationships or sexual contacts.

6. We sexualize stress, guilt, loneliness, anger, fear and envy. We use sex or emotional dependence as substitutes for nurturing, support and understanding.

7. We manipulate and control others with drama and sexuality.

8. We become immobilized or seriously distracted by sexual or romantic obsessions and fantasies.

9. We avoid personal responsibility by attaching ourselves to people who are emotionally unavailable.

10. We stay in denial about our addiction to emotional intensity, romantic intrigue and compulsive sexual activity.

11. To avoid feeling vulnerable, we may retreat from all intimate involvement, mistaking sexual and emotional anorexia for recovery.

12. We assign magical qualities to others. We idealize and pursue them, then we blame them for not fulfilling our fantasies and expectations.

---

*The Characteristics are typically read at meetings of Sex and Love Addicts Anonymous.

RESOURCES

Because effective resources are frequently updated, please visit the Resource section of the Bethesda Workshops website (www.bethesda workshops.org) for a current list.

There you'll find the following types of resources:
- Twelve Step groups
- Organizations and ministries that work with sexual addiction
- Recommended reading
- Links to organizations that provide lists of counselors

ACKNOWLEDGMENTS

This book would never have become a reality without the help and support of many people. Their names will mean nothing to most readers, of course, but it's important to me to honor them. Compiling this long list of treasured people reminds me of the importance of community. It's one of the things I teach, and I'm blessed to enjoy it in a deep way in my own life.

My shepherds at the Woodmont Hills Church in Nashville and my coworkers at the affiliated Bethesda Workshops program have been wonderfully supportive. Rubel Shelly, the former preaching minister at Woodmont Hills, saw me at my worst at the beginning of the journey and believed in me when I didn't believe in myself. Rubel's integrity and compassion helped heal my view of preachers, just as the family of God at Woodmont Hills helped heal my view of church. From both I learned to replace religion with spirituality, for which I am eternally grateful.

My first therapist, Dr. LaRue Moss, literally saved my life physically and emotionally. She immediately recognized my trauma history buried beneath the presenting addiction. LaRue first helped me picture a redeemed life and taught this "little bird" how to fly. She's been my biggest cheerleader, first as a recovering woman and now as a clinician.

I owe a tremendous debt of gratitude to Dr. Mark Laaser. This book is full of his teaching, and he opened numerous doors for me professionally. I learned invaluable lessons about recovery and integrity through our years of working together.

A few special women have been incomparable friends. First, my sister-in-law Yvonne Craig has helped me more than she'll ever know. She was the first person to hear my terrible secret, and she loved me through my pain. She's a spiritual giant for me and a wonderful prayer warrior on my behalf. My dear friends Angela Thompson and Barbi White have become the sisters I never had. They are my accountability partners, my colleagues in ministry and my constant sounding boards.

Other women are also treasures in my life. Bernie Arnold mothered me at certain critical times. She and her husband Buddy, along with others, shared memories of my own mother and allowed me to know her through their stories about my mother's life and death. My mother-in-law, Lorene Ferree, has never wavered in her kindness and support despite the pain I've caused her son. She intuitively practices what I outline in the chapter for families of addicts. I'm grateful. My sister-in-law Mary Lou Craig is another inspiration. Her gentle spirit and wisdom teach me about being a woman of God, especially in the area of motherhood.

Many recovering women have allowed me to share their journeys. Each one has touched my life in a special way and taught me many valuable lessons. Some I know as clients and others as fellow seekers in recovery. Their cries for this book haunted and motivated me. Though their identities must remain unrevealed, their contributions are priceless.

A few "brothers" have also been safe and important men in my life. My colleague Eli Machen especially blesses me with safe friendship. He and others from the Healing for Men workshop staff and the Woodmont Hills Church allow me to relate to men purely as other people created in the image of God. Many males from my childhood and adolescence were honorable in their interactions with me when it would have been easy to exploit my loneliness. Today, I'm keenly aware of that powerful gift. When I'm tempted to focus on the other guys who made different and harmful choices, the memories of a dozen trustworthy faces provide a balance to the pain.

God's providence also supplied a special angel to care for my brothers and me during our childhood. "Mama Bess" came to live with our family when my mother died, and she stayed until her own death when I was a sophomore in college. She wasn't equipped to help with some of the problems I faced growing up, but her love was unmistakable. Without her dependable presence, I'm convinced I'd be certifiably crazy. Thank you, dear Bess, for being the only mother I ever knew.

I'm deeply grateful for my father and my two brothers. "Doc" is now suffering from Alzheimer's disease, and I grieve to see him slowly slipping away. My commitment is to love him well through this final stage of his life's journey. I pray he'll feel peaceful and comforted. My brothers, Larry and David, provide immense support and enrich my life greatly. I love our talks about our shared history and the healing we've experienced. I'm so glad we're family!

As I complete this project which has been a lifetime in the making, I honor my mother and her influence in my life. It's a mystery how clearly I've felt her presence from beyond the grave. I don't understand how that happens, but I'm immensely grateful.

I'm thankful for my children, E. A. and Matt, and I'm humbled to be their mother. In different ways each was harmed by my addiction, yet I'm blessed to have a positive, meaningful relationship with them both. Now young adults, they are a constant source of pride and inspiration. E. A.'s husband, Chris, is a wonderful addition to our family, and I appreciate who he is and how well he loves our daughter. I look forward to the continued unfolding of my children's stories.

Finally, I've saved the most important acknowledgment for last. Words fail me when I try to express my gratitude for my wonderful husband, David. He's lived out the vows of faithful commitment. His forgiveness and grace constantly remind me of God's love. His devotion to our children amazes me. He quietly keeps the home fires burning while I'm out in the spotlight. I could never pursue my work without his steadfast support and servant heart. He is truly the wind beneath my wings. David moved far outside his comfort zone in sharing some of his own experiences in this book, and for that stretch I can never thank him enough.

NOTES

CHAPTER 2: MESSAGES ABOUT BEING FEMALE

[1]Doug Rosenau and Michael Todd Wilson, *Soul Virgins: Redefining Single Sexuality* (Grand Rapids: Baker, 2006).

[2]Kelly McDaniel, *Ready to Heal: Women Facing Love, Sex, and Relationship Addiction* (Carefree, Ariz.: Gentle Path, 2008), esp. pp. 35-41.

CHAPTER 3: DEFINITION OF ADDICTION

[1]Patrick Carnes, *Out of the Shadows* (Minneapolis: CompCare Publishers, 1983), p. 4.

[2]Jennifer Schneider and Richard Irons, "Differential Diagnosis of Addictive Sexual Disorders Using the DSM-IV," *Sexual Addiction & Compulsivity* 3, no. 1 (1996): 7-21.

[3]Carnes, *Out of the Shadows.*

[4]Harvey Milkman and Stanley Sunderwith, *Craving for Ecstasy: The Consciousness and Chemistry of Escape* (Lexington, Mass.: Lexington, 1987).

[5]Ralph Earle and Mark Laaser, *Pornography Trap: Setting Pastors and Laypersons Free from Sexual Addiction* (Kansas City: Beacon Hill, 2002).

[6]Charles Swindoll, "Lessons from a Tavern," *Leadership Journal* 4, no. 1 (1983).

CHAPTER 4: FEMALE PRESENTATIONS OF SEXUAL ADDICTION

[1]Al Cooper, David Delmonico and Ron Burg, "Cybersex Users, Abusers, and Compulsives: New Findings and Implications," *Sexual Addiction & Compulsivity* 7, nos. 1 and 2 (2000).

[2]Internet Filter Review (September 2008) <http://internet-filter-review.topten reviews.com/internet-pornography-statistics.html>.

[3]Jennifer Schneider, "A Qualitative Study of Cybersex Participants: Gender Differences, Recovery Issues, and Implications for Therapists," *Sexual Addiction & Compulsivity* 7, no. 4 (2000).

[4]Paige Padgett, "Personal Safety and Sexual Safety for Women Using Online Personal Ads," *Sexuality Research and Social Policy* 4, no. 2 (2007).

[5]Archibald Hart, Catherine Hart Weber and Debra Taylor, *Secrets of Eve* (Nashville: Word, 1998), p. 35.

[6]Jennifer Schneider and Burt Schneider, *Sex, Lies, and Forgiveness: Couples Speaking Out on Healing from Sex Addiction* (Tucson: Recovery Resources, 1999), p. 267.

[7]Mark Laaser, *Healing the Wounds of Sexual Addiction* (Grand Rapids: Zondervan, 2004).

[8]Patrick Carnes, *Facing the Shadow: Starting Sexual and Relationship Recovery* (Wickenburg, Ariz.: Gentle Path, 2001).

CHAPTER 5: CONSEQUENCES AND CYCLE OF ADDICTION
[1]Patrick Carnes, *Out of the Shadows* (Minneapolis: CompCare Publishers, 1983).

CHAPTER 6: DIAGNOSIS OF SEXUAL ADDICTION
[1]Sexaholics Anonymous Self-Test. (September 2008) <http.//www.sa.org>.
[2]Patrick Carnes and Sharon O'Hara. Women's Sexual Addiction Screening Test (September 2008) <http.//www.sexhelp.com>.
[3]American Psychiatric Association, *Diagnostic and Statistical Manual of Mental Disorders*, 4th ed. (Washington, D.C.: American Psychological Association, 1994).
[4]Patrick Carnes, *Out of the Shadows* (Minneapolis: CompCare Publishers, 1983).

CHAPTER 7: UNHEALTHY FAMILIES
[1]Mark Laaser, *Faithful and True Workbook: Sexual Integrity in a Fallen World* (Nashville: LifeWay, 1996).
[2]Patrick Carnes, *Don't Call It Love: Recovery from Sexual Addiction* (New York: Bantam Books, 1991).

CHAPTER 8: TRAUMA OF ABUSE
[1]Patrick Carnes, *Don't Call It Love: Recovery from Sexual Addiction* (New York: Bantam Books, 1991).
[2]Mark Laaser, *Healing the Wounds of Sexual Addiction* (Grand Rapids: Zondervan, 2004).
[3]Administration for Children and Families, a Division of the U.S. Department of Health and Human Services <http.//www.acf.dhhs.gov>.
[4]Linda Sanford, *Strong at the Broken Places: Overcoming the Trauma of Childhood Abuse* (New York: Avon Books, 1990).

CHAPTER 9: TRAUMA OF ABANDONMENT
[1]Mark Laaser, *Faithful and True Workbook: Sexual Integrity in a Fallen World* (Nashville: LifeWay, 1996).
[2]Beth Moore, *Breaking Free Workbook* (Nashville: LifeWay, 1999).
[3]Mark Laaser, *Talking to Your Kids About Sex* (Colorado Springs: WaterBrook, 1999).
[4]A. Grunseit et al., "Sexuality Education and Young People's Behavior: A Review of Studies," *Journal of Adolescent Research* 12, no. 4 (1997).
[5]"There Is a Balm in Gilead," African American spiritual.
[6]John Bowlby, *Attachment,* Attachment and Loss (New York: Basic Books, 1973), p. 1.

CHAPTER 10: LONG-LASTING EFFECTS OF TRAUMA
[1]Patrick Carnes, *The Betrayal Bond: Breaking Free of Exploitative Relationships* (Minneapolis: Hazelden, 1997).

[2]Ibid.
[3]Mark Laaser, *Faithful and True Workbook: Sexual Integrity in a Fallen World* (Nashville: LifeWay, 1996).

CHAPTER 11: ADDICTS' CORE BELIEFS, EMOTIONS AND COPING
[1]Patrick Carnes, *Out of the Shadows* (Minneapolis: CompCare, 1983).
[2]Chip Dodd, *The Voice of the Heart* (Franklin, Tenn.: Sage Hill, 2001).
[3]Marilyn Murray, *Prisoner of Another War: A Remarkable Journey of Healing from Childhood Trauma* (Berkeley, Calif.: PageMill, 1991).

CHAPTER 12: SURRENDER AND SOBRIETY
[1]*Sexaholics Anonymous* (the White Book) (Simi Valley, Calif.: SA Literature, 1989), p. 204.
[2]Ibid., pp. 191-92. In SA's sobriety definition, the term *spouse* refers to one's partner in a marriage between a man and a woman.
[3]Ibid., p. 204.

CHAPTER 13: DISCLOSURE
[1]Jennifer Schneider, Deborah Corley and Richard Irons, "Surviving Disclosure of Infidelity: Results of an International Survey of 164 Recovering Sex Addicts and Partners," *Sexual Addiction & Compulsivity* 5, no. 3 (1998).

CHAPTER 14: HEALTHY RELATIONSHIPS AND REBUILDING TRUST
[1]Mark Laaser, *Faithful and True Workbook: Sexual Integrity in a Fallen World* (Nashville: LifeWay, 1996).
[2]Rubel Shelly, "The Longing to Belong," *New Wineskins* 5, no. 4 (2001).

CHAPTER 15: TOOLS OF RECOVERY
[1]*Alcoholics Anonymous.* (New York: AA World Services, 1976), p. 63.
[2]Ibid.

CHAPTER 16: HEALING FROM TRAUMA
[1]Mark Laaser, *Faithful and True Workbook: Sexual Integrity in a Fallen World* (Nashville: LifeWay, 1996), p. 199.
[2]John Bowlby, *Attachment,* Attachment and Loss (New York: Basic Books, 1973).
[3]Patrick Carnes, "Toward a New Freedom: Exploring Healthy Sexuality," keynote presentation at National Council on Sexual Addiction and Compulsivity national conference, Louisville, Kentucky, May 1998.
[4]Charles Whitfield, *Healing the Child Within* (Deerfield Beach, Fla.: Health Communications, 1987).
[5]Marilyn Murray, *Prisoner of Another War: A Remarkable Journey of Healing from Childhood Trauma* (Berkeley, Calif.: PageMill, 1991).
[6]Laaser, *Faithful and True Workbook.*

[7]Ralph Earle and Mark Laaser, *Pornography Trap: Setting Pastors and Laypersons Free from Sexual Addiction* (Kansas City: Beacon Hill, 2002).

[8]Sandra Wilson, *Into Abba's Arms: Finding the Acceptance You've Always Wanted* (Wheaton, Ill.: Tyndale House, 1998).

CHAPTER 17: FOR HUSBANDS AND OTHERS (INCLUDING CLINICIANS)

[1]Jennifer Schneider, *Back from Betrayal* (Tucson: Recovery Resources, 2001).

[2]Peter Steinglass, Linda Bennett, Steven Wolin and David Reiss, *The Alcoholic Family* (New York: Basic Books, 1987).

[3]Schneider, *Back from Betrayal*.

[4]Ibid.

[5]Patrick Carnes, *Don't Call It Love: Recovery from Sexual Addiction* (New York: Bantam, 1991).

[6]Patrick Carnes, Debra Laaser and Mark Laaser, *Open Hearts: Renewing Relationships with Recovery, Romance & Reality* (Wickenburg, Ariz.: Gentle Path, 1999).

[7]Patrick Carnes and Kenneth Adams, eds., *Clinical Management of Sex Addiction* (New York: Brunner-Routledge, 2002).

[8]Patrick Carnes, "Task Centered, Competency Based Approach to Treatment" (1998) <http.//www.sexhelp.com>.

[9]Charles Swindoll, "Lessons from a Tavern," *Leadership Journal* 4, no. 1 (1983).

[10]Marnie Ferree, "Spoken Secrets: Breaking the Silence About Sexual Abuse," *The Tennessean,* August 15, 1993, sec. F, p. 4.

[11]Henry Cloud and John Townsend, *Safe People* (Grand Rapids: Zondervan, 1995), pp. 164-65.

[12]Nancy Hopkins and Mark Laaser, eds., *Restoring the Soul of a Church: Healing Congregations Wounded by Clergy Sexual Misconduct* (Collegeville, Minn.: Liturgical, 1995).

CHAPTER 18: LIVING HAPPILY EVER AFTER

[1]Mark Laaser, *Healing the Wounds of Sexual Addiction* (Grand Rapids: Zondervan, 2004).

[2]H.G. Spafford, "It Is Well with My Soul" (1873).

[3]Ginger Manley, "Healthy Sexuality: Stage III Recovery," *Sexual Addiction & Compulsivity* 2 (1995).

ABOUT THE AUTHOR

Marnie C. Ferree is a licensed marriage and family therapist in Nashville, Tennessee, where she directs Bethesda Workshops, an outreach program of the Woodmont Hills Church. She has a national reputation as a leader in the field of sexual addiction, particularly as it presents in women. In 1997, Marnie established a workshop program for female sex addicts that was the first of its kind in the country and today draws participants from across the United States and Canada. She has directed Bethesda Workshops since 2000. Previously, Marnie provided for sexual recovery (both from sexual abuse and sexual addiction) through the Woodmont Hills Counseling Center, a sister ministry at the church.

Marnie is a frequent lecturer at professional and recovery conferences, churches and schools. She also consults with Christian organizations and churches about sexual integrity, especially in cases where a leader has fallen into sexual sin. Marnie is a member of several professional organizations including the American Association of Marriage and Family Therapists (clinical member), the American Association for Christian Counselors, and the Society for the Advancement of Sexual Health, where she is on the editorial board of the professional journal *Sexual Addiction & Compulsivity*. She is a Certified Sexual Addiction Therapist (CSAT).

Marnie received a B.A. in English education from Lipscomb University in 1977 and an M.A. in counseling from Trevecca Nazarene University in 1996. Both schools are located in Nashville, Tennessee.

In addition to articles in peer-reviewed journals, Marnie has published dozens of essays and articles in a variety of magazines and newspapers. Of particular note is a comprehensive series on childhood sexual abuse published in 1993 in *The Tennessean.* "Spoken Secrets" was one of the first in-depth treatments of sexual abuse in a major U.S. newspaper, and it broke new ground for its use of on-the-record, first-person stories of survivors.

Marnie and her husband, David, have been married since 1981 and live in Nashville, Tennessee. They're the parents of a married daughter and a young adult son.

Marnie may be contacted through Bethesda Workshops:

Bethesda Workshops
3710 Franklin Pike
Nashville, TN 37204
Toll-free: 866-464-4325
Local: 615-467-5610
www.bethesdaworkshops.org
mferree@bethesdaworkshops.org

ABOUT BETHESDA WORKSHOPS

MISSION AND VISION

The mission of Bethesda Workshops is to encourage sexual whole-ness by ministering to those damaged by sexual addiction. We seek to provide a place of healing where people can begin a process of restoration with God, with themselves, with others and within their marriages. We use the best clinical strategies, coupled with Christian principles, to achieve spiritual, emotional, behavioral and relational healing.

GENERAL INFORMATION

Bethesda offers intensive workshops for recovery from sexual addic-tion and co-addiction. Most workshops are Wednesday through Sat-urday. Clinical intensive workshops include:

Healing for Men: for male sexual addicts

Healing for Women: for female sexual addicts

Healing for Partners: for partners of addicts
(wives, husbands and ex-spouses)

Healing for Couples: for addict/co-addict couples

Bethesda Workshops ~ *a place for healing*

3710 Franklin Pike, Nashville, TN 37204
Toll-free: 866-464-HEAL • Local: 615-467-5610
www.bethesdaworkshops.org
mferree@bethesdaworkshops.org